300 QUESTIONS ON QIGONG EXERCISES

Compiled by   Lin Housheng
              Luo Peiyu
Translated by   Yu Yaosheng
                Ding Tingmin
                Zhu Rui
Translation reviewed by   Zhuo Dahong
Copy editor   Chen Sushi   Huang Daquan

GUANGDONG SCIENCE AND TECHNOLOGY PRESS

First Edition 1994
ISBN 7—5359—1269—9/R · 232

Published by **Guangdong Science and Technology Press**
13F. , No. 11 Shuiyin Road, Huanshidong Road, Guangzhou
510075, China
Printed by **Guangdong Xinhua Printing House**
45, Yongfu Road, Guangzhou 510070, China
Distributed by **China International Book Trading Corporation**
35, Chegongzhuang Xilu, P. O. Box 399, Beijing 100044, China

Printed in the People's Republic of China

Lin Housheng   Luo Peiyu

INTRODUCTION

This book is meant for popularizing the common knowledge, basic forms and therapeutic patterns of Qigong exercise. It contains an introduction to Qigong's features, principles, and essentials for practice; and also on Qigong exercise forms, therapies for diseases and methods to correct deviations. There are illustrations in the sections of Qigong forms and movements.

The book is composed of questions and answers, rich in content and fit for practical needs. Qigong learners will find it easy to understand and medical workers of therapeutic Qigong exercise will find useful materials for reference in the book.

WRITER'S NOTE

Qigong (breathing exercise), a splendid heritage of Chinese medicine, is a medical treatment and exercise for the body. This science of controlling and training the body and mind has a long history and has been accepted and performed by many people. As a method of health preservation, Qigong aids in warding off diseases, strengthening the body and prolonging life.

Chinese scientists and doctors of both traditional Chinese and Western medicine have cooperated in their researches on clinical practice and scientific theory of Qigong. The study of the psychological and physical nature of Qi (vital energy) has involved several branches of learning, and utilized modern scientific methods to examine the essence of this energy. There has been much progress in popularizing the basic forms of Qigong exercise, and applying 'external Qi' to medical treatments. Qigong has broven to be a useful tool in preventing and curing diseases.

In July 1981, Qigong Brings Health was published by Guangdong Science and Technology Press. The book was a summary of the predecessors' experience and the writer's own years of Qigong practice. Qigong Brings Health has aroused great interest in both Chinese and foreign readers, and has received their enthusiastic support.

Many readers have sent letters or approached us to ask questions on Qigong exercise. To meet the readers' requests, we have compiled Three Hundred Questions on Qigong Exercise.

We have consulted materials from Shanghai Research Institute of Traditional Chinese Medicine, Liu Gui—zhen and several other researchers for explanations to the questions.

We would like to thank the scientists and researchers at the Traditional Medical College of Shanghai and the Shanghai Research Institute of Traditional Chinese Medicine for their support during our research and clinical practice of Qigong. We are also grateful to Lin Hai, Xue Weiban, Xiao Huibeng, Xu Wenbin, Wang Jian—cheng, Li Chengjian and Chou Yanlin for their help during the preparation of this book.

LIN HOU SHENG
LUO PEI YU
JUNE 1982 IN GUANGZHOU

CONTENTS

HISTORY AND INTRODUCTION

RESEARCH ON QIGONG PRINCIPLES

MATERIAL FOUNDATION

CHARACTERISTICS AND PRINCIPLES

ESSENTIALS FOR EXERCISE

6

INTRODUCTION ON EXERCISE FORMS

QIGONG EXERCISE FOR COMMON DISEASES

CLINICAL PRACTICE

THE DIRECTING-QI THERAPY

ANESTHESIA WITH EXTERNAL QI

TECHNIQUES OF BIONICS

MISCELLANEOUS

12

14

18

CORRECTION OF DEVIATIONS

INTERNATIONAL TRENDS

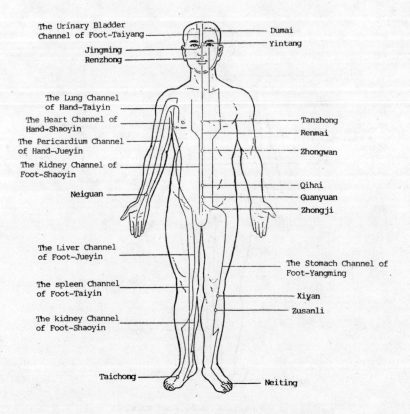

The Urinary Bladder
Channel of Foot-Taiyang —

Jingming —
Renzhong —

Dumai
Yintang

The Lung Channel
of Hand-Taiyin —

The Heart Channel of
Hand-Shaoyin —

The Pericardium Channel
of Hand-Jueyin —

The Kidney Channel of
Foot-Shaoyin —

Neiguan —

Tanzhong
Renmai

Zhongwan

Qihai
Guanyuan
Zhongji

The Liver Channel
of Foot-Jueyin —

The spleen Channel
of Foot-Taiyin —

The kidney Channel
of Foot-Shaoyin —

Taichong —

The Stomach Channel of
Foot-Yangming

Xiyan
Zusanli

Neiting

Front View of the Fourteen Channels and Acupoints

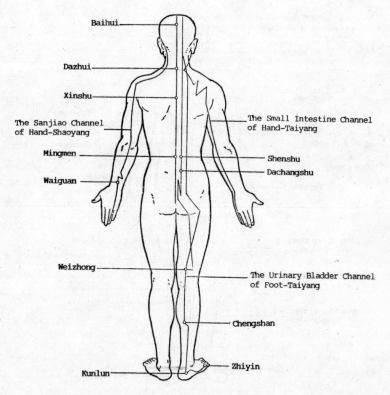

Baihui

Dazhui

Xinshu

The Sanjiao Channel
of Hand-Shaoyang

The Small Intestine Channel
of Hand-Taiyang

Mingmen

Shenshu
Dachangshu

Waiguan

Weizhong

The Urinary Bladder Channel
of Foot-Taiyang

Chengshan

Zhiyin

Kunlun

Back View of the Fourteen Channels and Acupoints

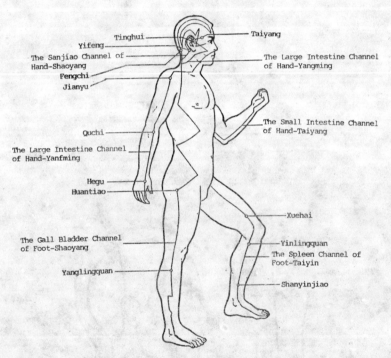

Tinghui — Taiyang

Yifeng

The Sanjiao Channel of
Hand-Shaoyang

Fengchi

Jianyu

The Large Intestine Channel
of Hand-Yangming

Ouchi

The Small Intestine Channel
of Hand-Taiyang

The Large Intestine Channel
of Hand-Yanfming

Hegu

Huantiao

Xuehai

The Gall Bladder Channel
of Foot-Shaoyang

Yinlingquan

The Spleen Channel of
Foot-Taiyin

Yanglingquan

Shanyinjiao

Lateral View of the Fourteen Channels and Acupoints

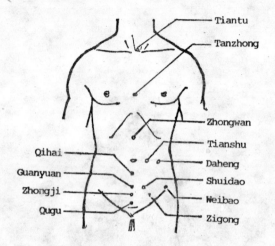

Acupoints at the Chest and Abdomen

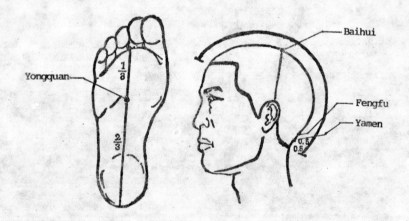

Common Acupoints for Qigong

HISTORY AND INTRODUCTION

1.   What Is Qigong?

Qigong, or breathing exercise, is a wonderful gem in the treasure-house of traditional Chinese medicine and a splendid heritage of Chinese medical literature. It is a keep-fit exercise characterized of the Chinese nation. It is also a summary of the experience of the Chinese people in their struggle against nature and diseases and in their self-adaptation to the process of life. This exercise is quite unique in its way of training both body and mind through cultivating one's vital essence, vital energy and vital spirit.

Qigong can be simply defined as the art of training one's Qi (vital energy) and mind (mental consciousness). The Chinese character "Qi" means respiration while "Gong" means continuous regulation of one's respiration and posture with the mind conducting the process. To do Qigong exercise is to train Qi and mind, with mind leading Qi to circulate along the network of channels, to promote and enhance functional activities of viscera and to develop Yuan Qi (intrinsic energy). This can help cure diseases and keep good health. Learners of Qigong can choose the type and form of the exercise in keeping with their state of disease, age, physique and specific conditions. They may practise the Qigong exercise in motion, in stillness or in motion and stillness alternately so as to keep the main and collateral channels in good shape, regulate circulation of the blood and vital energy, maintain balance of Yin and Yang, and strengthen one's physique. As a result, it cures diseases and brings good health. Therefore, Qigong is a self-training exercise of both body and mind with the help of mental direction. It is a science to keep fit and prolong life through self-regulation and self-control of the process of life. It is also an art of cultivating "intrinsic energy" of human body and building up health.

2.   How Did Qigong Originate?

Qigong is an exercise worked out, developed and gradually perfected by the Chinese people in their long struggle against nature. It has become an effective measure to prevent and cure diseases, improve health and keep fit, and prolong life.

The Chinese people started exploring the law of life thousands of years ago. On some copperwares from Shang Dynasty and early Zhou Dynasty there are pictures which vividly reproduce various postures of ancient people doing "Qigong". This shows that Qigong came into existence long before the invention of written language. In order to survive, man had to overcome all kinds of difficulties enforced on him by nature through training his body organs and adapting himself to the changing natural environments. Besides taking advantage of natural conditions to protect himself, man had to train his body to meet with various difficulties and sufferings created by nature. In the course of time, man came to realize the importance of self-protection and self-training, and to improve his ability to prevent and cure diseases. For example, when one is tired he yawns for rest or sleep. When he feels a pain, he groans to relieve of it. When he toils, he will utter a sound of "Hey" to support his effort. When he is hungry he desires for food, and so on. Similarly, when the weather is cold, he will take shelter from the wind and manage to face the sun for warmth. He will sit with limbs withdrawn close to the body, and hands on abdomen (the acupoint of Dantian) and mouth closed for keeping warm. Wherever the air is thin, he has to breathe deeply and form the habit of abdominal breathing. When he sits undisturbed, he feels vitalized and comfortable. These exercises, having proved beneficial to both body and mind, have been practised conscientiously, and gradually developed into various types and forms. The ancient exercises of Tuna, Daoyin and Xingqi have been constantly practised, improved, perfected and evolved into Qigong.

3.   How Was Qigong Named?

Qigong was referred to in various terms because there were in China different schools, including Confucianist school, Medical school, Taoist school, Buddhist school, and school of Martial Arts. There were various styles and forms such as Tuna, Daoyin, Xingqi, Liandan, Xuangong, Jinggong, Dinggong, Xinggong, Neigong, Xiudao, Zhoshan, Neiyanggong, Yangshenggong, etc. Varied as they were in name, they were all the predecessors of Qigong. According to textual research, *Jing Ming Religious Record* written by Xuxun, a Taoist, of Jin Dynasty included the "Elaboration of Qigong". *Special Therapy for Tuberculosis — Qigong Therapy* written by Donghao and published by Hangzhou Xianglin Hospital in 1934, and *Secret of Success of Shaolinquan* published by Zhonghua Press in 1935 and some other books, all mentioned the two characters "Qi Gong", but no explanation of the meaning was made, nor was the name be formally recognized. It was not until 1953 when Liu Guizheng wrote and published *Practice On Qigong Therapy* after discussion with some other people did Qigong be given a full explanation and recognized as a formal name instead of various terms used by different schools.

Why is it called "Qigong Therapy"? The book *Practice On Qigong Therapy* says, "Qi means respiration while Gong means continuous regulation of breathing and taking in postures." Now it is believed that besides regulation of breathing and postures, Qigong includes mental activities. In the light of medical knowledge, different styles of Qigong exercise have been sorted out and studied, and applied to the cure of diseases and preservation of health. With superstitious dross in them rejected, there comes Qigong Therapy. This therapy being so called is true to the fact and easy to understand. Thus, Qigong or Qigong Therapy has come to be accepted by the common workers and has enjoyed popularity throughout the country.

4.   What Records Were Made About Qigong During the Spring-and-Autumn Period and Warring States Period?

Qigong has had a history of thousands of years in China. In the ancient Spring-and-Autumn Period, people had already practised Qigong for building up health and curing diseases. Many records about Qigong can be found in classics. The oldest medical classic of ancient China *Medical Canon of Huang Emperor* brought forth the idea of "practising Qigong for prevention of diseases", which gave first priority to the preservation of health. In *Su Wen: Natural Truth In Ancient Times* it is said, "The ancient people who knew the way to keep fit. They followed the law of Yin-Yang and the art of breathing, kept moderate in eating and drinking. They led a regular life and did not get exhausted, and thus managed to keep both the body and mind healthy, enjoy a full lifetime and die a natural death." It is also said, "When one can evade external pathogens, keep free of wishes and ambition, gather genuine vital energy and concentrate his mind internally, he cannot be struck down by disease. As he is free from wishes and desires, he is calm and fearless; he works hard without feeling tired." In another chapter of *Su Wen*, it is said, "The folk eat assorted food and lack physical activities, they suffer from flaccid paralysis, faint, heat and cold. Daoyin and Anqiao may be the proper cure of their diseases." It is also said, "If one suffers from chronic kidney disease, he should face south early in the morning, keep in quiescence, regulate his breathing, lead the Qi downward and swallow the saliva. Repeat the cycle seven times."

The terms mentioned in the classics, such as "Daoyin", "Anqiao", "Breathe in essence", "Swallow saliva", "Hold breath", "Concentrate the mind", and "Keep in quiescence", all refer to Qigong exercise.

The well-known doctor Bian Que recommended breath-counting to be used in Qigong exercise as a way to regulate breathing and induce meditation.

The ancient scholar Lao Zi said in his *Canon of Morality* that when practising Qigong exercise, one should keep in a calm state, concentrate the mind at Dantian, breathe softly and in a long-drawn manner, and lead the Qi to flow through Dantian. That is, one should pay attention to exercising "mind" and "Qi"

It is pointed out in *Zhuang Zi: On Painstaking*, "To exhale and inhale, to get rid of the stale and take in the fresh, to walk like a bear and stretch like a bird, all this is for attaining longevity, and is what the Daoyin exercisers and health preservers are doing." This statement makes it clear that Qigong exercise can help build up health and prolong life.

5. What Records Were Made About Qigong During the Two Han Dynasties?

Ancient Qigong was further developed in Han Dynasty. The Pictures of Daoyin of the Early Period of Western Han Dynasty unearthed from the No.3 Han Tomb at Mawangdui late in 1973 show many human figures doing exercises. One of the colored silk paintings contains more than 40 figures taking different postures: sitting with closed eyes, holding head with hands, squatting with abdomen drawn in, bowing with the small of the back bent, standing with head lifted, or bending knees with hands pressing downward. This is a valuable finding for the study of the origin and development of Qigong.

It is recorded in *Huai Nan Zi: On Spirit*, "... Inhaling and exhaling, getting rid of the stale and taking in the fresh, walking like a bear and stretching like a bird, bathing like a wild duck and hearing like an earwig, looking around like an owl and glancing about like a tiger, this is the exercise for health preservation."

In *Brief Extracts of the Golden Chamber* Zhang Zhong-jing mentioned, "Man should manage to prevent wind pathogens from invading the channels and collaterals, or find a cure for them before they do harm to parenchymatous viscera. If he feels limbs heavy and unable to move, he should do breathing exercise (Daoyin and Tuna), make use of acupuncture, moxibustion, ointment or massage before the nine apertures get blocked.'' The statement makes it clear that practising internal or external Qigong exercise can bring both preventive and curative effects.

In *History of Later Han Dynasty: Biography of Hua Tuo* it is recorded, ''Hua Tuo had a good knowledge of several classics and understood very well how to keep fit. At the age of 100 he was still healthy. The folk took him for God.'' On the basis of Zhuang Zi's ''walking like a bear and stretching like a bird'', he worked out ''Five-Animal Play'' — tiger, deer, bear, ape and bird. He said, ''Man has to labour but cannot get exhausted.'' And he explained through practising the ''Five-Animal Play'', man can get blood flowing freely in vessels, ears and eyes clear and bright, teeth complete and firm; thus he will not fall ill easily and can cure his own disease.'' As the legend goes, his disciple Wu Pu who persevered in doing the 'Play', lived to the age of more than ninety, with good hearing and sharp eye-sight, and firmly-rooted teeth. Another disciple Fan Ah who practised the same 'Play' lived to the age of over one hundred with hair still black.

In *History of Later Han Dynasty: Biography of Wang Zhen* it was recorded, ''Wang Zhen lived to the age of over one hundred, but looked like a man of fifty with ruddy complexion, for he could breathe and eat in the manner of the foetus.'' That is to say he was skilled in sitting in quiescence to regulate his breathing and to swallow mouth fluid.

Besides, some of Zhi Guan Exercise and the exercises of sitting in quiet meditation adopted in Buddhism are acceptable even nowadays.

6. What Records Were Made About Qigong During the Period of Two Jin Dynasties and Northern and Southern Dynasties?

In the two Dynasties of Jin and Northern and Southern Dynasties, people already had much experience in preserving health.

Ji Kang wrote some articles on preservation of health.

Ge Hong in his writings gave detailed explanation on the same topic.

Bao Pu Zi: On Principles says, "Although taking medicine can help one live a longer life, practising Qigong will bring quicker results. Even without medicine, practising Qigong following the guidelines can also help one attain longevity. Man lives in Qi, and Qi exists in man. Nothing in the universe can exist without Qi. Hence, those who are skilled in cultivating Qi can nourish internal organs inside and resist external pathogens outside."

Bao Pu Zi: On Miscellany says, "Those who preserve health according to principles practise Qigong exercises morning and night so that they can enhance resistance against diseases and seldom fall ill. But those who have no will to stick to the exercise are usually not constant in practice and can achieve no good results."

Bao Pu Zi: On Preserving Health says, "Try to avoid long duration of sitting, walking, seeing and hearing. Do not eat when you're not hungry. Do not drink when you're not thirsty. You should do some physical labor but never get exhausted, you should eat less, but never cause hunger. When you are clear minded, you can keep genuine spirit to its place. When your Qi is gathered, you can resist pathogens. ... if you are indifferent to fame and free of desires, you'll keep in the state of tranquility and away from harmful disturbances. That is the principle for preserving good health."

Bao Pu Zi: On Avoiding Temptation says, "... Daoyin can prevent possible diseases and cause disharmonized Qi to circulate. With exercise, the Qi will circulate freely through all the organs."

By summing up the experience of health preserving before the Six Dynasties, Tao Hong-jing compiled *Collection on Preserving Health and Prolonging Life,* which includes many principles and methods of health preservation. For example: "Quiet people can attain longevity and nervous people are apt to die young. However, to be quiet without preservation will reduce one's age, whereas to be nervous yet with preservation can bring longer life. To keep in a state of calmness helps develop Qi, while to be always nervous makes it difficult to accumulate Qi. Take exercise to preserve one's health, to keep in quiescence and to develop one's Qi." This statement explains that when taking Qigong exercise, attention should be paid to inner nourishment, which is most helpful to bring good health and longevity. Another writing states, "If you are practising Qigong to cure disease, say some words in the mind against the diseased part, whether it is on the head or at the foot. Muster up the Qi to attack this part." This statement means saying words in the mind can relieve pain. Another writing says, "There is only one way of taking in Qi, which is inhaling. There are six ways of breathing out Qi shown in six Chinese characters: "Chui", "Hu", "Xi", "He", "Xu", and "Si". "Chui" expelling wind, "Hu" removing heat, "Xi" driving away annoyance, "He" leading down the Qi, "Xu" dispersing stagnation and "Si" relieving extremes..." This statement tells us that the exercise of saying the six Chinese characters in the mind has become a method to cure diseases ever since that time.

7. What Records Were Made About Qigong in Sui and Tang Dynasties?

In Sui and Tang Dynasties, health-preserving methods such as Daoyin and Tuna were further developed.

Cao Yuan-fang in the book of *Causes and Symptoms of Diseases* listed 260 forms of Daoyin and Tuna under most of symptom complex. The book was taken for a summary of Qigong therapies even before Sui Dynasty. For examples, "For limb trouble or stagnation of Qi in abdomen, you are required to lie flat on back in a steady bed, and to take a supine posture. Put under head a pillow about 3 inches thick, and hold hands gently. ... Calm the mind, regulate the breath, expel distracting thoughts, concentrate the mind with mind leading the Qi, let the tongue touch teeth slightly and rinse the mouth gently with saliva and swallow it. Exhale slowly and inhale through nose, warm up gradually and do not pursue the effect with effort. With the breath well-regulated, effect will be felt and disease cured after breathing one hundred to two hundred times." This shows that practising Qigong exercise helps cure disease in the limbs or abdomen.

Sun Si-miao in the chapters of *Prescriptions of Value* talked about Daoyin exercise. He mentioned, "For preserving health, one must do some exercise." "When one has the breath well-regulated, he can avoid diseases... Regulation of the breath helps to build up health." "The way to harmonize spirit and energy is to do exercise in a quiet room.... Lie supine, close eyes, hold breath so that even a goose feather can not stir before the nostril. Breathe slowly and gently three hundred times without hearing anything, seeing anything, or thinking about anything..." He also gave an account of the Six-Character Exercise, the Boluomen Eighteen Forms Posture Massage And Exercise of India, and the 49-Movements of Lao Zi's Massaging Method.

In *Wai Tai Secret Recipe,* Wang Tao usually listed methods of Daoyin and Tuna exercises for a particular disease before the section of prescriptions for the disease. For example, before the description of the ten prescriptions for pain in heart or abdomen, or distention and fullness, he said, "Often keep quiet. Lie supine early in the morning, rinse the mouth and swallow the fluid three times. Regulate the inner organs so as to prolong life and cure pain in the heart or abdomen." Before the two prescriptions for phlegm and excessive fluid, he said, "Lie on the right side or left side, regulate the breath twelve times. This will cure phlegm and excessive fluid."

Besides, Bai Ju-yi wrote a poem on quiet meditation, which reads:
You sit with eyes closed and away from noise,
    Harmony of Qi helps build up skin and muscles.
You seem drunk with fine wine,
    stirring only slightly as if in hibernation.
You look calm

while blood and Qi flow freely throughout.
You think no more,
with heart and mind in a state of nothingness and
emptiness.

The poem makes clear the state of one in tranquility.

8. What Records Were Made About Qigong in Song, Jin and Yuan Dynasties?

In Song Dynasty, efforts were made on a comprehensive and systematic check and compilation of medical classics, including writings on health preservation.

In the last chapter of the book *Sheng Ji Summary,* there are three sections on exercises of swallowing saliva, Daoyin and taking in Qi, which mainly deal with the methods of Qigong training.

On swallowing saliva, it is said, "Open the mouth with tongue touching the upper teeth, draw saliva and swallow it. Repeat the process 360 times a day."

On Daoyin, it is said, "One's Qi usually circulates through the parenchymatous and hollow viscera, all the bones and apertures. Free circulation of Qi brings health while stagnation of Qi causes diseases. Daoyin exercise helps circulate blood and Qi, actuate joints, keep external pathogens away from the body." "For pathologic changes of the Viscera and the Triple Heater, resort to Six-Character Qigong Exercise. "Xu" is good for the liver, "He", for the heart, "Hu", for the spleen, "Si", for the lungs, "Chui", for the kidneys and "Xi", for the Triple Heater... . The Six-Character Qigong Exercise usually promote purging but produce less effect on tonifying. Do the exercise when you feel Qi is in stagnation, stop it when the disease of the particular vicera is cured."

On taking in Qi, it is said, "Practise taking in Qi during midnight and early morning: Drink mouth fluid; breathe out the stale and take in the fresh; perform Daoyin and Anjiao; draw in essence from the moon and the sun. Qi exists in the body and the body is filled with Qi. When one's Qi is abundant and in harmony with the body, one can live a long life … ."

The treatises on health preservation during this period included *Keep-Fit in Four Seasons* by Zhao Zi-hua, *A New Book on Longevity* by Cheng Zhi, and *Su Shen on Prescriptions* compiled by Su Dongpo's descendents with many of his treaties in it. Lu You in his poem described:

> My heart is as calm as still water
>> without the least wind stirring,
> I sit undisturbed
>> Taking thousand breaths.
> Suddenly in the midnight, I enter a wonder land,
>> With rolling waves and rising sun in sight.

This is a vivid description of the man's special feelings in a state of unperturbedness.

Zhang An-dao in his *Formula of Keep-Fit* said, "Get up in the midnight with clothes on, sit cross-legged, face east or south, chatter teeth thirty-six times, hold hands gently, hold breath, and look at viscera inside with mind's eye… . When the abdomen is filled with Qi, exhale gently and slowly. When the breathing becomes even, rinse the lips and teeth with tongue until the mouth is full of fluid, and then swallow it with head lowered slightly. Lead the Qi down to Dantian… ." This detailed explanation of Qigong exercise is of value even for today's reference.

Eight-Section Exercise by an anonymous person of Song Dynasty is one of the earliest treatises on keep-fit and Daoyin exercises. Taijiquan is said to be a summary written during the period of Northern Song Dynasty.

In the Jin and Yuan Dynasties, Liu Wan-su in his treatises mentioned the Six-Character Formula and talked about methods of keep-fit. Zhang Zi-he in his book recorded the cure of external injuries by means of blowing. He said, "Think of the east and the rising sun, inhale a mouthful and blow on the injured part."

Li Gao in his treatise said, "If one is subject to changing mood and lives an irregular life, harm will be done to the body and Qi. Decline of Qi induces fire, with manifestations of being disinclined to talk or move about, shortness of breath, exterior heat, spontaneous sweating, restlessness, etc. In this case, one should sit quietly taking in Qi; use sweet and cold drugs to purge the fire; use sour drugs to gather the dispersed Qi; use sweet and warm drugs to warm the central Qi." This statement explains that overwork does harm to spleen and results in diseases, and these cases can be treated by means of "sitting in quiescence" in combination with drugs.

Zhu Dan-xi in his *Supplementary Comment of Ge Zhi* mentioned, "Prescribe Daoyin exercise for stagnation of Qi, flaccid paralysis, sudden fainting and fear of cold." "Regulating the breath and physical body with change of seasons is the foundation for curing diseases." What he said is a correct illustration of Qigong's function of curing diseases.

9. What Records Were Made About Qigong in Ming and Qing Dynasties?

In the middle period of Ming Dynasty, Xu Chun-fu compiled the *Complete Volume of Ancient Medical Classics,* including the experiences of practising Qigong by ancient medical men. He verified, through textual research, that health preservation had become one of the thirteen medical specialties since Song and Yuan Dynasties.

In the *Study on Eight Extra Channels* Li Shi-zhen said, "Only those who constantly observe the internal channels with mind's eye can see them clearly." This shows the close relationship between Qigong exercise and the body channels.

In *Secret to Keep-Fit* Cao Yuan-bai listed 46 diseases to be treated with Daoyin exercise. He brought forth the idea of combining exercises in motion and in stillness as one of the Qigong styles.

In *Views on Keep-Fit,* Chen Ji-ru considered "essence, energy and spirit" to be a sort of top-grade medicine, and "keeping essence", "cultivating energy" and "developing spirit" to be the best prescription for longevity. He suggested that one should distinguish deficiency, excess, cold and heat, and suit the exercise to specific case, saying, "Qigong exercise is the method to cure diseases. For deficiency syndrome, the exercise of concentrating the mind on the interior is appropriate tonification. For excess syndrome, massage and Daoyin and deep-inhaling and external release of Qi are considered to be good measures to disperse it. For heat disease, it is advisable to get rid of the stale and take in the fresh, to exhale with mouth and inhale with nose so as to cool it. For cold disease, one should hold breaths and store Qi and to warm it up with the mind. They are all good measures to cure diseases, much more effective than taking medicine."

In Zhang Jing-yue's *Canon of Classification,* it is said, "Health preservation usually results from breath regulation ... ," pointing out the relationship between preservation of health and regulation of breathing.

Fu Ren-yu in his *Treasure Notes on Eye Diseases* first recorded the use of the Six-Character Qigong Exercise for curing glaucoma, which is valuable even for today's reference.

Wang Ken-tang in his *Criterion of Cure: On Glaucoma* mentioned, "If you can cultivate and accumulate intrinsic energy, diseases can be cured without much treatment." He brought forth the idea of curing glaucoma through practising Qigong.

Wang Yang-ming was skilled in sitting in quiescence. He wrote the book *Notes on Instruction and Practice* for his students to learn the art.

In the early Qing Dynasty, Wang Ren-an wrote *Explanation on Medical Prescriptions,* including in it some exercises practised by his predecessors. One of the records says, "You can practise regulating the breath at any time. Sit anywhere with torso erect. Undo the tight clothes and belt. Move the tongue in the mouth several times, exhale through mouth and inhale through nose gently three to five times, or once or twice. Swallow fluid, chatter teeth several times, let the tongue touch the palate, close mouth and teeth, drop eyelids. Breathe gently and smoothly. Count the number of exhaling or inhaling from one to ten , and up to a hundred for regulating the breath.''

Shen Jin-ao wrote *Volume of Shen's Way to Keep Fit*, in which he talked about the methods of Qigong exercise and brought forward twelve rules. For example, ''If you feel unwell, do some exercise at once, so that you can avoid becoming seriously ill because of long delay.'' He also recommended the methods to expel distracting thoughts, which are similar to the method of concentrating the mind on a certain point such as Dantian and the like.

In late Qing Dynasty, Wang Zu-Yuan compiled *Internal Exercises With Illustrations,* including the formula and pictures for Twelve-Section Exercise and pictures for the Canon of Changing Tendons, massage of body parts, Daoyin and so on. He suggested practising both moving and quiescent exercises.

Xi Xi-fan compiled the internal and external exercises of ancient times with illustrations, which introduced the cure of diseases by means of Daoyin, Eight-Section Exercise, Canon of Changing Tendons, massage and regulating the breath. It was entitled as *Internal And External Exercises With Illustrations* classified into 28 items with 124 pictures. Besides, Zheng Guan-ying in his *Main Ideas on Health* gave a brief account on removal of distractions leading to quiescence during Qigong practice.

Before liberation, Jiang Wei-qiao wrote *Yin Shi-zhi Exercise of Quiet Sitting,* in which he briefly explained the methods of training the breath and preserving health through concentration of the mind. His writing was helpful to the learners of Qigong at that time. Ding Fu-bao also compiled books on exercises of quiet sitting, which can serve as reference for study of Qigong exercises.

10. How Has Qigong Developed Since Liberation?

Since liberation, under the leadership of the Party, Qigong has developed greatly. In 1955 Liu Gui-zhen and some others made a survey of the clinical practice of Qigong therapy at the Qigong Sanatorium in Tangshan. They did well in their work and received praises from the Ministry of Public Health. The Qigong Sanatorium in Tangshan was the first to apply Qigong to the cure of ailments, marking a new stage in its development. Liu Gui-zhen, by adopting other people's experience incorporated with his own knowledge of Qigong exercise, wrote the book of *Practice of Qigong Therapy,* in which he summed up the Qigong exercises practised at Tangshan and put them into three groups. They are: Intrinsic-Nourishing Qigong, Tonic Qigong and Keep-Fit Qigong. From 1956 on, special classes were set up in Tangshan and Bei Daihe to train personnel in this field. This greatly helped the popularization of the therapeutic Qigong exercise.

On July 1,1957, a Qigong Sanatorium was set up in Shanghai. Guided by the Party, Qigong therapy was accepted in many medical institutions in Shanghai in the ensuing two years. Some institutions and organizations began to cooperate in research of the principles governing Qigong. In 1958, the Shanghai Qigong Sanatorium started two courses on the therapeutic Qigong exercise and published *Lecture Notes on Qigong Therapy.* The book consists of ten lectures, which give brief accounts on Qigong's origin, exercising styles, guiding principles, points for attention and nursing methods. It is worth mentioning that through abundant clinical practice, they found "relaxation" to be the key to Qigong exercise (including relieving mental tension and relaxing muscles and joints of the whole body). Relaxation also proved to be effective in preventing deviations in doing Qigong exercise. It was thus grouped as one of the Qigong exercises, the Relaxing Qigong, and taken for the essential step of learning and practising Qigong.

From then on, many hospitals and convalescent institutions in China began to include Qigong in clinical treatment. They discovered more Qigong styles and applied them to the treatment of more ailments. The Tangshan Qigong Sanatorium, Xingcheng Sanatorium, Beijing Xiaotangsham Sanatorium, Tianjin Worker's Sanatorium and Gansu Workers' Sanatorium all achieved good results in applying Qigong to the treatment of peptic ulcers, tuberculosis, chronic hepatitis, etc.

In August 1959, the Ministry of Public Health authorized the City Party Committee of Qinhuangdao to hold a meeting for exchange of Qigong experiences in Beidaihe, with 64 units (including 9 medical colleges and institutions) from 17 provinces, cities and autonomous regions taking part. There they exchanged experience, introduced their successful application of Qigong in the treatment of various ailments, such as peptic ulcers, neurasthenia, gastroptosis, tuberculosis, chronic hepatitis, silicosis, rheumatoid heart disease, bronchial asthma, hypertension, low blood pressure, diabetes, nephritis, postgastrectomy dumping syndrome, topple over after gastrectomy, chronic colonitis, chronic cholecystitis, liver cirrhosis at an early stage, sequelae of schizophrenia, impotence, ankylosing spondylitis, radioactive reaction, thrombocytopenic purpura due to radioactive disorders, pulselessness, prolapse of gastric mucosa, etc. This meeting helped Qigong therapy to go forward. Qigong training courses were started in succession in Tangshan, Beidaihe, Shanghai, Tianjin and other cities. In 1960, the Ministry of Public Health entrusted Shanghai with the work of conducting a course for training Qigong teachers who left their regular work for a short time study. 39 persons from different parts of the country received the training, making preparation for an all-out development of the therapeutic Qigong exercise. According to an incomplete statistics, 86 institutions in Shanghai started Qigong training, and the data from 45 institutions revealed that Qigong was used as a basic cure in treating more than 50 ailments such as hypertension, tuberculosis, ulcer, glaucoma, toxemia of pregnancy, essential uterine haemorrhage, chronic pelvic infection, rheumatism and cancer, etc. 20 cases of acute appendicitis were prescribed with therapeutic Qigong exercise. All this shows that Qigong has proved to be a cure of acute diseases as well as chronic ones, a cure of organic pathological changes as well as functional disturbances.

Beginning in 1978, research of application of Qigong to clinical treatment was started and observation of the therapeutic Qigong exercise was carried out in Shanghai, Beijing and other cities. It is noteworthy that the Traditional Medical College of Shanghai, the Shanghai Traditional Medical Research Institute and the Atomic Nucleus Research Institute of Chinese Academy of Science came to cooperate in testing the External Qi emitted by Qigong performers with the help of modern scientific instruments. They discovered that the Qi (vital energy) emitted through exercising Qigong is material. This marks a new stage in the scientific research of Qigong, changing it into a science, and making it a new subject in the exploration of life process. In July 1979, a meeting on Qigong practice was held in Beijing by the National Science Commission, the National Physical Culture and Sports Commission, the Ministry of Public Health, the Chinese Academy of Science, the Chinese Association of Sciences, and other organizations. The meeting attracted the attention of the circles of medicine, science and technology, and the press; and greatly promoted the popularization and scientific research of Qigong. Later in Beijing, Qingdao, Zhangjiakou, Guangzhou, Shanghai and some other cities, scientific workers imitated Qigong masters emitting a kind of far infrared ray radiation by means of bionics. Meanwhile they made an instrument, a receiver of Qigong infrared ray and successfully applied it to clinical treatment. In recent years, reports on Qigong researches have proved that the science of Qigong benefits people in understanding the fundamental principles of the Chinese traditional medicine (such as the main and collateral channels, vital energy and blood, etc.), medical and health care, health protection of the aged, physical culture and sports, the functioning of human body, and so on. The popularization of various styles of Qigong exercise is really inspiring. On September 12, 1981 the Qigong Scientific Research Society of the Chinese National Association of Traditional Medicine (abbreviated as The Chinese

18

Qigong Scientific Research Society) was established. For the first time the Qigong circles have had a national leading organization, which is bound to play a leading role in organizing and spreading Qigong clinical practice and scientific experiments in the days to come.

11. Why Is Qigong Regarded As A Therapeutic Exercise of the Chinese Tradition?

Qigong has a long history in China. According to textual research there were already records on Qigong (though not called Qigong then) in the inscriptions on bronze objects from the Zhou Dynasty (11th century B.C. — 77 B.C.). The cultural relic, a jade column with twelve phases from the early Warring States Period had the inscription of the principles and forms of Qigong practice. The earliest medical classic available in China *Medical Canon of Huang Emperor* included descriptions of Qigong as well. More details on Qigong were recorded during the later dynasties.

In China, Qigong has a firm rooting in the folks. From the ancient time till today, hundreds and thousands of people have taken part in the exercise and through which they found their power of preventing and curing illness enhanced, physical conditions improved and health built up.

The Chinese Qigong is varied in style and abundant in exercising form. There are lying form, sitting form, standing form and walking form. They can be exercised in motion, in stillness and in motion and stillness alternately.

Qigong is different from other sports in the way that it demands no strenuous exercise of the body in a short time, but requires slow regulation of the physiological functioning of the body by conscious application of the principles.

Qigong exercise demands one to lay emphasis on internal movement. In other word, it is the regulation of the functional movements inside the body and the cultivation of vital essence, vital energy and vital spirit that count.

In the treatment of ailments, Qigong is based on the traditional Chinese medicine. In the light of the theories of Yin Yang (The two opposite aspects in nature), and Xu Shi (deficiency and excess), and the treatises of Qi Xue (vital energy and blood), and Jing Luo (main and collateral channels), Qigong is applied to diagnosis and treatment of diseases on an overall analysis of the patients' conditions. For instance, for Yang Xu (deficiency of Yang), the patient is required to think of a certain acupoint; for Yin Xu (deficiency of Yin), the patient should shift his/her attention repeatedly between two or more acupoints. A patient suffering from high blood pressure is required to concentrate on the point of Yongquan, while the one suffering from low blood pressure on the point of Baihui. In short, Qigong is prescribed selectively according to the seriousness of a disease, the different phenomena of different cases, different conditions of the same disease, the varying stages of a disease of the same patient, etc. Qigong exercise has to suit the patient conditions, to be practised in different forms and with definite purposes. There is no doubt that Qigong is among the treasure of the traditional Chinese medicine inherited from the ancestors and is a therapeutic exercise of Chinese tradition.

12. Why Were There Ups and Downs in the Development of Qigong?

Qigong has a history of thousands of years, abundant in content and varying with different schools. It is firmly rooted in the folks and has become a science for preventing and treating diseases and building up health. But why did it undergo high tides as well as low ebbs in its development? In the authors' opinion, there are several reasons.

(1) The Qi(vital energy) of Qigong is something that can neither be seen nor be felt. Those who practise Qigong may have the feelings of tingling, soreness, swelling, warming up and the like, but most people consider it to be elusive and mysterious, and are hesitating to accept

it as an effective means of preventing and curing disease and improving health.

(2) Different schools practice different forms of Qigong. There were Toaist school, Buddhist school, Confucianist school and others. They had contributed to its popularization and health preservation, but mixed in it with such superstitious elements as immortality, mastering the essence and entering the Heaven, meeting ghosts and gods, and so on. All this puzzles people greatly.

(3) As Qigong is an exercise of improving health and curing disease, some traveling swindlers made use of it to bluff and swindle by giving demonstrations of hard Qigong, or to defraud people of their money by selling spurious medicine. As a result, they ruined the reputation of Qigong.

(4) Schools and sects stood in great number. They were conservative of their own styles while excluding and attacking others. As a result, all of them suffered.

(5) Some people were eager to attain quick results and impatient for success. They neglected the essentials and failed to follow the principles and points for attention in practice. When deviations occurred, they became sceptical and half-hearted.

(6) Although Qigong can help to prevent and cure disease and improve health, in publicity it was exaggerated as "all-powerful", "curing every ailment", and the like. Not only is this unfavorable to its popularization, but places people under bad impression and makes them take an aversion to it.

(7) Some leading cadres always had a prejudice against Qigong, regarding it as a trade of itinerant entertainers with neither learning nor scientific foundation. During the "ten chaotic years", Qigong was further reduced to superstitious activities and totally repudiated. As a result, very few people kept on practising Qigong exercise.

Now people's views of Qigong have changed and more people have come to realize the curative effects of this exercise. It is believed that with people's experiences continually summarized, sorted out and raised to higher levels, the therapeutic Qigong exercise will enjoy greater popularity.

13. What Is Meant by "Qi" in Qigong?

Qi (vital energy) is something by which the ancient people understood the phenomena of nature. They considered Qi to be the essential substance forming the world and though its movement and change to be the cause of things coming into existence in the universe. In the light of this viewpoint, medical workers tend to think that Qi is the fundamental substance to constitute the human body and that its movement and change account for the activities of life. It is mentioned in *The Whole Volume of Jing Yue*," Human life solely depends on Qi"; and also in *The Law of Medicine*, "A thing takes shape when Qi accumulates, and the thing dies out when Qi dissipates."

Qigong is the way for cultivating Qi inside human body. The Qi inside the body is referred to in different terms such as Zhen Qi, Yuan Qi, Zheng Qi, Jing Qi and Qi of Zhen Yuan.

Zhen Qi consists of the essence in kidney (essence inherited from the parents), the essence of water and grain absorbed and transformed by spleen and stomach (nourishment taken in and transformed) and the air inhaled through the lungs. Qi is a sort of delicate and vigorous substance circulating around and permeating every part of the body. Its movement is referred to in the traditional medical classics as the mechanism of Qi, manifesting itself in the forms of moving upward, downward, outward and inward. The viscera, main and collateral channels and other body organs are places where Zhen Qi comes and goes. It can be said that Zhen Qi flows here and there inside the body, exhibiting the physiological activities of different body organs, and thus referred to by different terms:

Visceral Qi: The Qi present in the viscera is called visceral Qi, including the Qi of the heart, the lungs, the spleen, the stomach, the liver and the kidney.

The Qi of channels: Zhen Qi circulating in the main and collateral channels is referred to as the Qi of channels, abbreviated as Jing Qi in Chinese.

Ying Qi: The Qi circulating in blood vessels is called Ying Qi.

Wei Qi (the Defense Principle): Wei Qi circulates outside vascular tissue of the body. It is of violent and agile nature, not kept in vascular vessels but circulating freely outside them.

Zong Qi: Zong Qi is the Qi stored in the thorax.

The circulation and distribution of Qi manifests its functioning in five aspects:

Motivating function: It is the Qi that stimulates and promotes the growth and development of human body, the physiological and biochemical activities of viscera and channels, the circulation of blood, and the conveyance and distribution of body fluid. Deficiency of Qi will weaken its motivating force, slow down the growth and development of the body and reduce the functioning of the viscera and channels. And what is more, pathological changes such as stagnation of blood or fluid will take place.

Warming up function: Normally Qi acts to regulate and maintain body temperature. If it fails to do so, you will fear cold and your limbs won't warm up.

Protective function: Qi can protect the body against invasion of external pathologic factors. *Su Wen: On Heat Diseases* mentioned, "Presence of external pathologic factors leads to deficiency of Qi." Here the Qi refers to its protective function. When this function weakens, certain pathogens will invade the body and cause diseases. In that case, Zhen Qi (the vital energy) will act against and eliminate the pathogens and restore one's health.

Astringent function: Qi acts as astringent which helps to control blood and prevent it from overflowing blood vessels; to control sweat and urine and make the discharge moderate; to control seminal fluid and prevent emission, etc. The motivating function and astringent function of Qi are in contradiction as well as in harmony with each other. For example, Qi functions to stimulate and at the same time check the flow of blood so as to normalize its circulation. Deficiency of Qi will weaken its force and slow down the flow of blood, resulting in blood stasis. Meanwhile, deficiency of Qi will reduce its astringent function and lead to bleeding.

Transformation of Qi: it is believed that Qi can be transformed into essense or fluid, or blood, and vice versa. *Sun Wen: On the Theory of Yin-Yang* says, "Essence turns into Qi." Wang Bing interpreted this statement, saying, "Transformation of Qi promotes the increase of essence, and moderation of tastes promote growth of body organs," referring to the mutual promotion of transformation and growth of essence and Qi. In another sense, it denotes the functional activities of the viscera. *Su Wen: On The Secret of Ling Lan* says, "Bladder is the chief organ where fluid stores. Its activity causes discharge." Here the activity of the bladder means its function of discharging urine.

The above-mentioned functions are different but cooperative in their activities.

In short, Qigong exercise aims at cultivating Qi. In one sense, it is the fine substance that constitutes the human body and maintains life activities. In another sense, it means the physiological functioning of the viscera. The two aspects are related to each other. Therefore, it is said in the traditional medical classics that Qi is the essential substance that maintains the activities of human life. Qigong exercise of cultivating Qi is taken as an important means of preventing and curing disease. The cultivation of Zhen Qi (vital energy) contributes a great deal to human health.

14. What Is the Relationship between Qi and Blood?

Qi and blood are substances essential for life activities of human body. They are separable but closely related through interdependence and interaction.

Qi as the commander of blood:

Blood contains nutrients derived from liquid and grain by spleen and stomach and combined with pulmonary Qi. Blood is led by Qi to circulate through the blood vessels. The heart controlling blood circulation, the liver storing blood, and the spleen regulating blood all result from the activities of the visceral Qi. Apparently, blood depends on Qi in its formation and circulation. Qi helps to produce and regulate blood and stimulate its circulation. That is why Qi is said to be the commander of blood.

Blood is the mother of Qi:

"The flow of Qi brings along the flow of blood."

The statement means it is the Qi that stimulates and leads blood circulation as a commander leads his army. On the other hand, Qi must rely on blood for sufficient nutrients to develop its function of promoting physiological activities of the body organs.

Mutual Dependence of Qi and Blood:

Qi and blood are interdependent. They rely on each other and jointly constitute the essential substances for life activities of human body. *Canon of Difficult Questions: The Twenty-second Difficult Question* says, "Qi gives warmth while blood gives moisture." They act on each other in continuous circulation through the body in the process of metabolism, in the growth, development, physiological activities and life activities of the body. The ancient people said, "Stagnation of Qi or blood results in disease while free circulation of Qi and blood cures the disease." "Disturbance of the relationship between Qi and blood induces pathologic changes." All this denotes the close relationship between Qi and blood and their important role in life activities of the body.

15. What Is the Viscera?
What Is the Relationship between Qi and the Viscera?

The traditional medical theory on the viscera is called the visceral Manifestation Theory. According to the theory, the word viscera is a general term for the five parenchymatous viscera: heart, liver, spleen, lungs and kidney; and the six hollow viscera: gallbladder, stomach, small intestine, large intestine, urinary bladder and the Triple Heater. It is the five parenchymatous viscera that derive and store essential materials, and it is the six hollow viscera that decompose liquid and grain, and to transform the dross. In *Su Wen: On Five Viscera* it is mentioned that "The five parenchymatous viscera with essential materials stored are full but not substantial. The six hollow viscera with materials transformed but not kept are substantial but not full." This is how the five parenchymatous viscera and the six hollow viscera differ in their physiological functioning.

The functioning of the viscera depends on the visceral Qi, which is so called when Zhen Qi (the vital energy) goes to the viscera through the main and collateral channels and produces effects. Insufficiency of Zhen Qi results in the impairment of visceral Qi and weakens its functioning. For example, if one lacks cardiac Qi he feels restless with the symptoms of anxiety, palpitation, insomnia and dreaminess. If the case is serious, there appear the symptoms of lethargic sleep, coma, dementia, delirium, restlessness and the like. Deficiency of cardiac Qi results in blood stasis with the symptoms of pallor, cold limbs, dizziness, weariness, shortness of breath, profuse sweat, etc. Deficiency of the pulmonary Qi causes impairment of the pulmonary functioning and affects the growth of Zhen Qi (the vital energy), resulting in the deficiency of Qi of the whole body, accompanied by weariness, shortness of breath, and perspiration. Disturbance of the pulmonary Qi in regulation of water-flow of the lungs results in stop-up of the muscle and skin and no sweating. Upward reverse flow of pulmonary Qi results in edema, dysuria and little urine. Concerning the splenic and stomach Qi, Ye Tian-shi of the Qing Dynasty said, "The stomach is concerned with reception and the spleen with transmission and digestion. It is normal for the splenic Qi to ascend and the stomach Qi to descend."

The splenic Qi ascends, transporting nutrients (the essence derived from water and grain) upward to the heart and lungs. The stomach Qi propels downward, sending the chyme to the intestines. Failure in sending nutrients upward affects sending the chyme downward, and vice versa. As a result, there appear symptoms of anorexia, abdominal distension, nausea, belching, indigestion, diarrhea, glossy coating of tongue, and the like. In short, deficiency of visceral Qi puts the viscera out of normal functioning and induce various pathological changes. To reinforce the visceral Qi, you must first strengthen the accumulation, circulation and storage of Zhen Qi, Qigong exercise can help achieve this purpose.

16. What Is Yin-Yang?
What Is the Relationship between Qi and Yin-Yang?

Yin and Yang are general terms used by the ancient people for two opposite aspects of matters and phenomena in nature. In the usual sense, matters and phenomena, which are dynamic, external, upward, ascending, warm, brilliant, hyperactive, or pertaining to functional activities, belong to the category of Yang. Those which are static, internal, downward, cold, dull, hypoactive, belong to that of Yin.

In the light of the Yin Yang theory, the constituent parts of human body are also included in these two categories. The upper part, the exterior of the body, the back of the exterior, the outer sides and the six hollow viscera belong to the category of Yang. The lower part, the interior of the body, the abdomen, the inner sides and the five parenchymatous viscera belong to that of Yin. In *Su Wen: On Cherished Life and Whole Figure* it is said that "The complexity of the human anatomy represents exclusively by Yin and Yang."

The Yin-Yang theory has much to do with Qi in its explanation of pathological changes. According to the theory, a disease results when

Yin and Yang loses their relative balance due to excess or deficiency of one aspect or the other. The occurrence and growth of a disease is closely related with the vital principle and the pathogenic factor. The defensive factor of the body and the external pathogenic factor, and their interaction and mutual struggle can be explained with Yin Yang theory. The pathogenic factor includes the Yin pathogens and the Yang pathogens while Zhen Qi (the vital energy) includes the Yin essence and the Yang principle. The Yang pathogens will cause pathologic changes in which excess of Yang results in impairment of Yin, and heat manifestations are predominant. The Yin pathogens lead to pathologic changes in which the excess of Yin causes impairment of Yang, and cold manifestations are predominant. Deficiency of Yang principle leads to excess of Yin with manifestations of weak and cold. Insubstantial Yin Liquid leads to a relative excess of the Yang Principle, with pathologic manifestations of weak and heat. Complex and varied as the pathologic changes are, they exhibit the results of disharmony of Yin and Yang. "Predominant Yin produces cold while excessive Yang produces heat. Deficiency of Yang results in cold while deficiency of Yin induces heat."

In medical diagnosis, insufficiency of Yang principle causes Yin diseases, while insufficiency of Yin principle causes Yang diseases. Yang diseases involve exterior, heat and excess symptoms while Yin diseases involve interior, cold and deficiency symptoms. In diagnosing a disease, you must first distinguish primordial Qi from evil Qi, and Yin from Yang. For example, in inspection of the patient's facial complexion, bright color belongs to Yang while dull color to Yin. In auscultation and olfaction, loud voice belongs to Yang, while low and weak voice to Yin. In palpation and feeling pulse, superficial, rapid, slippery and substantive pulses belong to Yang while deep, slow, irregular and deficient pulses to Yin.

Disharmony of Yin and Yang will lead to pathologic changes. In case Yang pathogens cause diseases with manifestations of heat syndrome and excess syndrome, take care to direct the Qi downward in practising Qigong, or prescribe purgation. If Yin pathogens cause the disease with the manifestations of cold syndrome or deficiency syndrome, direct the Qi upward through Dantian when practising Qigong, or prescribe tonification. Hence Qigong practice not only helps to reinforce body resistance and eliminate pathogens, but also restores the balance of Yin and Yang and improve health.

17. What Is Sanjiao? What Is the Relationship between Sanjiao and Qi?

Sanjiao (the Triple Heater) is one of the Six Hollow Viscera and the largest of the twelve viscera in human body. It is thus called the Solitary Hollow Viscus. As is described in *Lei Jing*, "The Triple Heater is a general term for the Upper Heater, the Middle Heater and the Lower Heater. The notion of the three heaters now commonly used is somewhat different from the original idea of the Triple Heater as one of the six hollow viscera. Presently, the upper, middle and lower heaters are mainly used to mean the sections of the body cavity. That is, the segment above the diaphragm, including the heart and lungs, belongs to the Upper Heater; that between the diaphragm and umbilicus, including the stomach and spleen, belongs to the Middle Heater; and that below the umbilicus including the liver, kidneys, small and large intestines and bladder, belongs to the Lower Heater.

The Triple Heater controls the functional activities of the viscera and tissues and commands the activities or the mechanism of Qi (vital energy) of human body. It serves as a passage for Yuan Qi (the primordial principle) and water and grain. Yuan Qi rises in the kidneys and permeates the entire body by way of the Triple Heater, so as to stimulate and promote the functional activities of the viscera and tissues and organs. *Canon of Difficult Questions: The Thirty-eighth Difficult Question* says, "The Triple Heater is the passage of Yuan Qi, and is in command of other Qi." In the Sixty-sixth Difficult Question it is said that "The Triple Heater is the passage of Yuan Qi and governs 3 Qi, and runs through the five parenchymatous viscera and the six hollow viscera." Yuan Qi circulates freely throughout the body by way of the Triple Heater, that is, by way of the Upper, Middle and Lower Heaters and the Viscera. All the way through, it promotes their functional activities of digestion, assimilation, distribution and discharge of food, drink, water and grain. The Upper Heater (the heart and lungs) transmits and distributes nutrients of the grain and water to all parts of the body, to warm and nourish the muscle, skin and tendon, and to reinforce the juncture between muscle and skin. *Ling Shu: On Nutrition* mentioned, "The Upper Heater is like mist and fog," describing the state of the fine nutrients of the water and grain spreading evenly like mist and fog. The Middle Heater governs digestion of water and grain. That is, food and drink are digested, absorbed and transformed into nutrients and blood chiefly by the Middle Heater (spleen and stomach). In *Ling Shu: On Nutrition* it is mentioned that "The Middle Heater is concerned with maceration," vividly describing the characteristics, of which food is digested, decomposed and fermented. The Lower Heater is concerned with discharge, excreting unwanted liquid and food residues. This refers to the excretion of urine and stool through the functioning of the kidneys, bladder and intestines. In *Ling Shu: On Nutrition* it is mentioned that "The Lower Heater acts as the drain," describing the continual discharge of unwanted water like the functioning of a drainage system. The Triple Heater is the passage for transmitting water and grain. It is through the Triple Heater that Yuan Qi (the vital energy) circulates freely and the Heater is thus in a position to govern the activities of Qi and the functional activities of the viscera.

To sum up, the Triple Heater has the function of clearing up water passages and keeping Yuan Qi, water and grain flowing freely. Therefore, cultivation of Qi in Qigong exercise has much to do with the Triple Heater.

18. What Is Jing Luo?
What Is the Relationship between Qi and Jing Luo?

Jing Luo (main and collateral channels) are the passages through which Qi (vital energy), blood and fluid circulate, correlating and reaching all parts of the body. In *Canon of Difficult Questions* it is said that "Jing Luo harmonizes blood and Qi, regulates Yin and Yang, and is helpful to physical health." The main and collateral channels correlate and connect various viscera, organs, apertures, skin and hair, muscles and bones, making the body an organic whole.

Jing Luo is composed of Jing Mai (the channels) and Luo Mai (the collateral channels). Jing Mai is the trunk lines of the Jing Luo system which lead to the deep parts of the body along definite channels. Luo Mai is the branches of the channels. In *Access To Medicine* it is mentioned that "Jing means channels, and their branches are referred to as collateral channels." Jing Mai, the channels are classified into Zhen Jing (the Regular Channels) and Qi Jing (the Extra Channels). The Regular Channels include: the lung channels of hand-Taiyin, the large intestine channel of hand-Yangming, the stomach channel of foot-Yangming, the spleen channel of foot-Taiyin, the heart channel of hand-Shaoyin, the small intestine channel of hand-Taiyang, the urinary bladder channel of foot-Taiyang, the kidney channel of foot-Shaoyin, the pericardium channel of hand-Jueyin, the sanjiao channel of hand-Shaoyang, the gall-bladder channel of foot-Shaoyang, and the liver channel of foot-Jueyin, twelve in all. The extra channels include: Renmai (the anterior midline channel), Dumai (the posterior midline channel), Chongmai (the straiegic channel), Daimai (the girdle channel), Yinqiaomai (the motility channel of Yin), Yang-qiaomai (the motility channel of Yang), Yinweimai (the regulating channel of Yin) and Yangweimai (the regulating channel of Yang), all together eight extra channels. Among the collateral channels, the larger branches are called

Bie Luo, the minute branches are called Sun Luo and those located superficially on the skin are called Fu Luo (the floating collateral channels). The Qi circulating along the channels is generally referred to as the channel Qi, which manifests the reaction and conduction of the channels. During acupuncture, the "Needling sensation" is a manifestation of the channel Qi.

The external pathogenic factors invade the human body usually by way of the channels and collateral channels through the skin into the viscera. In *Su Wen: On Miu Ci* it is said, "Pathogenic factors invading the body first stay on the skin and hair, then get into the minute branches of the collateral channels, and further into the collateral channels and again into the channels leading to the five parenchymatous viscera, and disperse in the stomach. With excess of Yin and Yang, the viscera is injured. It is through the skin that evils get in and do harm to the viscera." The description makes it clear that Qi is closely related to the Jing Luo System. The channel Qi circulates along the main and collateral channels which in turn serve as the main passage for the circulation of Qi.

The Qigong exercise to promote free circulation of Qi in the twelve channels is called Large Zhou Tian Circulating Exercise. The exercise to promote free circulation of Qi in Renmai and Dumai is called Small Zhou Tian Circulating Exercise. To lead the Qi to flow from Dantian throughout the whole body along the channels and collaterals is called Dantian Circulating Exercise. Varied as the methods are, Qigong practice is aimed at clearing up the channels and collaterals, harmonizing Qi and blood and building up health. Channels and collaterals are the passages for Qi and blood. They serve to circulate Qi and blood, connect Yin and Yang, nourish the viscera and actuate the joints, playing an important role in the activities of life.

19. What Is Meant by Seven Emotions? What Is the Relationship between Qi and

Seven Emotions?

The Seven Emotions is a term for man's emotional reactions. In traditional Chinese medicine the emotional reactions are included in seven groups, i.e., joy, anger, anxiety, worry, grief, apprehension and fright. Usually they are within the scope of physiological activities which are unlikely to cause disease. However, long term mental disorder or sudden and intense emotional shock may cause the emotions to exceed the normal limit of physiological regulation. Emotional disturbances may cause imbalance of Yin and Yang, disharmony of the viscera and Qi and blood, which is called Internal Injury in the traditional Chinese medicine. The Seven Emotions have much to do with Qi. The abnormal changes of the Seven Emotions will injure the viscera, that is, the mechanism of Qi will be affected and the functional activities of Qi and blood disturbed. Abnormal functioning of the viscera manifests itself as follows: Anger arousing ascent of Qi, Joy inducing sluggishness of Qi, Excessive sorrow dissipating Qi, Fear causing descent of Qi, Fright causing disturbances of Qi and Worry causing stagnation of Qi.

By anger arousing ascent of Qi it is meant that in great anger, the Hepatic Qi flows abnormally upward, and brings along the blood up as well, hiding clear apertures and resulting in fainting. Overjoy or overexcitement would adversely induce sluggishness of Qi and absentmindedness. Hence, Joy inducing sluggishness of Qi. Excessive sorrow leads to demoralization, as well as dissipation and loss of the Pulmonary Qi. Hence, Excessive sorrow dissipating Qi. Excessive fear may cause instability and descent of the Renal Qi, with the symptom of fecal or urinary incontinence. This is known as that fear causes descent of Qi. Sudden fright results in restlessness, mental confusion and bewilderment, this means that fright causes disturbances of Qi. Excessive Worry and over anxiety may suppress the splenic and stomach functions, causing disturbance of transmission and digestion. Hence, worry causes stagnation of Qi. In short, seven emotions are closely related with Qi. To prevent disturbance and injury of the Seven Emotions and preserve health, one must be optimistic, broadminded and free from selfish ideas. As to the effect of optimism, it was mentioned in *Canon of Placidity* "Happy mood helps enhance the harmony of Yin and Yang." Qigong exercise helps one to quiet mental activities, expel personal considerations and relieve worries. It is an important means to remove the Seven Emotions and bring health.

20. What Is Meant by Six Excesses? What Is the Relationship between Qi and Six Excesses?

Six Excesses refer to Six abnormal climates, viz., wind, cold, summer-heat, dampness, dryness and fire, or normally known as Six Qi which refers to six kinds of changes in climate. Through practice in life people come to know the feature of climate changes and have adapted to them. The six Qi is not the cause of disease in normal condition. Only when climate changes abruptly or body resistance declines does six Qi become pathogenic factor and cause disease. In that case, six Qi turn into Six Excesses. The Chinese word Yin (Excess) means too much. As six excesses are abnormal, they are sometimes referred to as Six Evils. They are the pathogenic factors likely to cause external affections.

Six Excesses causing diseases are noted for the following features:

They are related to the changes of seasons and environments. Causes of most diseases may be traced to wind in spring, heat in summer, dampness in long summer or early autumn, or damp environment, dryness in late autumn, and cold in winter.

Six Excesses act on human body either singly or collectively (two or more pathogenic factors act simultaneously), causing diseases with wind-and-cold syndrome, downward flow of damp and heat, and damp blockage of wind and cold.

In the process of a disease, Six Excesses can influence each other or transform into each other under certain conditions. For instance, cold pathogens getting into the interior of the body will induce fire and long time summer dampness will induce dryness and injure Yin.

Six Excesses invade the body usually by way of muscle and skin, or mouth and nose, causing external affections.

The occurrence, development and change of a disease are related to the patient's physique and the nature of the pathogenic factors. Six Excesses refer to the pathogenic factors of wind, cold, summer-heat, dampness, dryness and fire. When they invade human body, they encounter the body resistance. The traditional Chinese medicine regards this phenomenon as "the struggle between the Primordial Qi and the Evil Qi", and holds that the symptoms of external infections such as fear of cold, fever, shivering and sweating are the reactions of this struggle. The development of a disease depends on the change of the relative strength of both sides and their struggle. That is, when the Primordial Qi wins and the Evil Qi withdraws, the disease cures; when the Evil Qi flourishes and the Primordial Qi declines the disease grows serious.

Qigong exercise helps to reinforce body resistance against pathogens. It strengthens people's power to resist exteral pathogenic factors. That is why Qigong is an important method for physical fitness and cure of disease.

21. What Is Meant by Jing, Qi and Shen? What Is the Relationship between the Three?

Jing (Vital Essence), Qi (Vital Energy) and Shen (Vital Spirit) are fundamental materials to maintain life activities. The ancient people said, "Heaven has three gems — the sun, the moon and the star. Man has three gems — the Essence, the Energy and the Spirit."

The Vital Essence is the essential material in human body. In a broad sense, it refers to the fundamental material to constitute human body including that of the viscera. In a narrow sense, it refers to the Essence of reproduction. Essence is either congenital or acquired. The congenital essence is inherited from parents. *Ling Shu: Jing Mai* says, "Birth of man begins with Essence." The acquired Essence comes from transformation of food and drink. *Su Wen: On Jing Mai* says, "Food goes into the stomach ... transforms in Mai, ... goes into the stomach, and becomes essence." This is the acquired Essence. The Congenital Essence and the Acquired Essence supplement each other.

The Essence plays an important role in human body. The ancient people said, "Man is born with Energy and dies of exhaustion of Essence."

Vital Energy is the fundamental material to constitute human body and maintain activities of life. It includes Yuan Qi (the Vital Energy, or called Zhen Qi), Visceral Qi, the Qi of main and collateral channels, Zong Qi, Ying Qi, and Wei Qi, etc. Its importance is mentioned in *Complete Volume of Jing Yue*, "Man's life depends on vital energy."

Vital Spirit is another substance, a production of Essence and Energy. *Canon of Ling Shu* says, "The struggle of two Essences is called Spirit." In one of the chapters it is mentioned that "Spirit is the essence of water and grain." *Canon of Da Ping* says, "Man has spirit when he has energy. The spirit dies when energy exhausts." Vital spirit is generally considered to be a sort of mental activity, but regarded as an essential material for human life in traditional Chinese medicine. *Ling Shu: Change Essence Into Energy* says, "Things flourish with Spirit but die without it." That is why Qigong practice lays emphasis on cultivating, examining and keeping spirit.

Then, what is the relationship between the Essence, the Energy and the Spirit? In *Su Wen* it is said that "Energy is born in Essence and Spirit in Energy.," In *Canon of Lei* it is said, "Fullness of Essence results in the fullness of Energy. Fullness of Energy results in fullness of Spirit." In the light of this theory the Qigong masters in ancient times put forward the idea, "Cultivate Essence to attain Energy. Cultivate

Energy to attain Spirit. Cultivate Spirit to return to void," and "Accumulate spirit to produce energy and accumulate energy to produce essence." Qigong is an important method for cultivating essence, producing energy, keeping spirit and improving health.

RESEARCH ON QIGONG PRINCIPLES

22. Why Can Qigong Make One Healthy?

Qigong exercise is actually the training of Zhen Qi, cultivating of Yuan Qi, and developing of Zheng Qi. That's why it can build up vitality and ward off evils, and thus strengthen the body's immunity and resistance against pathogens. Qigong exercise requires one to relax, to be calm, natural and free from distractions, so that it can remove "stress", and dispel tension. Qigong exercise helps to keep the main and collateral channels in good shape to establish harmony between vital energy and blood, to balance between Yin and Yang, and improve coordination of the nervous system, so that protective inhibition of the cerebral cortex can be enhanced. Qigong exercise helps to reduce fundamental metabolism, increase the capacity of storing energy, apply massage to the abdomen and improve appetite and brings good digestion. Qigong exercise helps to tap the body potentialities, stimulate positive factors, and enhance one's self-control. Therefore, with no need of either medicine or injection and only by training the body and mind, Qigong exercise becomes a very effective measure to prevent and cure diseases and attain health and longevity.

23. Why Can Qigong Develop Resistance to Diseases and Eliminate Pathogens?

Some people are easily affected by influenza but others are not. Some people suffer from enterogastritis because of unhealthy food but others do not, why? Those who often go for Qigong exercise or sports have healthy complexion and strong body, fear neither cold in winter nor heat in summer, and seldom fall ill, why? Those who rarely take part in sports fear both cold and heat and are liable to diseases, why? Traditional Chinese medicine explains diseases in the light of the theory that Zheng Qi (the body resistance) is the primary aspect. "Pathogens dominate where the body resistance declines." "Pathogens fail to work where the body resistance grows." (Zheng Qi refers to body resistance against disease. Xue Qi refers to various pathogens.) The occurrence of a disease depends not only on pathogens, but on one's body resistance and health. Qigong exercise is effective for preventing and curing disease simply because it helps strengthen physique, cultivate Zhen Qi (or Yuan Qi, the vital energy), and reinforce Zheng Qi (the body resistance or vital principle) against pathogens.

External infections are caused by external pathogenic factors, namely, wind, cold, summer-heat, dampness, dryness and fire. When they invade human body they encounter the resistance of Zheng Qi (vital principle) leading to a struggle between the two parties. In traditional Chinese medicine, it is called "the struggle between the vital principle and the pathogens." Normally the primary aspect of the contradiction is the body's Zheng Qi (vital principle) of which the defensive elements gradually overcome the pathogens, and the disease is cured. However, under certain conditions, the defensive elements of Zheng Qi (vital principle) fails to resist the invasion of the pathogens, and the struggle develops in a direction unfavorable for health. The disease turns for the worse or even leads to death. Therefore, changes of disease depend virtually on the relatively varying strength of the vital principle and pathogens and the development of the struggle between them. That is, when the vital principle dominates, the pathogens retreat, and the disease cures. When the pathogens flourish, the vital principle declines and the disease grows worse. Qigong exercise helps to foster Zhen Qi and develop Zheng Qi, so as to prevent disease before it occurs and to enhance one's immunity. If a disease does occur, Qigong exercise helps Zhen Qi to develop and pathogens to decline so as to restore health. In short, the purpose of Qigong exercise is mainly to eliminate pathogenic factors through reinforcing Zhen Qi (the vital energy).

24. Why Can Qigong Help Relaxation and Removal of Tension?

Qigong exercise demands conscious relaxation, calmness and freedom from distractions in the course of practice. This helps keep the doer relaxed and free from nervousness. Great amount of evidence from both home and abroad has proved that one's health is closely related to his mental activity. During the ten chaotic years in China, many people suffered or died as a result of excessive strain in the mind. More than two thousand years ago, our ancestors had noticed this problem. It is said in *Medical Canon of Huang Emperor* that "Anger, injuring liver; great joy, injuring the heart; worry, injuring the spleen; sorrow, injuring the lungs, and fear, injuring the kidneys." Scientific experiments have also proved that "reaction to excitement" results in an increase of adrenaline secretion, speed-up of respiration and heartbeat, rise of blood pressure and increase in blood sugar. Qigong exercise will do the reverse. According to American researchers, practising Qigong makes one enter a state of relaxation response, which lessens the behavior of the sympathetic nerves. Stone and Drewe have advanced the research and pointed out: Practising Qigong helps decline of activation of plasma dopamine β-hydroxylase and reduce the behavior of renin. This shows that a change in the secretion system of angiotensin takes place and leads to relief of tension of blood vessels and fall of blood pressure. Qigong exercise also causes changes of the central nervous transmitter and endocrine system. According to reports from Maharishi European Research Institute in Switzerland: The serotonin metabolism of Qigong performers is 2-3 times higher than the ordinary people, and the concentration of prolactin in plasma rises. This means that as the transmitter of the central nerve, the dopamine behavior is lowered. That is why after Qigong exercise, one feels relaxed, peaceful and free from nervousness. Qigong exercise helps remove emotional disturbances, reduce reactions to external stimuli so that the physiological and biochemical activities are kept in the best state, the cerebral cortex is relieved of its stress reaction, providing favorable conditions for rest, restoration and regulation of one's organism and thus bringing in health.

25. Why Can Qigong Keep the Channels in Good Shape and Keep Qi and Blood in Harmony?

It is said in *Ling Shu: Jing Mai*, "Channels are decisive to both death and living, and to hundreds of diseases. They control insubstantiality and substantiality, and thus must be kept in good shape. In *Study of Eight Extra Channels* Li Shi-zhen said, "Only those who observe the channels inside with mind's eye (sitting in quiet meditation) can see them clearly," which means practising Qigong is closely related to the channels. The performers often have the feelings of soreness, swelling, tingling at hand or foot or somewhere in the body; or feel a warm stream moving along the route of channels. These feelings take place either at a certain point, or a certain section, or along a certain channel; mostly moving in Renmai (the anterior midline channel) and Dumai (the posterior midline channel), or in any of the eight extra channels, esp. in Daimai. These feelings of sensations experienced by the doer are similar to radiation of the needling sensation experienced by a patient. This is referred to as "Internal Qi" in Qigong. When the internal Qi is abundant enough as to emit out of a certain point of the body, it is called "External Qi". Both circulation and emission of the internal Qi take place along the channel route. In traditional Chinese medicine, it is said, "When the channels are unimpeded, you feel no pain; when impeded, you feel pain." That is why Qigong exercise helps to clear up channels and remove pains, and bring in good health.

Qigong exercise usually leads to rise of skin temperature of the hand by 2-3°C, which gradually return to normal only 20-60 minutes after finishing the exercise. The picture taken with a thermograph shows that the skin temperature at the Laogong point in the palm is 2.8⁰C higher in Qigong exercise than before it, and there is a bright ring around the point. After Qigong exercise, it is discovered in the plethysmogram there appear such phenomena as dilatation of blood vessels in the hands, increase of vessel capacity, speed-up of phosphorus assimilation and improvement of the vessel transmissibility. And what is more, peripheral blood flow is found increased, with activation of dopamine β-hydroxylase in plasma declined, eosinophilic granulocyte increased, red blood cells and haemoglobin somewhat increased, phagocytosis of white blood cells raised, secretion amount of plasma cortin reduced by half. It is thus clear that Qigong exercise helps to clear up channels, harmonize blood and Qi and thus prevent and cure disease.

26. Why Can Qigong Help Cerebral Cortex to Achieve Protective Inhibition?

Man's emotional changes greatly affect the frequency and length of brain waves. When one is over excited or worried, waves of high frequency and low amplitude occur in the brain. When he keeps clam, brain waves remain slow. In order to find out the effects of Qigong exercise on the function of the brain, both the Chinese and overseas scientific workers have made measurements of the varying electroencephalogram. They have discovered that records of the ordinary people when they are clear-minded exhibit waves of high frequency and low amplitude, of which few are synchronous; while records of Qigong masters who have had much training exhibit synchronous waves of low frequency with amplitude three times higher than that of ordinary people. Brain waves result from Qigong exercise are different from the electroencephalogram taken when one is clear-minded, or in respose with closed eyes, or in sleep. They are peculiar in some ways: (1) α wave is of longer cycle, higher amplitude and lower frequency. (2) θ wave appears and spreads in the presence of α wave.

The electro-encephalogram taken of a Qigong exerciser indicates improvement of inhibition with the amplitude of the inhibitory α wave growing higher and its rhythm slowed down. This kind of protective inhibition will help the cerebral cortex cells to restore from functional disorder due to over-excitement, or bring the perpetual pathological excitation into inhibition, which is beneficial to the recovery of health. Protective inhibition can put right the functional disorder of the cerebral cortex resulting from over-excitement, for it gives part of the central nervous system a good rest so as to improve the coordination of excitation and inhibition of the central nervous system and their control of the functional activities of all the body organs. Hence, diseases can be prevented or cured.

27. Why Can Qigong Exercise Improve the Coordination of the Function of the Central Nervous System?

Sometimes a piece of sad news would make some people head swimming, eyes dazzling, hands and feet cold, and the whole body weak. This is because that the bad news has stimulated the nervous system and destroyed its power of coordination. In a healthy man, the sympathetic nervous system and the parasympathetic nervous of the autonomic nervous system usually keep in a state of relatively dynamic equilibrium. When one is ill or his irritating reaction becomes abnormal, the symphathetic nerves grow over-excited, resulting in fast heartbeats, higher blood pressure and decline of intestine and stomach movements. Qigong exercise can change this sort of abnormal reactions and improve the coordination of the sympathetic and parasympathetic nerves. Experiments have proved that when a patient of high blood pressure practises Qigong, his activation of dopamine β hydroxylase declines, a manifestation of the reduction of sympathetic nerve excitation. Experiments made in other countries have also proved that Qigong exercise leads to reduction of the EMG activity and the ECG-activity, the frequencies of heartbeat and respiration, indicating the decrease of sympathetic nerve reactions and increase of excited reaction of the parasympathetic nerves. What makes the nervous system perform regulation? When one is practising Qigong, his muscles and joints are relaxed, and the "proprioceptive sensation" of these parts is reduced. Experiments with animals have proved that the reduction can lower the reactions of hypothalamus and the visceral sympathetic nerves. Moreover, Qigong is usually performed in a peaceful, relaxed, natural and pleasant state, which effectively wards off evil influences from outside and reduces stress. As a result, abnormal reaction is further regulated and power of coordination raised. Health can thus be improved.

28. Why Can Qigong Reduce Basal Metabolic Rate and Enhance Energy-Storing Capacity?

From physiological point of view, reactions such as improvement of respiration, speed-up of heartbeat, excitation of sympathetic nerves, tension of skeletal muscle are called energy-consumptive reactions, where energy consumption tends to increase. On the contrary, reactions such as decrease of respiration, slow-down of heartbeat, inhibition of the sympathetic nervous system, relaxation of skeletal muscle are called energy storing reactions, where energy consumption tends to decrease. As Qigong exercise lays emphasis on mental tranquility, body relaxation and gentle respiration, it promotes energy storing reaction. When Qigong is being done in sitting or lying posture oxygen consumption of the body is reduced about 30% less than before the exercise, energy metabolism is also reduced, even less than during deep sleep; frequency of respiration and ventilation per minute also reduced. According to a psychologist-Wallace's measurements, energy consumption of common people in deep sleep is 10% less than being awake, whereas Qigong exerciser in training consumes oxygen 16% less than when they stay awake. Some Qigong masters with much training would reduce their oxygen consumption by 34%. The rate of the increase in entropy grows slower (when the rate of the increase in entropy is greater than the amount of discharged entropy, the organism is said to be senile). Qigong exercise helps to improve brain functioning, with basal metabolic rate lowered, body consumption reduced and energy storing capacity increased. Some people attribute this situation to the combination of iso-ion. That is, during Qigong exercise, one of the ions in human body absorbs one electron and turns into an excited atom, emitting the photon and releasing the residual energy; or, one ion colides into two electrons at the same moment and combines with one of them, resulting in an excited atom, whereas the other electron carries away the residual energy. As the iso-ion combining process emits energy, it helps to reduce energy consumption of organism, and thus achieve energy storage. Therefore, one's organism can again store and accumulate energy which is of importance in overcoming diseases and bringing in health.

29. Why Can Qigong Apply Massage to Abdominal Cavity?

Qigong exerciser usually have better appetite and digestion, simply because Qigong lays emphasis on regulation of respiration and the mind, especially on regulation of abdominal respiration and mind concentration on Dantian. Experiments have proved that abdominal respiration will increase saliva and gastric juice of digestive glands; raise abdominal temperature, and improve blood circulation in intestines and stomach; increase the amplitude of diaphragm movement by 3-4 times and alter the pressure in the abdominal cavity. Regular changes of the intra-abdominal pressure will apply "massage" to intestines and stomach, stimulate the movements and improve their functions of digestion and absorption. Hence, through Qigong training one can enjoy better appetite, put on weight, and have healthy complexion and robust health.

30. Why Can Qigong Enhance Self-Control?

People who seldom take part in physical activities will feel out of breath or tired after some exertion of effort. Those who often have physical training or Qigong exercise have no such feelings in spite of exertions. Qigong training makes those who are weak and weary become vigorous and energetic, because Qigong exercise can fully tap potentialities of the body. Experiments have proved that human body has great latent potentialities. Take brain nerve cells for example, 140,000 million or so constitute the brain, of which only a little more than 10,000 millions are in action while 80-90% stay idle. A great number of blood capillaries remains untapped either. Of the 750 million pulmonary alveoli, only a part is in action. Qigong exercise results in change of brain waves and increase, of pulmonary capacity and volume of blood capillaries. All this shows that Qigong exercise can fully tap one's latent potentialities and enhance control of oneself. Biocybernetics in modern science regards human body as a complete self-controlling system with the brain as the center, dealing with various message coming from inside or outside to maintain dynamic equilibrium of life activities. Recently many scientists have worked out a new self-control theory, confirming the existence of the self-controlling system in human body. The main part of this system is the signal transmitter and cell structure (compound) and their interaction. Cells transmit messages between them by releasing transmitter. The messages are got by receptor. Regulation of the mind, body or breathing in Qigong exercise is a sort of self-controlling activity, which can increase the content of plasma cyclic adenosine monophosphate (CAMP) and the media for transmitting message. For example, serotonin will increase 2-3 times more than ordinary persons. These media bring organic cells into conformity and order in their activities, which can cure diseases caused by communicative errors between cells. Qigong is regarded as a therapy for self-controlling and self-training. It is found to be an effective method to control heartbeats, blood pressure, EMG, EEG, and the like functional activities. Similar reports came from other countries. In the early 1970s, the English physicist and psychologist, E. Green tested a Qigong master Swamy and discovered that this man was able to control his skin temperature in the hand with the mind, creating a temperature difference of 12°F between the outer sides of the thumb and the small finger in 10 minutes. The Qigong master managed to change his heartbeat from 70/min into 300/min with the mind. In 1960, two American doctors Malinase and Hollander found out in their treatment of apoplexy and peripheral nerve injuries: if the EMG of the injured tissues are changed into signals receivable by sight and hearing and acting on the patient himself, the patient will soon recover through practising self-control exercise. In 1964, Dr. Andrews treated 20 hemiplegia patients in a similar way and found the same result. This attracted the attention of the American and Canadian medical circles. Since 1969, they have made a series of electronic monitors; skin resistance biofeedback machine blood pressure biofeedback machine, and EMG biofeedback machine. When the patient is doing Qigong, "messages" of changes in his body will feedback to him through these instruments, and cure his disease by regulating and controlling himself. This is called "bio-feedback method". According to reports from Gemens and Browns in Canada, thay have treated 200 patients in this way, of whom 60% were reported disappearance of symptoms, 32% recovered and only 8% with no effects. Bredley in the United States treated 114 patients in this way, most of them gradually recovered in 8-12 weeks, and they had already undergone long routine treatments without any good results. To sum up, Qigong exercise can fully tap one's body potentialities and play the role of regulation and control of oneself.

MATERIAL FOUNDATION

31. Is There Material Foundation for the "Qi" of Qigong?

Although the "Qi" of Qigong can neither be seen nor felt, it is material.

In the light of traditional medical classics, Qi is a sort of substance essential for maintaining life activities of human body. "The Theory of Qi and Blood" and "The Theory of Qi Activities all deal with the problems of Qi. The Chinese traditional medical theories are based on clinical practice over thousands of years. According to the theories, there is a channel system in human body for "circulation of Qi and Blood". The Internal Qi circulates in the channels whereas the External Qi emits through acupoints along main and collateral channels. The body movements inside and their connections outside all closely related with Qi. What is Qi after all? There has never been any definite answer to this question. To reveal the material nature of Qi, by the end of 1977. The traditional Medical College of Shanghai, Shanghai Research Institute of Traditional Chinese Medicine and Shanghai Atomic Nucleus Research Institute cooperated in their research on the External Qi emitted by the Qigong master with modern scientific instruments. The scientists found out that the External Qi was material. Modern instruments received messages of infrared, static electricity, magnetism and certain fluid. Whether the messages are the essence of Qi or the carrier of Qi is something that needs further research.

In order to verify the material nature of Qi, on July 15 and July 19, 1978, Chinese Academy of Science, National Science Commission, The Chinese Association of Science, Ministry of Public Health, and The National Physical Culture and Sports Commission invited 600 and more leading cadres concerned and notable scientists to examine the Qi of Qigong on the testing spot at the Xi Yuan Guesthouse in Beijing.

It was again proved that Qi was material. This occasion marked a new stage in the research of Qigong. This ancient exercise has been brought into the scope of science and has become a new subject in the science of life exploration. Now the research is just beginning. More modern scientific measures are needed and the research has to be carried on in coordinated branches so as to bring the true nature of Qi to light.

32. What Scientific Experiments Have Been Done on the Material Nature of Qi?

Infrared Detector Test:

HD-1 Infrared Thermometer (wave length of observation window 8-14 micrometer) was used. Lin Hou-sheng, the author of this book, placing his hand a meter away from the instrument and began emitting External Qi. The instrument indeed received infrared radiation signals coming from the Laogong point of Lin's palm centre. These signals are different from ordinary people's and different from Lin's infrared radiation when he is in normal state. They are infrared signals of low frequency and great fluctuation.

Static Current Detector Test:

In the process, Qigong master Cheng Zhi-jiu and Liu Jin-rong mustered up the Qi of their bodies to their respective emission points in a moment. The static detector, 2 cm away from the emission point Yintang of Chen Zhi-jiu and 5 cm away from the emission point Baihui of Liu Jin-rong, received abundantly- collected electric charge signals with static increment of 10^{-14} — 10^{-11} coulomb (equal to the electric charge of 100,000 to 1,000,000 electrons), and showed static current increment signals of different form, strength and extreme when the masters changed their forms of doing Qigong.

Magnetic Detector Test:

During the process, Qigong master Liu Jin-rong mustered up the Qi to the point Baihui while another man struck Liu's Baihui violently with a steel strip of 5 cm width, 76 cm length and 4 cm thickness. The steel strip bent with the violent strikes but Liu did not hurt. A magnetodiode detector received magnetic signals emitted from Liu's Baihui point.

Piezoelectric Ceramic Detector Test:

When Qigong master Zhao Wei-fa warmed up, his Qi moved the suspending thread and pushed the falling powder dust one meter forward. A niobium-lithium-aluminum piezoelectric ceramic detector discovered the signals from the Qigong master, which was of pulse type. The pulse rose from 50 millisecond to 150 millisecond, with vibrating frequency of 0.3 hertz at an interval of 2-20 seconds. The signal traveled 2-3 meters right in front of the Qigong master. In normal air it traveled at a speed of 20-60 cm/second, and passed through a laser grid with apertures 60 micrometer in diameter, but failed to get through glass. The signal was restricted by convestive conditions. In the piezoelectric ceramic test, the Qigong master emitted Qi at a distance of one meter from the probe of an instrument, producing signals entirely different from that of electric blower. This shows that Qigong's External Qi has a property different from airflow.

The Beijing Research Institute of Atomic Energy helped to measure Qigong master Zhao Wei's External Qi by means of a plastic crystal photoelectric multiplier. This instrument was only sensitive to light and particle, and received signals in a capacity test under three different conditions.

Moreover, The Research Institute of Acoustics of The Chinese Academy of Science made a test on Qigong master's External Qi and discovered subsonic signals. Their instrument showed a brilliant light ring over the master's head. The Soviet scientists noticed a sort of radiance around human body. With complicated X-ray apparatus they found out that the body's radiance increased with the rise of emotion and love, similar to display of fireworks on the screen. Infrared photograph shows that the Qigong master's Qi on the head is a mass of steam (See Fig. 1). Radiation field photograph shows that the radiance around Qigong master's finger is quite different from that

50

of ordinary people (See Fig. 2). The above-mentioned tests have proved that the Qi of human body is material, and the proofs are based on science.

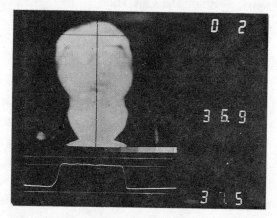

Fig. 1

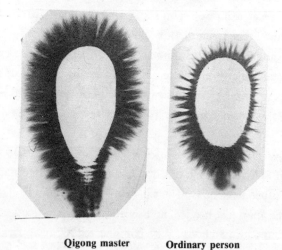

Qigong master   Ordinary person

Fig. 2

CHARACTERISTICS
AND PRINCIPLES

33. What Are the Characteristics of Qigong?

Qigong is a unique self-training method. It is a therapeutic and preventive exercise with national features in the Chinese medical heritage. Qigong can tap one's potentials. Through constant regulation of the body (posture), mind (consciousness) and respiration (breathing), it can cultivate the vital essence, vital energy and vital spirit; and through regulation of internal functioning of the body, it helps to strengthen one's physique and raise his resistance to diseases, and thus bring in good health. That is why Qigong is said to be a positive and multi-training therapy which is characterized by mental direction, external quietness and internal movement, and combination of quietness with movement. For example, when practising the Still Form Qigong the exerciser is quiet in appearance while his internal organs are stirring violently with saliva increasing, intestines making noises, diaphragm rising and falling, heartbeat, blood vessels and blood pressure undergoing changes.

34. Why Can Qigong Tap Potentialities of the Human Body?

Qigong exercise requires one to learn the essentials, pay attention to the principles, have faith, patience, perseverance and determination in it to achieve the best result. It regulates the functioning of internal organs, tap latent potentials and keep fit through one's own effort. It is different from other medical treatments in which drugs and doctor's skills are dominating factors and the patient is placed in a passive position. Qigong exercise requires the patient to strengthen his or her physique and resistance and overcome disease through self-training. This therapy depends neither on medicine nor injection. Therefore, it has no side-effects from use of them.

35.   Why Is Qigong An Exercise of Qi and Yi?

Qigong is practised to cultivate Zhen Qi (vital energy) of human body. In the light of the traditional medical theory, "Qi is the essential substance of human body." Here Qi refers to the primordial principle which includes three components: the congenital Qi (the primordial energy inherited from one's parents, the same as Yuan Qi), the Qi from water and grain (the nutrients derived from food), and the Qi from heaven and earth (the oxygen the body needs). They are the substances essential for life activities. Sufficient Zhen Qi in the body can bring good health and longevity.

Cultivating Zhen Qi usually begins with training of pulmonary Qi. By practising different Qigong forms and different breathing methods, one has the Qi going deeper and slower, gradually forming the habit of abdominal respiration, with regular, fine, long and slow exhaling and inhaling. The breathing process is at first directed by the mind, and then becomes regular and natural. Internal Qi of the body can be brought into full play. It develops and circulates freely in the main and collateral channels. As a result, the channels are kept in good shape, Qi and blood harmonized, disease cured and health improved.

Qigong is an exercise of training Yi (the mind). It requires removal of distracting thoughts and tranquility of the brain, which provides protective inhibition. On the other hand, it requires mind concentration which leads to free circulation of internal Qi and causes changes of the whole organism. To enter the state of tranquility is difficult for beginners. It takes time to practise. Mind concentration is important. The quicker you master the art, the better will be the result, or vice versa. To enter tranquility and to concentrate the mind are unified. The sooner you quiet down, the easier you can concentrate the mind. The better you concentrate your mind, the easier it is to remove distracting thoughts. You should choose suitable and correct postures. Through training coordination of Qi and Yi you can achieve the goal of strengthening Zhen Qi to prevent and cure diseases and prolong lifetime.

36. Why Is Qigong An Exercise for Essence, Energy and Spirit?

According to the traditional medical theory, essence, energy and spirit are essential substances for maintenance of life activities. When a man has vital essence, energy and spirit, he is healthy. The ancient people put the methods of Qigong exercise into two groups, that is, internally, exercise for essence, energy and spirit and externally, exercise for tendon, bone, and skin.

In traditional medical theory, it is said that, "through exercises, essence turns into energy, energy turns into spirit and spirit returns to void."

Through exercise of regulating the body, respiration and the mind, functions of internal organs can be improved and the essence, energy and spirit developed, hence, strong physique and good resistance result. Qigong lays emphasis on inner exercise. It is the exercise of developing essence, energy and spirit.

37. Why Is Qigong Suitable for Patients with Chronic Diseases?

An old saying goes, "Life lies in motion." When patients of chronic diseases cannot go in for strenuous exercise, Qigong is suitable for them.

Qigong is varied in style and form. It is chiefly an exercise for training internal organs. Patients with chronic diseases who cannot do strenuous exercise can choose suitable styles and forms of

Qigong according to their state of disease, physique and conditions. Stronger patients may practise standing posture and the weak ones sitting posture or lying posture. Those who can walk may do the exercise out of doors for fresh air, and those who have difficulty in walking may do the exercise indoors. Whatever form or posture you choose and wherever you do the exercise, you can achieve good results. Therefore, Qigong is said to be suitable for patients of chronic diseases.

38. Why Must A Qigong Exerciser Have Perseverance and Not Give Up Halfway?

Qigong is in fact an exercise of Qi (vital energy) and Yi (mind concentration). In practice, one must have confidence, determination and constancy of purpose, and keep on practising perseveringly. In this way, one's physiologic functioning can be transformed from illness to health. Those who practise by fits and starts, as "to go fishing for three days and dry the nets for two" cannot attain good results. Similarly, anyone who goes heating water by fits and starts will never boil it. Therefore, we hope those who have a will to do Qigong will persevere in practising and do not give it up halfway.

39. Why Must One Keep A Correct Posture in Qigong Exercise?

The methods of practising Qigong are various, including postures of lying, sitting, standing and walking, and the combination of movement with stillness. To take correct and comfortable posture, one must be careful from beginning to end in practice. If you fail to take postures in the correct manner, you cannot obtain expected results. Take standing posture for example. It requires you to sink shoulders and drop elbows, draw in chest and keep the back erect and keep the vertical line of the knees in line with the tips of toes. Otherwise, you will not attain good results even though you have done the exercise over a long time. That is why you must pay attention to the correctness of postures all the time.

40. Why Must One Keep Relaxed, Calm and Natural in Qigong Exercise?

In Qigong exercise, it is important to be relaxed, calm and natural. That is, to keep the whole body relaxed, the mind calmed down, and the posture and consciousness and respiration going naturally.

"Relaxation" involves not only the whole body but one's consciousness and mood. When one is relaxed, his oxygen consumption decreases, energy metabolism reduces, reaction to energy storage improves, regulation and coordination of sympathetic nerves and parasympathetic nerves develop. All this helps to keep the main and collateral channels in good shape, to harmonize Qi and blood, to regulate and recover the body's functioning, and to bring good health.

"To keep calm" means to calm the mind, not to let the thoughts go wild, or to think of one pleasant thing only. This can help restrain one's cerebral cortex, regulate and recover the functioning of the nervous system and thus strengthen the mechanism of the body organs, hence, benefit both the body and the mind.

"To be natural" means to keep natural posture that is correct and relaxed, natural thinking that is cheerful, and natural respiration that is smooth and regular. In Qigong exercise one must not pursue the effects by wishful thinking, nor make noise during exhaling and inhaling. Try to appear perfectly at ease.

Only by keeping relaxed, tranquil and natural in exercise can one master the essentials of the art and achieve expected results.

41. Why Must One Maintain A Positive Mood and Calm State of Mind in Qigong Exercise?

One's mood is the reaction to the influence exerted by external matters on the body organism. Disturbances of the mood tend to cause disease even if one is in good health. It is favorable for a patient to recover health if he is in a less anxious state of mind. Clinical observations have proved that one's spiritual state has much to do with health and disease. It is said that "Happy mood leads to health." Generally speaking, carefree and happy people are relatively healthy. On the contrary, sentimental and nervous people fall ill relatively easily. To be nervous usually leads to increase of stress response, which affects the normal functioning of human body. Practising Qigong can overcome "irritating reaction" resulting from nervousness. Therefore, one must keep good mood and calm state of mind and expel distracting thoughts in order to obtain health and get rid of disease.

42. Why Must Qigong Exercise Be Based on An Overall Analysis of the Performer's Conditions?

Qigong is varied in style and form. Choice of styles and forms should be made according to one's state of disease, physique, age, Yin and Yang, substantiality and insubstantiality, and the function of the viscera. That is, different cases are prescribed different Qigong forms so as to achieve good results and bring health. The following are some principles for proper choice of Qigong forms and postures.

Firstly, choice should be made on the basis of the state of disease: Seriously ill persons should choose lying posture and sitting posture. Relatively better persons may choose standing posture, walking posture or Taiji Qigong.

Secondly, choice should be made on the basis of different diseases: Sufferer of ptosis of stomach or spleen should choose lying posture and concentrate the mind on Dantian point, while sufferer of heart disease or pulmonary emphysema should choose Taiji Qigong.

Thirdly, choice should be made according to different patients of the same disease: Some patients of hepatitis who like walking may take a walking posture while others of the same disease may practise Taiji Qigong if they like this exercise.

Only by practising Qigong exercise according to one's specific condition and disease, can he achieve better results.

43. Why Is Qi the Basis of Qigong? How Does Qi Follow Yi?

In Qigong exercise, Qi (the vital energy) and Yi (the mind) are interrelated and interdependent. The one activates the other. Qi is the substance essential for maintaining activities of life and physiological activities of the channels, the viscera and other body organs. Qigong exercise is chiefly for the training of Qi. If the "Internal Qi" is not brought into play, nor accumulated, nor stimulated to circulate in the channels unhindered, it cannot follow the direction of the mind. On the other hand, attention should be paid to training of the mind in the process of training Qi. In Qigong exercise, it is the mind that conducts the body to relax, the channels to keep good shape, the Qi and blood to harmonize, and the Qi to follow up. It is also the mind that combines motion with tranquility, and exercising with cultivating. In the process of training the mind, take care not to use much effort, nor in pursuit of the special feelings. Don't be anxious for "opening up the points", that is, to open up "Large and Small Zhoutian".

44. Why Must One Proceed Step by Step and Guard Against Impatience for Success in Qigong Exercise?

It is certain that Qigong exercise can help to strengthen physique and bring health, and its curative effects on some diseases are good. Therefore, many people, especially those suffering from chronic diseases are confident and determined in doing this exercise for the cure

58

of their diseases. Nevertheless, some of them do not follow a scheme of gradual progression and fail to achieve good results. For the exercisers, the right path to success is one of understanding correct method, following gradual progression with perseverence and preventing anxiety for success.

They must allow gradual increase of exercise amount, degree of difficulty, number of times, and time spent on the exercise according to their physical conditions. Thus, they can learn the process step by step.

As people are different from one and other in physique, disease and degree of proficiency in the skill of the exercise, the time they need for bringing results and the degree of effectiveness are also different.

With constant practice leading to deeper understanding and finer mastery of the art, the curative effects will become greater and more noticeable. An exerciser's impatience for success is likely to result in loss of confidence.

45. Why Must Consideration Be Given to Both Training and Rest in Qigong Exercise?

Taking into consideration both training and resting here means to be reasonable in planning one's practice and rest. This is important for the patients of chronic diseases in particular.

During each time of practice, one may stop regulating both the mind and breathing for a while after doing a sequence of exercise and rest quietly in a state of relaxation for 10-20 minutes before going on with the practice. For the beginners, it is effective to recuperate from time to time during the process. When one has had more training and become more experienced, he may keep on practising without the repeated recuperations.

46. Why Must Qigong Exercise Be Combined with Other Medical Treatments?

Some people regard Qigong as "curing all diseases" and become exclusive of other medical treatments when they take up Qigong. Their viewpoint is unfounded and mistaken. We think it effective to combine Qigong with other therapeutic measures (including both the Chinese and the Western medical treatments) and make them supplement each other in bringing good results. Injection or medicine helps to recover the functioning of body organs through curing of pathologic changes in them. This is to "get rid of what is bad" so as to "foster what is good". On the other hand, Qigong exercise is aimed at regulating the balance of the functioning of body organs, enhancing resistance against diseases and bringing good health. That is to say, the process is to "foster what is good" so as to "get rid of what is bad".

For the sufferers of chronic diseases, it is necessary to take injection and medicine in order to relieve of pains more quickly and to prevent disease from turning worse. As it takes them longer time to recover from chronic diseases, greater amount of medicine is needed, which is likely to produce ill effects. Therefore, to take up Qigong as part of overall treatment of chronic diseases will bring better curative effects.

47. Why Is It Easy to Popularize Qigong?

Qigong can be done in motion or in stillness or in motion and stillness alternately. Doing Qigong in stillness is mostly the exercise of a single movement combined with the training of the mind. Movements in motion are also very simple, usually one movement at one beat. Qigong exercise is varied in form and posture, including lying, sitting, standing and walking postures and combination of moving and stationary forms. They are simple and easy to learn. That is to say, Qigong is simple in movement which is easy to learn and to understand. Qigong is varied in form which can be chosen in accordance with specific conditions of the performers. These advantages facilitate its popularity.

ESSENTIALS FOR EXERCISE

48. What Are the Three Essentials in Qigong Exercise?

The three essentials in Qigong exercise are the mind, the respiration and the posture (Disciplining of the mind, the breathing and the body).

Mind-intent (Disciplining of the mind):

Disciplining of the mind means that in practising Qigong one must cease the activities of thinking, feeling and consciousness gradually, and expel distracting thoughts so that the brain will enter into a state of tranquility, emptiness, and cheerfulness. As a result, muscles, nerves, blood vessels and other organs of the body will get relaxed and recover from fatique, Qi and blood get harmonized, and the channels get cleared up, so that the latent potentials can be brought into play and the physiological functions of the body can regulate themselves. This is the way to improve health and cure disease. The methods of disciplining the mind includes relaxing, saying words in the mind, counting the breaths, concentrating the mind on a certain acupoint, shifting attention between two or more acupoints, thinking of something pleasant, and so on.

Respiration (Disciplining of breathing):

Disciplining of breathing means to stimulate the internal Qi by regulating one's respiration. The Qi gradually accumulates and circulates freely along the main and collateral channels, bringing along the flow of blood. Methods of disciplining breathing includes natural breathing, deep breathing, abdominal breathing, inhaling and exhaling, mouth inhaling and nose exhaling, foetal breathing, hiberanation breathing, etc.

Posture (Disciplining of the body):

It means to regulate the posture of the body to make one feel relaxed and comfortable. This is the first step to the regulation of the mind and breathing. It is said in the Chinese medical classic: "If the posture is not correct, the Qi will not circulate freely. If the Qi does not circulate freely, the mind will not become calm. If the mind is not calm, the Qi will disperse." Therefore, disciplining of the body is of primary importance in Qigong exercise. Methods include lying posture (lying on the back or lying sideways), sitting posture (sitting upright or sitting with back supported), standing posture (natural standing, three-circle standing, standing with hands pressing down and mixed type standing), Taiji Qigong, and walking exercise. These can be done in stillness, in motion or in stillness and motion alternately.

49. What Is Mind Concentration? How to Practise It?

Mind concentration is to focus one's mind on a certain area of the body, or to think of a certain acupoint of the channels, or to think of an external scene or object. That is to replace all other thoughts with only one thought, to expel all distracting thoughts and enter a state of tranquility and comfort.

Mind concentration is usually done by directing the mind to the following acupuncture points: Dantian, which is said to be the root of life, the locale where the vital energy accumulates, and the source where the internal energy rises. Here Dantian refers to the lower abdomen. Mingmen (the vital portal): It is the area where Dumai and Daimai converge and functional activities of the two kidneys meet. It is said to be the "Gate of Life". Huiyin: It is the point located in the middle of the perineum, where Ren Mai, Chong Mai, Du Mai start and converge, and where primordial energy takes root. Yongquan: This point is on the sole of foot, where the renal Qi takes root and vital Qi descends. Focusing the mind on this point helps to tonify the Yin and restrain the Yang. Mind-intent can also be directed to a specific object or scene of nature. For sufferers of indigestion, it is advisable to focus the mind on Dantian; for sufferers of high blood pressure on Yongquan. To avoid exertion of the mind, one may think of external scenes such as pine-trees or flowers. In focusing the mind on a certain area of the body, one should not overdo it, or do it with effort. It is better to be less exerted than more for the mind. Exertion of the mind will cause ill effects. For sufferer of indigestion, it is better to focus the mind on Dantian. He will first feel the lower abdomen warming up, then the intestines making noises and the intestines and stomach wriggling. All this is normal. If he focuses his mind with too much effort, too much Qi will sink to the area of Dantian and distention of Qi will take place. He will even find the area of Dantian bloated and suffer from it.

In focusing the mind on external scenes, the doer must choose the ones beneficial to his health, such as green pines, flowers, the sea, the sky, etc.

50. What Is Meant by Focusing the Mind on "Internal Scene" and "External Scene"?

One's mind may either be focused on "internal scene" or "external scene". Internal scene refers to a certain area of the body, the acupoints of Dantian, Yongquan, Beihui, Zuqiao, etc. External scene refers to fine scenes such as garden with blossoming flowers, field with beautiful views, bright and clear moon or blue seas. For beginners to focus the mind on "internal scene", it is better to start with Dantian or Yongquan. To start with upper points such as Beihui or Zuqiao first might cause the Qi to flow upward and produce ill effects. Take care not to exert the mind too much so as to avoid deviations. The mind is focused gently and naturally as if it were lingering around the point without restraint. When focusing the mind on "External scene", choose the lovely and pleasant things instead of the ones that will make you sad and uncomfortable. Following the principles, the doer will find the exercise bringing good effects, beneficial to both his body and mind.

51. What Is Meant by Thinking of Fine Things and How to Do it?

One's spiritual state and mood have much to do with his health. To think of fine things in Qigong exercise means to think of the things that will create fine feelings and maintain merry mood, such as beautiful scenery, pleasant events, or satisfying matters. You may think of the joys in work, the beautiful flowers, far-reaching fields, fresh air or lovely child. One must avoid thinking of things that are terrible, fearful, irritating, or disturbing such as fighting or quarreling with others; troubles in work, etc. In short, to think of fine things in practising Qigong will remove ill feelings and develope cheerful mood and optimistic spirit, which will bring good health.

52. What Is Meant by "Supposition"?

In Practising Qigong, to suppose some delightful scenes or recall some pleasant and meaningful events is what we refer to as "supposition". For instance, let's suppose entering a garden to enjoy the sight of blossoming flowers, watching playful animals, enjoying the boundless blue sea on board a ship, recalling one's success in work or in scientific experiments. This kind of supposition gives you fine feelings and help you to remove distracting thoughts and evil ideas. "Supposition" cannot be made in association with distressing situation such as graveyard, death, car accident, fire alarm, etc., which arouse only evil feelings and are harmful to health.

53. What Is Meant by Mind-concentration "With Effort" and "Without Effort"?

In practising Qigong, there have always been two different views on mind concentration, that is, concentration with effort or without effort. Some people maintain that there is no need to use effort when concentrating the mind. You do not have to think of anything if you can enter into tranquility, that is, to expel all thoughts and come to a state of unperturbedness and emptiness. Some other people on the contrary insist on the use of effort. You have to use one thought to replace or expel all other thoughts no matter whether you focus your mind on the internal scene or external scene. There are some elements of truth in both these views. It is better for the two to merge, each taking the other's reasonable element and making up for its own deficiencies for better results of Qigong exercise.

The view of using effort in concentration of the mind has its reasons. When you practise Qigong, especially in the process of stationary exercise, various distracting thoughts tend to arise and it is difficult to enter into quiet meditation or relaxation. Our predecessors found it helpful to use mind intent. To direct the mind to a certain acupoint, to say words in the mind, to count breaths, or to look at internal organs are methods of replacing all distracting thoughts with a single thought. They are experiences of proper use of the mind.

The other view insists on doing Qigong in a natural manner without the need of mind-intent. It is believed that improper use of the mind leads to a "rigid state" in which it is hard for one to relax or to quiet down. In this case, deviations such as distention of Qi, stagnation of Qi, deterioration of Qi, confusion of the mind, and disorder of breathing will occur.

We think that in the process of Qigong exercise, do not go too far in using mind-intent. The less you exert the mind the better. You seem to be using the mind but refrain from doing so at the same time, reaching a state of nothingness and emptiness. On the other hand, the state of nothingness and emptiness cannot be taken in its absolute sense. That is, not to let the mind leave the body (not to forget that you are doing Qigong), but keep at a proper extent so as to avoid falling into sleep or losing control of yourself.

54. What Is Meant by Six Knacks?

Six knacks are referred to as the correct method of regulating respiration. They are Counting, Following, Staying, Watching, Returning and Purifying.

Counting is to count the number of breaths. That is to harmonize respiration, to breathe smoothly, slowly, gently and with ease. You may count the exhaling times or inhaling times from one to ten, from ten to a hundred, and to a thousand. When you become proficient through long period of practice, your breathing and the counting will grow delicate and almost unreal.

Following means to follow your own breathing. You let the mind follow the breathing and the breathing follow the mind. They depend on each other going on in continuity and become delicate in the course of time, reaching a state of calmness and stillness.

Staying means not to follow the breathing but let the mind stay at the nose tip or the like point with some or no intent as if you were in a state of stillness.

Watching means to watch with the mind over the slight exhaling and inhaling which seem non-existent like wind. By and by you will find your mind's eye become clear and see the inhaling and exhaling flowing through out the body.

Returning means to watch breathing with the mind, to observe the mind-intent and the state of breathing. When mind-intent returns to its source, that is, when all distractions are removed the mind will reveal its genuine state in the way that water appears when waves calm down.

Purifying means to quiet down the breathing. Keep the mind as quiet as still water without the slightest disturbance of distractions. That is the genuine state of the mind. Mind without distracting thoughts reveals its genuine state just as waves subsiding down reveals water. This state of breathing is said to be purifying.

In the Six Knacks, Counting and Following are the first step exercises; Staying and Watching are principal exercises; Returning and Purifying are the results of the exercises.

55. What Is Meant by Listening to Breathing?

To listen to breathing means to keep calm and concentrate the mind on listening to inhaling and exhaling through the nose in the process of Qigong exercise. This method was first worked out by Zhuang Zi. It is his theory that in doing Qigong you should concentrate the mind from the very beginning without being disturbed by other thoughts. Through listening to breathing, you proceed to listen to the Qi and spirit, enter a primeval state where Qi and spirit come to merge into one without your awareness of it. You look as if you were sleeping but things in the body are changing, leading you to a state of nothingness. This situation comes naturally without your consciousness, nor is it created by the mind.

It is known that people with healthy respiration system produce no noise while breathing. However, you feel the exhaling and inhaling through the nose whether it is slow or quick, thick or thin. Even deaf people have such feelings. Listening to breathing can lead you to tranquility with all thoughts coming to one point. This method will produce good results in Qigong exercise.

56. What Is Relaxing Exercise?

It is an exercise of the mind. In practising Qigong, after taking a posture (sitting, lying or standing), you conduct the whole body to relax with mind-intent. This is the relaxing exercise. When the body is relaxed to the greatest extent, you feel like riding on the clouds and floating in the air, natural and comfortable. Relaxation helps you to fall into quiet meditation and brings good results in Qigong exercise.

57. What Is Meant by Part-by-Part Relaxation?

This is an exercise of the mind. In practising Qigong, after taking a posture, imagining relaxing the whole body part by part from head to foot. This is called part-by-part relaxation. You imagine relaxing the whole body part by part in the following order: head, neck, breast (including upper arms), stomach and abdomen (including arms and hands), thighs, legs, and foot. Do the relaxation slowly and in proper order from head to foot.

58. What Is Meant by Relaxation Along Three Lines?

This is a sort of exercise of the mind. After taking a posture, you relax the body in your mind along three lines:

First line (by two sides): The outer sides of the head — neck — shoulders — upper arms — elbows — wrists — palms — fingers.

Second line (front): Headtop — face — neck — breast — abdomen — thighs — knees — legs — ankles — toes.

Third line (back): Head — back of the neck — back — waist — backs of thighs — hollows of knees — backs of legs — heels — soles of feet.

This relaxing exercise begins with the first line, then the second and the third. It takes about three minutes to relax along each line. After finishing relaxation of the three lines, think of the navel or the diseased area for one minute. This is one cycle of the exercise, and each sequence of the exercise includes 1 — 3 cycles. During the process, if you do not feel relaxed, go on with the three lines in a natural manner without being impatient.

59. What Is Meant by Silent Saying?

Silent saying is to say some words in the mind as a form of Qigong exercise.

This is done in the following way:

Saying words in the mind to keep away distraction:

Select some words to say in the mind according to one's specific conditions. Those who suffer from neurasthenia or high blood pressure and get anxious easily may say the words or phrases such as "relax", "be quiet", "relax the body", "calm the mind", "lower blood pressure", "cheer up", etc. Meanwhile the body organs will undergo changes favorable to health. This is because these phrases can exert good effects on the doer through his second signal system and help him attain happy mood, relax the body, quiet the mind and finally bring good health.

Saying "be calm" when inhaling and "relax" when exhaling:

Saying words in the mind must be coupled with breathing. You should take regular, thin, deep and long-drawn breaths and say the words in mind with no effort.

Breathing out:

When doing exhaling, breathe out such words as Xu, He, Hu, Si, Chui, Xi (with no sound). This sort of Qigong exercise is applicable to the treatment of visceral excess syndrome.

60. What Is Meant by Counting Breaths?

This is the method of counting the number of breaths in continuity (each breath includes one exhaling and inhaling).

The famous doctor Pian Que of ancient China said counting breaths was an access to the regulation of breathing and to tranquility. It can help the sufferer of insomnia to go to sleep. When you concentrate the mind on counting, other distracting thoughts will recede and you will enter a state of calmness and relaxation. The counting usually goes up to several hundreds. When you feel calm and comfortable, you may stop counting in continuity and turn to follow the breathing. That is, let the mind follow the breathing and not to be distracted by other thoughts. This method can help to remove distractions and to regulate and train respiration.

61. What Is Meant by Guan Qi Method?

Guan Qi Exercise (shifting attention between acupoints) is exercised in two ways:

First, shift your attention from one part or one point of the body to another part or point with exhaling and inhaling. For example, sufferer of high blood pressure may think of the point of Dantian when inhaling and the point of Yongquan when exhaling. Shifting of the mind between different points with inhaling and exhaling is what this exercise means.

Second, imagine conducting Qing Qi (the Purified Principle) upward to the headtop and Zhuo Qi (the Turbid Principle) downward to the foot soles, leading the turbid principle from the soles three feet deep into the ground. This method of leading the purified principle upward and the turbid principle downward is also what the exercise means.

This exercise helps to clear up the main and collateral channels, activate Qi and blood, and reinforce body resistance to eliminate pathogens. But it doesn't suit the sufferer with low blood pressure or insufficiency of Qi in Zhongjiao (the Middle Heater).

62. What Is Meant by Zhi Guan Famen? How to Practise It?

'Zhi' means 'to stop', 'Guan' means 'to watch', and 'Famen' means 'access'. 'Zhi' requires discontinuity of one's thinking. There are three steps for one to stop thinking.

"Xi Yuan Zhi" (stop by fastening) — This is the first step leading to discontinuity of thinking. It implies that one should fasten all his thoughts as if to fasten a monkey with a lock.

This can be performed in two ways: The one is to stop on the tip of nose. That is, to think only of the nose tip and remove all distracting thoughts slowly. The other is to stop at the lower abdomen, the center of human body. That is, to think only of this part, imagining the nose inhaling and exhaling in a vertical line throughout the abdomen. In this way, one can keep away distracting thoughts and improve regulation of the breath.

"**Zhi Xin Zhi**" — "Xin" means heart or mind. This step requires one to concentrate his effort on the control of his mind after learning "Xi Yuan Zhi". That is, he has to discover the sources of distracting thoughts and break their connections.

"**Ti Zhen Zhi**" — This is the actual discontinuity of thinking. "Ti" means "to feel", "Zhen" means "truthfulness". This step requires one to realize his real thoughts and let them pass. His thinking will come to an end without effort. The absence of distracting thoughts is a state of truthfulness, where the mind stays. This is called "Ti Zhen Zhi".

"**Guan**" means "to watch". Here it does not mean to look outside but to watch the internal activities with closed eyes. There are three ways for this exercise.

Kong Guan — "Kong" means "vacancy", to see that things in the universe are forever changing: occurring, growing and dying. Looking in this way with mind's eye is what "Kong Guan" means.

Jia Guan — "Jia" means "to suppose". Imagine that things of the world come into existence when both the internal and external causes meet, and they die when the causes separate. It is true with one's thoughts in mind. Therefore, one should not pursue a thought with effort. This imagination is called "Jia Guan".

Zhong Guan — "Zhong" means "in the middle". Do not pursue the "vacancy" when you are doing "Kong Guan", and do not pursue the "supposition" when you are doing "Jia Guan". Keeping away from both "vacancy" and "supposition" and staying in the middle, you will see things clearly. This is what "Zhong Guan" means.

In the specific sense, "Zhi" means all thoughts coming into one and "guan" means seeing things clearly. They cannot be separated from each other. This is Zhi Guan Famen, an access to tranquility.

63. What Is Natural Breathing?

Natural breathing is indicated to beginners, general exercisers and those taking standing posture for Qigong exercise. One should breathe freely with usual frequency and in natural manner, at 15 — 18 breaths or so per minute.

Gradually the exerciser slows down his breathing speed, making the breath deeper and longer. This is called Deep Breathing, and it is usually used in Taiji Qigong Exercise and Ten-Section Exercises.

Natural breathing proceeds by taking breaths with the nose or with both mouth and nose. It is done in the usual and natural manner.

64. What Is Chest Breathing?

Chest breathing is to breathe by expanding and contracting the chest. That is, expand the chest and slightly draw in the lower abdomen while inhaling, and do the reverse while exhaling. When you inhale, the vital energy rises from the vertebra at the back of stomach pit, moving upward along the back bone to the chest, and lifting up the back ribs as if pumping the air from abdomen into chest, which in fact is the expanding of chest and contracting of abdomen. Inhaling until you feel it impossible to go on. You should not do it with effort so as to prevent discomfort.

When you exhale, imagine breathing out air from the back of stomach pit, with the chest contracted and slightly flattened, a bit larger than its usual shape. This process of varying the size of the chest through inhaling and exhaling is called Chest Breathing.

65. What Is Abdominal Breathing?

Expand your abdomen as you breathe in and contract your abdomen as you breathe out (Favorable Breathing). Or expand your abdomen as you breathe out and contract your abdomen as you breathe in (Reverse Breathing). This is Abdominal Breathing.

When you inhale, imagine the vital energy rising from back of the abdominal centre, with waist erect, abdominal muscles loosened and large amount of air drawn into the abdomen, as if to bring the air down to the anus along backbone. Inhale until you feel the abdomen full of air, expanded and comfortable. Hold the breath for a moment and then exhale slowly.

This suits people who suffer from indigestion and constipation.

66. What Is Meant by Inhale-Exhale Breathing and Inhale-Inhale-Exhale Breathing?

When practising a Qigong exercise, you inhale at one movement and exhale at another. This is Inhale-Exhale Breathing. If you take in two short breaths at one movement and breathe out at another, it is called Inhale-Inhale-Exhale Breathing.

This is usually used during Walking Qigong Exercise, and suits sufferer with cancer in reinforcing his resistance and immunity.

This sort of breathing exercise should be done in an environment with fresh air so that you can breathe in large amount of oxygen and breathe out large amount of carbondioxide. It helps to prevent and cure diseases and improve health.

67. What Is Meant by Long-Drawn Breathing?

This is a breathing exercise based on Tuna and Daoyin Exercises of ancient China. You inhale and exhale to the full with nose, or inhale with nose and exhale with mouth, with each inhaling and exhaling drawn as long as possible and producing loud noise (to be heard at a distance of 200 — 300 meters when it is quiet). This breathing exercise is aimed at increasing capacity of lungs. It helps to strengthen physique, activate activities of body organs and cure some complicated chronic diseases.

This exercise should be practised in open air and the noise produced during breathing tends to grow louder and louder in the process.

68. What Is Meant by Nose-Inhale and Mouth-Exhale Breathing, and Nose-Inhale-and-Exhale Breathing?

To breathe in with nose and breathe out with mouth is Nose-Inhale and Mouth-Exhale Breathing. It is usually used in Taiji Qigong and Walking Exercise.

To breathe in or out with nose only is Nose-Inhale-and-Exhale Breathing. It is a sort of Natural Breathing.

Most people use this kind of breathing in Qigong exercise. However, some exercisers breathe in with mouth and breathe out with nose, which is not as good as the above-mentioned breathing methods in view of physiological structure and health.

69. What Is Meant by Hold-Breath Breathing?

On the basis of Abdominal Breathing or Deep Breathing, you hold breath for a moment after inhaling and exhaling, or between inhaling and exhaling. You may also prolong the inhaling or exhaling, that is, longer inhaling and shorter exhaling, or shorter inhaling and longer exhaling with pauses in between them. This is called Hold-Breath Breathing, which produces only 2 — 3 times of long drawn breathing per minute.

This kind of breathing can help to store and activate Internal Qi, and is good for easing troubles in digestive system. However, it is not suitable for beginners, for it might cause stagnation of Qi in the process.

70. What Is Meant by Foetal Breathing?

This is a more advanced method of breathing with its frequency slowed down and the number of breaths reduced to the greatest extent.

Some skillful Qigong masters reduce the number of breaths to 1 — 2 times per minutes. They breathe in the manner of a foetus taking breaths in the womb. Hence, Foetal Breathing.

This takes place only at an advanced stage of Qigong exercise, reaching a state of "slight and thin breathing as if it were non-existent." Foetal Breathing comes naturally and cannot be attained with effort. It is good for cultivating vital energy, developing essence, energy and spirit, and curing the Five types of strains and Seven injuries. You will feel comfortable and lively all over the body after practising Foetal Breathing. It was first worked out by ancient Qigong masters for cultivating vital energy.

71.   What Is Meant by Hibernation Breathing?

This kind of breathing is very slight and gentle as if you were not taking any breath during Qigong exercise. It has been used in Yoga of India. Scientists have discovered through studying the Indian Qigong master Swamea that he managed to lie in a coffin buried underneath shallow earth and keep in a state of hibernation for seven days. It was found out that his lungs were at rest and his heart stopped beating as shown in electrocardiogram and test of lung capacity when he lay still in the coffin under the earth. This shows that Qigong exercise can bring protective inhibition on cerebral cortex, reduce basic metabolic rate, decrease energy consumption of the body and raise its power of storing energy. With the entire body in a state of hibernation and breathing slight and weak, it is called Hibernation Breathing. It is not suitable for beginners.

72.   What Is Meant by Supine Posture and Lying Sideways?

Lying Exercise is a form of practising Qigong. It includes two postures: supine posture and lying sideways.

Supine posture requires one to lie flat on the back in a bed. Keep the head naturally straight on a pillow of appropriate thickness, keep mouth and eyes gently closed, stretch limbs naturally with hands at both sides of the body. (See Fig. 3)

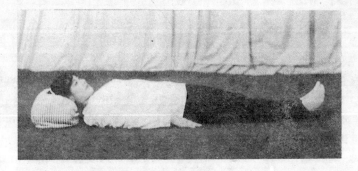

Fig. 3

Lying sideways usually requires one to lie on the right side. Bow the head a little and keep it steady on a pillow. Close mouth and eyes gently. Bend right arm naturally and place right hand on the pillow two inches from face, palm facing upward. Stretch right leg naturally and bend left leg with a 120-degree angle at the knee and place it above the right leg. Place the left hand gently on the left thigh. If you lie on left side, reverse the positions of limbs.

In short, keep body slightly bent with head bowing a little, always in a natural and comfortable manner. (See Fig. 4)

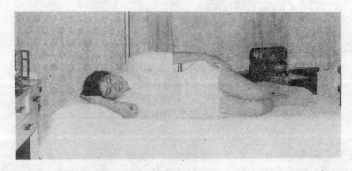

Fig. 4

Qigong exercise in lying form should be practised in coordination with proper methods of exercising the mind and respiration.

73. What Is Meant by Sitting Posture and Sitting with Back Supported?

Sitting Exercise is a form of doing Qigong. It includes sitting posture and sitting with back supported.

Sitting posture requires one to sit steady on a stool with head and neck straight, shoulders dropped and chest drawn in a little. Palms put lightly on the knees, keep lower limbs apart by shoulder width in parallel and pointing forward. Keep feet flat on the ground, keep the body and lower legs perpendicular to the ground with a 90-degree angle at the knees as well as at the hips. Keep mouth gently closed and eyelids dropped naturally. (See Fig. 5)

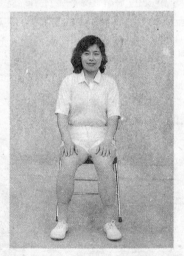

Fig. 5

Sitting with back supported by the back of a chair or a wall suits those who lack the strength to sit steady.

Doing Qigong in a sitting posture must be in coordination with proper methods of exercising the mind and respiration.

74. What Is Standing Posture?

This is one of the postures taken in Qigong exercise. Standing posture chosen for practising stationary exercise includes Natural Standing, Three-circle Standing, Pressing-down Standing and Mixed Type Standing. Correct choice of a standing posture in coordination with correct regulation of the mind and breathing is a sort of standing exercise.

75. What Is Meant by Alternating Moving Exercise with Stationary Exercise?

This is one of the postures taken in Qigong exercise. For instance, in the process of Involuntary Moving Exercise, you first take a sitting posture, or lying posture or standing posture in stillness to induce quiet meditation. Then you begin to move involuntarily. This is the exercise of alternating stillness with motion.

INTRODUCTION ON EXERCISE FORMS

76. What Is Intrinsic-Nourishing Qigong?

This is one of the main forms of stationary Qigong exercises. It requires the exerciser to regulate his posture, breathing and the mind, and meets the requirements of complete relaxation of the body, harmony of breathing, and tranquility of the brain. Therefore, this will help calm the mind, cultivate the primordial Qi, balance the two principles of Yin and Yang, harmonize the vital energy and blood, clear up main and collateral channels, and coordinate the functions of the viscera.

Intrinsic-Nourishing Qigong lays emphasis upon saying words in the mind, holding breath during respiration, moving the tongue up and down, and directing the Qi deep to Dantian. It is characterized by calmness of the brain and movement of the viscera.

Intrinsic-nourishing Qigong is the experience summed up and inherited from the predecessors by Liu Gui-zhen. He combined other's experience with his own clinical practice and put forward this form of exercise in 1947, and has it popularized ever since. This exercise is remarkable for its curative effects on visceral diseases, such as gastric ulcer, duodenal ulcer, gastroptosis, hepatitis and so on.

Methods of Intrinsic-Nourishing Form:

(I) Postures

There are four postures: Lying sideways, supine posture, sitting posture, and backing on chair posture.

(II) Breathing Methods

Intrinsic-nourishing Qigong requires combination of regulating breathing, holding breath, moving tongue and repeating some words in the mind.

There are three methods of breathing:

(1) Inhale — hold breath — exhale. Say some words in the mind. The commonly-used words are "relaxation", "quietness", "joy" and "good health".

(2) Inhale — exhale — hold breath. Say the above-mentioned words in the mind.

(3) Inhale — hold breath — inhale — exhale. Say the above-mentioned words in the mind.

(III) Concentrate One's Mind

Concentrate your mind on such acupoints as Dantian, Tanzhong, Yongquan, etc. Mind concentration must be performed only gently, without an effort.

(IV) Points for Attention

(1) Intrinsic-nourishing Qigong stresses on regulating the functions of liver and spleen. After doing the exercise, you'll find your digestion improved and enjoy good appetite. Therefore, you may appropriately increase your diet. Those who are under nourishment or emaciated need not restrict their diet.

(2) One should not perform intrinsic-nourishing Qigong while hungry.

(3) In clinical practice, selection of exercising forms, such as breathing, mind-concentration, repeating words in the mind, and postures, should be based on an overall analysis of patient's conditions, including the disease, the state of the disease and syndrome (deficiency syndrome and excess syndrome).

(4) Intrinsic-nourishing Qigong practised in coordination with other Qigong forms can produce better results.

77. What Is Relaxing Qigong? How to Practise It?

This is one of the forms of stationary Qigong exercise. It requires one to relax every part of the body consciously, and to repeat the word "relax" in the mind at the same time. Through gradual regulation it will make one feel natural, light and comfortable, relieve one of mental tension, remove his distracting thoughts, cause the attention to be gradually focused and the mind calmed down. As a result, the vital energy and blood become harmonized, the functions of the viscera coordinated, the main and collateral channels cleared up, the physique strengthened, and diseases prevented and cured.

Relaxing Qigong has certain curative effects on some chronic diseases, such as hypertension, intestine and stomach diseases, neurosis, neurasthenia and heart disease. Relaxing exercise was worked out by Chen Tao in 1957 through summing up other people's experience, and has become popular ever since.

Methods of Relaxing Qigong:

(I) Postures

Generally lying sideways, supine posture, sitting posture and backing on chair posture are used.

(II) Breathing

Natural breathing is commonly accepted.

(III) Mind Concentration

Directed by the mind, you can relax your body along three lines, relax the body part by part, relax a local section of the body, or relax the body as a whole. Say "calm" when inhaling, and "relax" when exhaling.

(IV) Points for Attention

Before taking exercise, one must concentrate his mind, be free of troubles and undo his tight clothes and belt. The exercise should be practised at a spot with fresh air and quiet environment. While practising, one must get rid of distracting thoughts, and keep every part of the body relaxed, only by doing so can the practice bring good effects.

78. What Is Tonic Qigong?

Tonic Qigong has been worked out by taking in the strengths of Confucian, Taoist and Buddhist exercises and rejecting the dross in them.

Detailed methods:

(I) Postures

There are free cross-legged posture, single cross-legged posture, double cross-legged posture, standing posture and free posture.

(II) Breathing

Methods include quiet breathing (natural breathing), deep-breathing, and reverse breathing.

(III) Mind Concentration

Tonic Qigong requires one to concentrate his mind on Dantian so that he can enter into a state of tranquility and expel distracting thoughts. He can also focus his mind upon scenery outside, such as beautiful landscape and delightful sights so as to increase positive stimulus, replacing evil ideas with fine ideas, getting rid of distracting thoughts and bringing in good health.

Tonic Qigong has certain curative effects upon hypertension, neurasthenia, neurosis, heart disease and arthritis.

79. What Is Keep-Fit Qigong?

Keep-Fit Qigong is a supplementary form of Qigong exercise. It is effective for keeping fit as well as curing diseases. It is especially good for infirm and elderly persons.

The Keep-Fit Qigong is also called Massage-and-Pat Exercise. Through self-massaging and self-patting it can achieve the purpose of clearing up the main and collateral channels, harmonizing Qi and blood, and improving health. This exercise can produce certain curative effects upon some chronic diseases, such as intestine and stomach diseases, heart disease, neurosis, liver disease, and spleen disease.

There are a dozen and more movements: massaging the ears, teeth chattering, tongue movement, rinsing the mouth with saliva, nose rubbing, eye exercise, massaging face, neck exercise, massaging the shoulders, rubbing the chest, massaging the abdomen, massaging the spine, rubbing the waist, rubbing the coccyx, rubbing Dantian point, massaging the knees, rubbing Yongquan point, bathing hands, bathing shoulders, bathing thighs, etc.

Points for attention in practising Keep-Fit Qigong:

Numbers of times for massaging and rubbing and the force applied may vary with different persons. It is desirable for the doer to feel comfortable and relaxed after the massage. Force applied should be appropriate. Too little force produces no effect at all, while too much force will injure the skin.

80. Can the Four Forms of Qigong Exercises Be Practised Alternately?

Intrinsic-Nurishing Qigong, Relaxing Qigong, Tonic Qigong and Keep-Fit Qigong are the exercising forms of Qigong. Their basic principles for training are the same, just as the training of high-jump, long jump, running, grenade-throwing, and the like field-and-track events, all for improvement of health. So these exercises can be practised alternately. But generally speaking, it is advisable to choose one exercise which best suits one's state of illness, physique and temperament, and supplement it with other exercises. For example, those who suffer from hypertension and heart disease are advised to take Relaxing Qigong,

83

those who have trouble in digestive system, Intrinsic-Nourishing Qigong supplemented with other exercise. Gravely weak persons are not advised to select sitting or standing posture of Keep-Fit Qigong. They may take the lying posture of Intrinsic-Nourishing Qigong and then turn to Keep-Fit Qigong when they feel better. Keep-Fit Qigong is usually practised only after learning Intrinsic-Nourishing Qigong, Relaxing Qigong and Tonic Qigong. Therefore, it is taken as a supplementary Qigong exercise.

81. What Is Standing Qigong Exercise? How to Practise It?

Standing Qigong is originated from the standing posture of the ancient Da Cheng Boxing. It includes health preserving exercise and skill attacking exercise. An introduction of health preserving exercise follows. Following the rule of trees growing up with roots deep into the ground, this exercise is applied to health care and medical treatment. It is practised only in standing posture, and needs neither special ground nor equipment. It can be done at any time and any place. That's why it has enjoyed great popularity as a health preserving method over many years. This exercise is characteristic by simple movement and prompt effect, and its curative effects are especially remarkable upon some chronic diseases, such as neurasthenia, neurosis, intestine and stomach troubles, coronary heart disease, physical weakness, and debility of the limbs.

(I) Postures

Postures of Standing Qigong varies greatly with different schools, yet they can be put into four groups: natural standing Qigong, three-circle standing Qigong, pressing downward standing Qigong and mixed type standing Qigong. According to the degree of difficulty, there are high-position standing posture, mid-position standing posture and low-

84

position standing posture. High-position standing posture, taken with the knees slightly bent, and consuming less energy, is suitable for the aged and the weak to practise. Mid-position standing posture, neither too high nor too low, with knees bent at an angle of about 130 degrees and consuming a moderate amount of energy, suits the patients of better physique. Low-position standing posture, low with knees bent at an angle of about 90 degrees and much energy consumption, suits those who are healthy or basically recovered from disease.

(1) Natural standing Qigong

Stand naturally upright with feet apart in parallel by a shoulder width, neck erect, draw chest slightly inward, knees bend slightly, hands overlap at abdomen with right hand on the left one and both palms facing inward, eyes look forward or slightly downward (Fig. 6).

Fig. 6

(2) Three-circle standing Qigong

It includes holding ball posture and embracing posture. They depend mainly on the bending degree of the arms. The posture with arms slightly bent is called holding ball posture; while with arms bent in greater degree embracing posture. (Fig. 7 and 8).

Fig. 7, 8

Movement of holding ball posture: upper limbs raised and bent in semi-circle manner as if you were holding a ball, palms facing each other, fingers pointing to each other about a foot in front of the eyes. Eyes look forward or slightly downward. Movement of embracing posture: upper limbs raised and bent in the manner of embracing a tree, palms facing inward about two feet away in front of the chest. Eyes look forward or slightly downward. The standing position may be high, middle or low, depending upon the condition of the exerciser.

(3) Standing Qigong with hands pressing downward

Arms are raised and bent, palms and fingers pointing forward, forearms parallel to the ground, palms facing downward, five fingers separated, eyes looking forward or alightly downward. The standing Qigong may be done at high, middle or low position (Fig. 9, 10 and 11) depending on specific condition of the exerciser.

Fig. 9, 10

Fig. 11

(4) Mixed type standing Qigong

1) Relaxing and drooping arms: Stand upright with two feet in parallel by shoulder-width, torso erect, head erect, eyes looking forward, lips and teeth closed gently, chest drawn slightly inward and back erect, shoulders drooping with two hands stretching and hanging at the sides of thighs, palms facing inward, muscles completely relaxed (Fig. 12).

Fig. 12

2) Arms raised forward like a flying dragon: On the basis of 1), the head, neck, chest and abdomon remain still. Raise hands horizontally, palms facing downward and hanging in a semi-circle, fingers kept together and relaxed. Meanwhile, bend legs slightly with knees at an angle of about 120 degrees (Fig. 13).

3) Palms facing each other like a symbol of good luck:

On the basis of 2), head, neck, chest, abdomon, legs and feet remain still. Turn palms to face each other as a ruyi, a symbol of good luck (Fig. 14).

4) Pigeon stopping in front of the chest: On the basis of 3), head, neck, chest, abdomen, feet and legs remain still. Draw hands inward

and near the chest, middle fingers of hands slightly touching each other, in the shape of a semi-circle (Fig. 15).

Fig. 13

Fig. 14

Fig. 15

5) Spreading wings in flight: On the basis of 4), head, neck, chest, abdomen, legs and feet remain still. Separate the two arms in front of chest and move them to two sides at the height of the shoulders, palms facing downward (Fig. 16).

Fig. 16

6) Pressing hands down in front of chest: On the basis of 5), head, neck, chest, abdomen, legs and feet remain still. Move the arms forward, and keep them straight, and then press them downward, palms facing downward about 30 cm away from the knees (Fig. 17).

Fig. 17

Finally resume the posture of Fig.12, stand upright for about three minutes, raise the hands before chest, and inhale simultaneously. Turn the palms to face downward, draw them to chest, press them downward in parallel, and exhale simultaneously. Repeat the circle three times before finishing the exercise.

For the above-mentioned movements, the exerciser can decide the time for exercising and degree of bending knees according to his physical conditions. Beginners who are weak physically and have difficulty in bending knees can bend slightly or just stand instead. With the physical condition improved, they can bend knees with greater degrees and prolong the exercising time. Generally, time for each movement can be increased from one minute to ten minutes, and the total time for each sequence of exercise be increased from 10 minutes to approximately an hour.

Points to remember for the standing Qigong: Feet in parallel by shoulder width, torso and head kept erect, eyes looking forward, lips and teeth closed gently, chest drawn in and back erect, shoulder drooping and arms hanging downward, muscle of the whole body completely relaxed. The vertical line of knees cannot exceed the tips of toes.

(II) Breathing

(1) Natural breathing (i.e., breathe as one usually does) is to breath freely when one begins doing the exercise.

(2) Abdominal breathing (Expand abdomen as you inhale and contract it as you exhale) should be practised repeatedly. Try to make your breath slow, even, soft, deep and long. It would be better to do it under instructor's guidance.

(3) Directing the Qi to run through Dantian and Yongquan. When you inhale, direct the internal and external Qi to Dantian, and when you exhale, direct the Qi from Dantian to Yongquan at the soles of feet, and again direct it up to Dantian when inhaling. Repeat the cycle many times to make vital energy circulate up and down through Dantian

and Yongquan. Try to make the breath soft and natural without using effort.

(III) Mind Concentration

(1) When you are not concentrating on any acupoint, think of something pleasant, such as the success in work, fresh air in the field, or blossoming flowers in the park, and so on. Never think of anything horrible, frightening, or unpleasant. This is the approach beginners should follow.

(2) Concentrating the mind on a certain acupoint such as Dantian, or Yongquan.

(3) Direct the Qi to run through different points with inhaling and exhaling. For instance, direct the Qi to run from Dantian to Yongquan, and again up to Dantian repeatedly.

(IV) Closing Form

(1) Raise hands while legs gradually straightened, palms facing upward, fingers pointing each other, and inhale simultaneously. When the hands are raised to the height of neck, turn over the palms, press them downward, and exhale at the same time. Repeat the cycle three times before closing the exercise.

(2) When gradually straightening the two legs, raise hands with palms facing upward, fingers pointing to each other. When hands are raised to the height of neck, turn palms to face the back of the head, go on raising them to the height of the head with palms facing upward, and inhale simultaneously. Turn over palms and press them down to in front of the abdomen, and exhale simultaneously.

After closing the exercise, rub the two hands hot, knead the hair and bathe face 20 times with the hands. This will bring better results.

(V) Points for Attention

(1) Take every posture in correct and comfortable manner. try to avoid neck stiffening, shoulders shrugging, chest thrown out, upper body

leaning forward or backward or bending sideways. When taking standing exercise, keep the vertical line of knees in line with the tips of toes, If you sense discomfort, you must adjust posture and correct the fault in time.

(2) When taking exercise, always remember to keep relaxed, with a light smile on the face. Try to avoid mental tension, and never to pursue the feelings with effort.

(3) For beginners or seriously ill persons, it is advisable to use natural breathing, to think of something pleasant and to take high-position standing posture with hands pressing downward.

(4) When taking exercise, it is important to keep with a certain posture from beginning to end. Do not change postures or do something else at will (except involuntary acting).

(5) If you have the feelings of warming up, soreness and tingling, throbbing of the muscles, especially slight jerking at the finger tips and legs, or even trembling, do not get nervous, as these are the common effects. You should neither pursue them nor fear them.

(6) Feeling warm in one shoulder and cool in the other, or warm in one half of the body and cool in the other half during the exercise is the result of disharmony of vital energy and blood. You should go on practising and it will diminish. But if you feel cool all over the body or even instantly shiver, stop practising immediately, wash hands and rub face with warm water, and do the exercise the next day.

(7) It is inappropriate to take exercise outdoors in windy weather. Stand with the wind if the wind is gentle. When you practise indoors, the room should have good ventilation.

(8) It is inappropriate to take exercise before meal when you are hungry, or within thirty minutes after meal. When you feel too tired to take standing exercise, you may choose sitting or lying posture instead.

(9) It's a good phenomenon for you to feel warm and to sweat a little during practice. But do not stand in the wind or drink cold water or have cold bath right after the exercise. If condition permits, drink

some warm water and have a warm bath.

(10) Take care not to stop abruptly. You should bring the movement to an end gradually.

82. What Is Walking Qigong Exercise? How to Practise It?

Walking Qigong Exercise is a combination of walking with breathing and walking movements.

Left foot steps first. Outer side of heel touches the ground first and then the toes. Both left and right hand move to the left, with elbows bent, left hand a bit forward, palm facing upward, right hand a bit behind, palm facing leftward, and inhale at the same time. Right foot steps. Outer side of the heel touches the ground first and then the toes, turn both left and right hand to the right, with elbows bent, right hand a bit in the front, palm facing upward; left hand a bit behind, palm facing rightward, and exhale at the same time. Walk 100 steps in this way (Fig. 18 and 19).

Fig. 18, 19

Effects: This exercise has certain curative effects on chronic diseases and cancers. Walking speed and the frequency of walking vary with the physical condition and disease of the exerciser. For instance, the sufferer of heart attack may take slow walking in coordination with even breathing, and less frequency. The sufferer of tuberculosis may take quick walking and more frequently depending on his physical condition.

83. What Is Taiji Qigong of Eighteen-Forms? How to Practise It?

Taiji Qigong of Eighteen-Forms is a combination of some forms of Taijiquan (Taiji Boxing) with regulation of breathing. Its movements are simple and easy to learn, and can produce good curative effects. It requires one to take a correct posture, make even and slow movements. Inhale with nose, and exhale with mouth. It is especially good for the weak and sick persons to practise.

Form 1 **Commencing and Regulating Breathing** (Fig. 20, 21 and 22)

Fig. 20, 21

Fig. 22

Stand naturally with feet in parallel by shoulder width or wider, torse erect, eyes looking forward, chest slightly inward and back erect, hands naturally hanging down.

(1) **Raise arms slowly forward** and a little over shoulder level, palms facing downward, and inhale at the same time.

(2) Keep torse erect, bend knees and squat down (at the angle of about 150 degrees, knees not exceeding the tips of toes), hands pressing down gently to navel level, palms facing downward, and exhale at the same time.

Points to remember:

Shoulders sunk and elbows drooped. Fingers bent naturally and slightly. Center of gravity at the middle of both legs, buttocks sitting downward but not protruding out, lowering of arms in coordination with squatting of torso.

Repeat the cycle six times (each cycle includes one inhaling and one exhaling). Say two numbers for each cycle of breathing, with odd number for inhaling when hands are raised, and even number for exhaling when hands are lowered. And then place hands at the sides of the body.

Form 2 **Broadening the Chest** (Fig. 23 and 24)

Fig. 23

Fig. 24

Follow the movements of Form 1:

(1) Raise the hands in parallel to the chest, straighten knees gradually, turn the palms to face each other, draw arms to two sides in parallel to their utmost length to broaden the chest, and inhale at the same time.

(2) Draw arms close to the chest in parallel with palms facing downward, bend the knees with palms pressing down, and exhale at the same time.

Points to remember:

Gradually stand upright when arms are stretched and raised to the chest level Squat down when hands are pressing downward. Raising and standing up, pressing and squating, exhaling and inhaling should be done continuously and coordinately.

Repeat the cycles 6 times (one exhaling and one inhaling as one cycle).

Form 3 **Waving Like Rainbow** (Fig. 25 and 26)

Fig. 25, 26

Follow the movements of Form 2:

(1) Raise hands to the chest level in parallel, while knees are straightened gradually. Go on raising hands to head top, arms straightened, palms facing forward, and inhale simultaneously.

(2) Shift the weight toward the right foot, with right knee slightly bent and the whole sole touching the ground. Straighten the left leg with toes touching the ground and heel raised. Turn the left hand from the headtop to the left side horizontally with palms facing upward. And bend the right arm in a semi-circle, right palm facing downward, bend body sideways to the right, and inhale.

(3) Shift the weight toward the left foot, the whole sole touching the ground and the knee slightly bent. Straighten the right knee with heel raised and the toe touching the ground. Turn the right hand from the headtop to the right side horizontally with palms facing upward. Raise and bend left elbow over the headtop in a semi-circle with left palm facing downward, bend body sideways to the left and exhale at the same time.

Points to remember:

Waving of the hands should be coordinated with movements of

body bending sideways and breathing, looking gentle and soft in manner.

Repeat the cycle 6 times (one exhaling and one inhaling as one cycle).

Form 4 **Waving Arms As Separating Clouds** (Fig. 27 and 28)

Fig. 27, 28

Follow the movements of Form 3:

(1) Shift the gravity of the body to the middle between two legs in "horse step", turn the left hand from above downward to the right in front of the body front, and turn right hand from right side downward to the left in front of the body, overlapping the left hand with both palms facing inward before abdomen.

(2) Turn the palms of the overlapped hands to face upward and raise them over the headtop when knees are straightened with palms still facing upward, and inhale at the same time.

(3) Turn the palms of the overlapped hands outward, straighten the arms and drop them to two sides horizontally with palms facing downward. Gradually overlap two hands before the abdomen with elbows slightly bent, and exhale at the same time.

Points to remember:

When waving arms, shoulder joints are taken as the centre of a circle, forming two big circles from lower point inside up to outside. When the hands are over headtop, raise head and throw out chest to help inhale. While inhaling, straighten the knees. While exhaling, bend the knees.

Repeat the cycle 6 times:

Form 5 **Whirling Arms on Both Sides** (Fig. 29 and 30)

Fig. 29, 30

Follow the movements of Form 4:

(1) Form a "horse step", turn the palms of the overlapped hands upward in front of the body, move one hand forward and the other backward, stretch the left hand forward and upward , and the right hand makes a semi-circle past abdomen and upward to shoulder level, turn torso slightly to the right and the eyesight to the right hand, and inhale at the same time. Then bend right elbow with palms facing forward and draw hand past the ear before pushing it ahead, and exhale at the same time. Draw the straightened left hand back before the chest, while right hand is turned up passing over at its point of Small Yuji.

(2) The left hand goes on making a semi-circle past abdomen and upward to shoulder level, turn torso slightly to the left and eyesight

100

to the left hand, and inhale at the same time. Then bend left elbow
with palms facing forward and draw hand past the ear before pushing
it ahead, and exhale at the same time. Draw the straightened right hand
back before the chest, while the left hand is turned up passing over
at its point of Small Yuji. Turn the two hands alternately in this way.

Points to remember:

Overlap two hands just before the chest, inhale while drawing back,
and exhale while pushing forward.

Repeat the cycle 6 times.

Form 6 **Rowing in Lake Centre** (Fig. 31)

Fig. 31

Follow the movement of Form 5:

(1) When the left hand is pushed to in front of the chest and
passing over the right hand, turn both palms upward and make a circle
from the abdomen upward. Straighten the arms and raise them upward
horizontally with palms facing forward, straighten the legs and inhale
at the same time.

(2) While bending the waist, turn the straightened hands above,
downward and backward making a circle, and exhale at the same time.

(3) When the hands reach thhe lower back to the utmost length,

stretch the waist and raise the arms, turn the hands to both sides making a circle, and raise the hands over the headtop with palms facing forward, and inhale at the same time.

Points to remember:

Arms should be straightened, exhale when bending the waist, and inhale when stretching the waist.

Repeat the cycle 6 times.

Form 7 **Holding A Ball Before the Shoulder** (Fig. 32 and 33)

Fig. 32, 33

Follow the movements of Form 6:

(1) When waist bent and both hands reaching the lower back, straighten waist with left hand remaining still, and right hand raised to the left with palms turning upward in the manner of holding a ball. When raised to shoulder level, shift weight on left foot, right toes touching the ground and right heel slightly raised. Inhale while holding a ball, and exhale when right hand resuming its position downward on the right.

(2) Shift body weight to right foot, stand on left tiptoes with left heel raised. Raise left hand from left lower position up to right upper

102

position. When at right shoulder level, form the manner of holding a ball, and inhale at the same time. Resume left hand to the position downward on the left, and exhale at the same time.

Points to remember:

When forming the manner of holding a ball by left or right hand, eyes look at the ball, and press ground with tiptoes on the same side. Holding a ball, pressing ground and inhaling should be done coordinately.

Repeat the cycle 6 times.

Form 8 **Turning Torso to Look at the Moon** (Fig. 34)

Fig. 34

Follow the movements of Form 7:

(1) Stand naturally with hands hanging at the sides. When swinging hands upward to the left back, turn torso to the left, with head raised to the left back as if looking at the moon, and inhale at the same time. And then resume the posture of natural standing and exhale.

(2) Straighten both hands and swing them upward to the right back, turn torso to the right, with head raised toward right back as if looking at the moon, and inhale at the same time. And then resume

the posture of natural standing and exhale at the same time.

Points to remember:

Hand swinging, waist turning and head turning should be done coordinately. While looking at the moon, turn hand and waist and head to their extreme, and do not raise heels.

Repeat the cycle 6 times.

Form 9 **Turning Waist and Pushing Palms** (Fig. 35 and 36)

Fig. 35, 36

Follow the movements of Form 8:

(1) Form a "horse step" with hands at waist sides, clench fists with palms upward and hukou (part of the hand between thumb and index finger) outward. Draw back left elbow, turn torso to the left, turn right fist into palm, and then push out with inner strength, inhale at the same time. And then resume to original posture and exhale at the same time.

(2) Turn torso to the right, push left palm forward, inhale at the same time. And then resume to original posture and exhale at the same time.

Points to remember:

104

Palm pushing in fact is stretching wrist, so turn palm and fingers upward and small Yuji facing forward with one hand pushing forward and the other drawing backward, using opposite force.

Repeat the cycle 6 times.

Form 10 **Waving Hands Like Clouds with Legs Astride** (Fig. 37 and 38)

Fig. 37, 38

Follow the movements of Form 9:

(1) After pushing forward, turn left palm inward at the eye level. Turn right hand forward with palm facing leftward at the navel level. Turn both hands parallelly leftward while turning waist to the left, and inhale at the same time.

(2) When left turning to its extreme, turn right hand upward and palm inward at the eye level, turn left hand downward and palm rightward at the navel level. Turn both hands parallelly rightward while turning waist to the right, and exhale at the same time.

Points to remember:

Hand movements should be soft and gentle with eyesight always moving with the movement of one upper palm.

Repeat the cycle 6 times.

Form 11 **Dredging from the Sea and Looking at the Sky** (Fig. 39 and 40)

Fig. 39, 40

Follow the movements of Form 10:

(1) Left foot steps forward about half a step length forming a "bow step", torso slightly forward, both hands crossing before left knee, and commence inhaling.

(2) When torso leaning backward, raise the crossed hands over headtop and separate and stretch them as if looking up at the sky, with palms facing each other, and go on inhaling. When torso leaning forward, descend both hands from the sides to knee front and cross them, and exhale at the same time.

Points to remember:

Exhale when torso leaning forward and both hands pressed down and crossed, and inhale when both hands raised over headtop and stretched as if looking up at the sky. While looking up at the sky, stretch both hands as comfortably as possible.

Repeat the cycle 6 times.

Form 12 **Churning Up Waves and Billows** (Fig. 41 and 42)

Fig. 41, 42

Follow the movements of Form 11:

(1) Push the raised hands forward and upward, bend elbows at the chest front with palms facing outward, shift weight to right foot, heel of the forward foot touching the ground, and toes raised, and inhale at the same time.

(2) Shift body weight to left foot, the whole sole on the ground, torso moving slightly forward, right toes on the ground and heel raised. Push palms forward at the eye level, and exhale at the same time.

Points to remember:

While withdrawing the hands, shift the body weight backward, and inhale. While pushing palms forward, shift the body weight forward, and exhale. The movements show waves churning in the sea.

Repeat the cycle 6 times.

Form 13 **Pigeon Spreading Wings** (Fig. 43 and 44)

Fig. 43

Fig. 44

Follow the movements of Form 12:

(1) Stretch the arms straight in parallel with palms facing each other, shift body weight to right foot, raise forefoot, draw both hands back horizontally to the sides, and inhale at the same time.

(2) Shift body weight to left foot, raise right heel, withdraw both hands in front of the chest horizontally, and exhale.

.Points to remember:

When torso leaning back, arms spread like wings. Inhale while both arms spreading backward, and exhale when they withdrawing forward.

Repeat the cycle 6 times.

Form 14 **Straightening Arms and Pounding Fist** (Fig. 45 and 46)

Fig. 45, 46

Follow the movements of Form 13: turn "bow step" into "horse step", form two fists and put them at the sides of waist with centers of fists facing upward.

(1) Inhale while right fist pushing forward, and exhale when resuming to original position.

(2) Inhale while left fist pushing forward and exhale while resuming to original position.

Points to remember:

When turning "bow step" into "horse step", make exhaling soft and long. When pushing the fist forward with inner strength, inhale with eyes looking at the fist.

Repeat the cycle 6 times.

Form 15 **Wild Goose in Flight** (Fig. 47 and 48)

Fig. 47

Fig. 48

Follow the movements of Form 14, stand upright with hands raised at two sides to shoulder level.

(1) Squat as low as possible, press two hands downward like wild goose in flight, and at the same time exhale.

(2) Stand up and raise two hands in balance and inhale at the same time.

Points to remember:

Wrist joints should be soft. Squatting down and standing up, hands pressing down and raising up, and inhaling and exhaling should be done coordinately.

Repeat the cycle 6 times, one squatting-down and one standing-up as one cycle.

Form 16 **Revolving Like Flyingwheel** (Fig. 49 and 50)

Fig. 49, 50

Follow the movements of Form 15. Stand up with two hands before abdomen.

(1) Straighten two arms and revolve them upward to the left and over headtop with turning of waist, and inhale. Turn the hands downward to the right and exhale. Repeat the cycle 3 times.

(2) Reverse the revolving direction and repeat the cycle 3 times.

Points to remember:

When revolving hands round, turn waist simultaneously. Hand revolving and waist turning, and exhaling and inhaling should be done coordinately.

Form 17 **Stepping on the Spot and Bouncing A Ball** (Fig. 51)

Fig. 51

Follow the movements of Form 16:

(1) Raise left leg and right hand, forming the manner of bouncing a ball in front of right shoulder, and inhale at the same time.

(2) Raise right leg and left hand, forming the manner of bouncing a ball in front of left shoulder, and exhale at the same time.

Points to remember:

Raising hand, pouncing the ball, pressing down the foot, and inhaling and exhaling should be in unison. While marking time, i.e. stepping on the spot, steps should be light and nimble.

Repeat the cycle 6 times, with bouncing the ball by both left and right hands as one cycle.

Form 18 **Palms Pressing Down to Smooth Breathing** (Fig. 52 and 53)

Fig. 52, 53

Follow the movements of Form 17. Stand up with two hands before abdomen.

(1) Fingers of both hands facing each other, palms facing upward and raised from before chest up to eye level, and inhale at the same time.

(2) Turn over palms, fingers of both hands facing each other, palms facing downward, and pressed down from in front of the eye to the abdomen level, and exhale at the same time.

Points to remember:

Inhale while raising the hands, and exhale while pressing them down at slow speed.

Repeat the cycle 6 times, with a raising and pressing down as one cycle.

84. How to Practise Qigong Shiduanjin (Ten-Section Exercise)?

Qigong Shiduanjin (Ten-Section Exercise) includes Ten-Section

Exercise on Bed and Ten-Section Standing Exercise. It is suitable for the weak and the sick. Ten-section Exercise on Bed is especially suitable for the sick persons lying in bed. Its movements are simple and gentle. You can do the exercise according to the beats in the mind and in coordination with breathing. It is easy to learn and patients with chronic diseases will benefit from it.

(I) Ten-Section Exercise on Bed

It is good to do the Ten-Section Exercise in a sitting posture on bed without quilts, or better still to do it on a plank bed. Details follow:

(1) **Loosening Neck** (Fig. 54, 55 and 56)

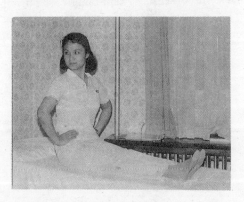

Fig. 54, 55

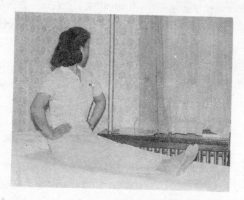

Fig. 56

Sit on the bed, legs naturally straightened, arms akimbo, head and torso erect, and eyes looking forward. Turn head to the left as far as possible, and inhale at the first beat. Resume original position, and exhale at the next beat. Turn head to the right as far as possible, and inhale at the third beat. Resume original position, and exhale at the fourth beat. Repeat the exercise in two octuple beats. (Say the beats in the mind. If practise it collectively, give the beats in word of command.)

Points to remember:

Turn the neck with other parts kept unmoved. Turn the neck with movements in coordination with breathing.

(2) **Turning Over Palms and Expanding Chest** (Fig. 57 and 58)

Fig. 57

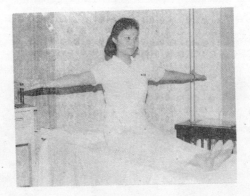

Fig. 58

Follow Section (1), raise two arms with elbows bent, two palms pointing to each other horizontally and facing downward. When counting 1 in the mind, expand chest with the help of two arms, and inhale at the same time. When counting 2 in the mind, turn over palms and straighten the arms outward, and expand chest by stretching the arms forward and outward, and exhale at the same time. Repeat 4 ocutaple beats.

Points to remember:

Expand chest with effort. Inhale when bending elbows and expanding chest, and exhale when straightening elbows and expanding chest. The movements should be practised at a horizontal level.

(3) Holding Up Heavy Weight with Both Palms (Fig. 59 and 60)

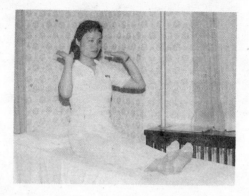

Fig. 59

Fig. 60

Follow Section (2), bend two arms and separate them to the sides of chest at the same level. When counting 1 in the mind, push arms upward with force, lift head looking up and inhale at the same time. When counting 2 in the mind, resume original posture, and exhale. Repeat 8 beats four times.

Points to remember:

1) Stretching arms, inhaling and lifting head should be done simultaneously.

2) Dropping the arms, looking straight forward and exhaling should be done coordinately.

(4) Turning Head and Aiming at Vulture (Fig. 61, 62 and 63)

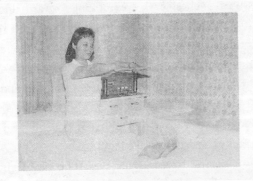

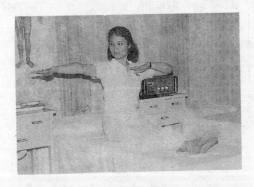

Fig. 61, 62, 63

118

Follow Section (3). When counting 1 in the mind, straighten and raise two arms forward at chest level, eyes looking forward, and inhale. When counting 2 in the mind, turn over left palm and turn the hand to the left horizontally, with the head also turning to the left, eyes following left palm. Simultaneously bend right elbow in front of the chest with palm downward, and pull it rightward with force, and exhale. When counting 3 in the mind, resume the position with two arms at chest level, eyes looking forward and inhaling. When counting 4 in the mind, turn over right palm and turn the hand to the right horizontally, with the head also turning to the right, eyes following right palm. Simultaneously bend left elbow in front of the chest with palm downward and draw it leftward with effort, and exhale. Repeat 8-beats 4 times.

Points to remember:

1) Movements of head and left and right hands and breathing should be in coordination.

2) While taking the posture of aiming at a vulture, draw the bent elbow leftward or rightward as far as possible, and expand chest with effort.

(5) **Holding Head and Bending Waist** (Fig. 64 and 65)

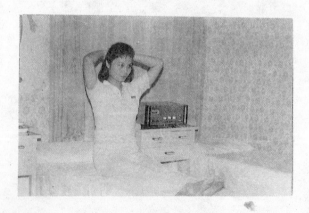

Fig. 64

Fig. 65

Follow Section (4), clasp hands behind the hand with palms facing forward and thumbs pointing downward. When counting 1 in the mind, contract abdomen and bend waist forward, and at the same time inhale. When counting 2 in the mind, resume head to original position, torso erect naturally, and exhale at the same time. Repeat 8-beats 4 times.

Points to remember:

1) Take vertebra as axis when bending forward and leaning backward.

2) Movements and breathing should be in coordination.

(6) **Kneading Chest and Abdomen** (Fig. 66 and 67)

Fig.66

Fig. 67

Follow Section (5), overlap both hands with left palm pressing right breast and fingers pointing rightward. When counting 1 in the mind, move palms leftward horizontally and then move downward to the left lower abdomen, and inhale at the same time. When counting 2 in the mind, move palms from left lower abdomen to right lower abdomen, and move them upward to right upper abdomen horizontally, and resume the original position at right breast, and exhale at the same time. Repeat 8-beats 4 times.

Points to remember:

Move clockwise left palm in the manner of even and soft massage, that is, from right breast to left breast to left lower abdomen to right lower abdomen and back to right breast.

(7) **Turning A Millstone with Both Hands** (Fig. 68 and 69)

Fig. 68, 69

Follow Section (6), bend two arms before the belly with palms facing downward. When counting 1 in the mind, stretch both hands left forward, and inhale at the same time. When counting 2 in the mind, move both hands as if turning a millstone in the direction from left forward to right forward to right backward to left backward, and exhale at the same time. Repeat 8-beats 4 times.

Points to remember:

Movements of turning a millstone with both hands should be done horizontally and evenly.

(8) **Massaging Ribs and Waist** (Fig. 70 and 71)

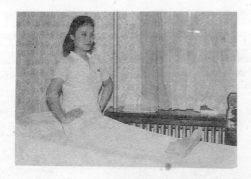

Fig. 70, 71

Follow Section (7), set arms akimbo with hukou facing downward. When counting 1 in the mind, raise hands in parallel upward to back ribs (raise as far as possible), and inhale at the same time. Move two palms downward in parallel massaging the waist, and exhale. Repeat 8-beats 4 times.

Points to remember:

1) Raising upward and moving downward should be done at even speed, applying massage with moderate force.

2) Raise upward with effort, and move downward with moderate force to apply massage to the waist.

(9) **Turning Two Legs Outward** (Fig. 72 and 73)

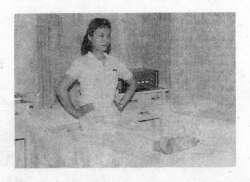

Fig. 72, 73

Follow Section (8), set both arms akimbo. When counting 1 in the mind, straighten and lay two legs flat, and turn two feet outward with heels as axes (stretching outward), and inhale at the same time. When counting 2 in the mind, turn the feet inward (stretching inward), and exhale at the same time. Repeat 8-beats 4 times.

Points to remember:

1) When turning two feet, keep torso erect and still.

2) Two knees should be turned outward or inward as far as possible.

(10) **Drawing Legs Inward and Loosening Knees** (Fig. 74)

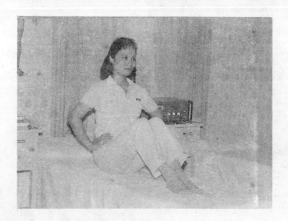

Fig. 74

Follow Section (9), set arms akimbo or palms pressing on the bed, fingers pointing forward at the sides of thighs. When counting 1 in the mind, draw and bend knees backward, and inhale at the same time. When counting 2 in the mind, straighten knees and resume original posture, and exhale at the same time. Repeat 8-beats 4 times.

Points to remember:

1) While bending knees, draw legs backward as far as possible.

2) Keep the inner sides of the knees and legs close together when doing knee-bending and knee-stretching movements.

124

(II) Ten-Section Standing Exercise

(1) **Standing Upright with Hands Up and Feet Steady on the Ground** (Fig. 75 and 76)

Fig. 75

Fig. 76

Stand naturally upright with feet apart by shoulder width, torso erect, eyes looking straight ahead, hands clasped with palms naturally before chest. When counting 1 in the mind, turn palms outward and then raise them upward from in front of the chest to headtop, lift head and inhale simultaneously. When counting 2 in the mind, move the clasped hands horizontally downward from headtop, passing chest front to the front of abdomen, turn palms outward and put them on abdomen, keep head erect, and exhale at the same time. Repeat 8-beats 4 times. (Say all the beats in the mind. If the exercise is practised collectively, give the beats in word of command.)

Points to remember:

1) Raising and lowering of palms should be perpendicular to the ground, that is, as close to chest and face as possible.

2) Raise palms to the highest point, as if you are lifting slightly upward with effort.

(2) **Picking Fruit and Pulling Downward** (Fig. 77 and 78)

Fig. 77, 78

Follow Section (1), separate the clasped hands at abdomen and raise them over head with fingers separated, palms facing forward and upward, hands separated by shoulder width. When counting 1 in the mind, do the movement of picking fruit, clench hands and pull them downward in parallel to the front of shoulders, palms facing forward, and inhale at the same time. When counting 2 in the mind, raise two fists upward in parallel to the highest point, and exhale at the same time. Repeat 8-beats 4 times.

Points to remember:

1) Raise hands upward naturally. Pick fruit and pull them downward with effort.

2) Raising upward and pulling downward are done with head erect, do not look up.

(3) **Thrusting Fists Sideways** (Fig. 79 and 80)

Fig. 79, 80

Follow Section (2), clench hands into fists at the waist sides with palms facing upward and hukou facing outward. When counting 1 in the mind, turn over two fists and thrust them upward to the sides horizontally at shoulder level with palms facing downward, and inhale at the same time. When counting 2 in the mind, withdraw the fists to waist sides, and resume original posture, and exhale at the same time. Repeat 8-beats 4 times.

Points to remember:

1) Thrust fists with force.

2) Thrusting fists outward and drawing them inward are done with fist palms turning downward, or upward.

(4) **Holding Head and Bending Sideways** (Fig. 81, 82 and 83)

Fig. 81

Fig. 82

Fig. 83

Follow Section (3), clasp hands with palms holding the back of the head. When counting 1 in the mind, protrude waist to the right side and bend body to the left side, and inhale at the same time. When counting 2 in the mind, resume the original posture, and exhale at the same time. When counting 3 in the mind, protrude waist to the left side and bend the body to the right side and inhale. Resume original posture at the fourth beat and exhale.

Points to remember:

Bending is done only at the waist, with other parts following the bending. Keep knees straight. Bending sideways is done as far as possible.

(5) **Bending Forward and Leaning Backward** (Fig. 84 and 85)

Fig. 84

Fig. 85

. Follow Section (4), move the clasped hands from the back of the head downward and set arms akimbo. When counting 1 in the mind, contract belly and bend forward at waist to horizontal level, and inhale. When counting 2 in the mind, lean backward, throw waist forward as far as possible, and exhale at the same time. Repeat 8-beats 4 times.

Points to remember:

1) Bending forward and leaning backward are done only at the waist, the rest of the body follows the movements.

2) While bending forward or leaning backward, keep two knees straight.

(6) Thrusting Fist with Legs Astride (Fig. 86)

Fig. 86

Follow Section (5), set legs astride with two hands clenched into fists at sides and palms facing upward and hukou facing outward. When counting 1 in the mind, turn over right fist and thrust it forward with force, palms facing downward, elbow straightened. Keep torso still, eyes looking at the fist, and inhale at the same time. When counting 2 in the mind, draw the right fist back to original position, and exhale at the same time. When counting 3 in the mind, turn over left fist and thrust it forward with effort, palms facing downward and elbow straightened. Keep torso still, eyes looking at the fist, and inhale at the same time. When counting 4 in the mind, draw the left fist back to the original position, and exhale at the same time. Repeat 8-beats 4 times.

Points to remember:

1) Thrust fist with force, and withdraw it naturally.

2) Keep torso and two legs still.

(7) **Horizontal Raising and Half-Squatting** (Fig. 87 and 88)

Fig. 87

Fig. 88

132

Follow Section (6), stand upright naturally, with two hands at the sides of thighs and palms facing inward. When counting 1 in the mind, squat down halfway with the vertical line of knees not exceeding the tips of toes. At the same time raise two hands horizontally in front of the chest with palms facing downward, and inhale. When counting 2 in the mind, resume natural standing posture, and exhale at the same time. Repeat 8-beats 4 times.

Points to remember:

1) Raising hands horizontally and bending knees should be practised simultaneously and in coordination.

2) Aged and weak persons may bend knees with smaller degrees.

(8) **Circling Knees with Hands on Them** (Fig. 89 and 90)

Fig. 89

Fig. 90

Follow Section (7), stand with feet together and torso bent forward, knees slightly bent and palms on them. When counting 1 in the mind, circle knees from right backward to left backward, and inhale at the same time. When counting 2 in the mind, circle them from left backward to left forward to right forward and right backward, and exhale at the same time. Repeat 8-beats 2 times. Then, circle knees in reverse direction, that is, from right forward to left forward, and inhale at the same time, and from left backward to right backward, and exhale at the same time.

Repeat 8-beats 2 times.

Points to remember:

1) Knees should be circled evenly and smoothly.

2) Mainly exercise knees, the other parts of the body follow the movements.

(9) **Kicking Left or Right Foot** (Fig. 91 and 92)

Fig. 91

Fig. 92

Follow Section (8), stand upright naturally with arms akimbo and hukou facing inward. When counting 1 in the mind, kick right foot upward to the left, toes stretched, and inhale at the same time. When counting 2 in the mind, resume right foot to its original position, and exhale at the same time. When counting 3 in the mind, kick left foot upward to the right, toes stretched, and exhale at the same time. When counting 4 in the mind, resume left foot to its original position, and inhale. Repeat 8-beats 4 times.

Points to remember:

1) Kick the foot upward with as much effort as possible.

2) While kicking, do not bend torso forward, exercise only the hip joints.

(10) **Waves Moving Forward** (Fig. 93 and 94)

Fig. 93

Fig. 94

Follow Section (9), take half a step forward with left foot, keep arms akimbo. When counting 1 in the mind, move torso forward, with weight shifted to left toes, throw out hipjoint forward to the left with right heel raised, and inhale at the same time. When counting 2 in the mind, move torso backward to the right, weight shifted to right heel, left toes raised and exhale at the same time. Repeat 8-beats twice. When counting 3 in the mind, take half a step forward with right foot, and go on repeating 8-beats another 2 times.

Points to remember:

1) Shift weight and move forward and backward as if waves are moving gently in the sea, and you'll feel comfortable with a sense of rhythm.

2) Movements should be coordinated and gentle.

85. How to Practise Massage and Patting Exercises?

This exercise is to apply massage to some parts or some acupuncture points of the body with one's own hands so as to clear the main and collateral channels, activate Qi and blood, and finally bring good health.

(I) Self-Massage

(1) **Massaging Forehead** (Fig. 95 and 96)

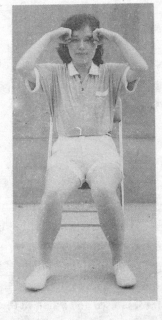

Fig. 95, 96

Clench hands into fists with hukou inward, press the point between eyebrows at the forehead with mid-joints of index fingers. Draw the finger joints apart sideways up to Taiyang points and massage the points 20 times (Taiyang acupoint is at the hollow place by the side of the end of eyebrow).

Good for:

Ache at forehead and sense of heaviness between two eyebrows.

(2) **Rubbing Neck** (Fig. 97)

Fig. 97

Clasp the fingers with palms pressing on the back of head and thumbs pointing downward. Rub gently down to Dazhui point; repeat the rubbing 20 times (Dazhui point is the seventh cervical vertebra, the most protruding part of the back neck).

Good for:

Ache at the back of the head, and relaxation of the neck muscle.

(3) **Bathing Face** (Fig. 98 and 99)

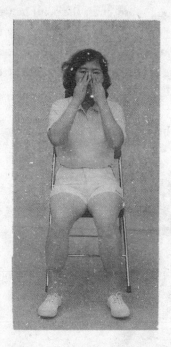

Fig. 98

Fig. 99

Rub palms till they are warm. Press both sides of nose with mid-fingers bringing along other fingers upward. Move sideways across forehead and downward across cheeks. Repeat the rubbing 20 times.

Good for:

Blood circulation in the face, and ruddy complexion. Prevention of catching cold and face getting wrinkled too early.

(4) Rubbing Ear Sides (Fig. 100)

Fig. 100

Fig. 101

Hold ears with mid-fingers, ring-fingers and small-fingers in front and thumbs and index-fingers at the back, that is, three fingers in front and two fingers at the back, rubbing ears up and down and rubbing the ear roots 20 times.

Good for:

Prevention of dizziness and tinnitus.

(5) **Rubbing Nose Sides** (Fig. 101)

Clench hands gently into fists, and rub both sides of nose up and down for 10 times. Rub with both hands simultaneously up to the lower parts of eyes and down to the sides of nostrils.

Good for:

Blood circulation in nasal cavity, keeping a certain temperature, and preventing cough and cold.

(6) **Bathing Hands** (Fig. 102)

Fig. 102

Rub palms together till they are warm. Rub the back of right hand with left palm, and then rub the back of left hand with right palm. Repeat the cycle 10 times.

Good for:

Flexibility of fingers, harmonization of Qi and blood and promotion of functioning of main and collateral channels.

(7) **Bathing Arms** (Fig. 103 and 104)

Fig. 103

Fig. 104

Press inner side of left wrist with right palm. Rub with effort along the inner side of arm upward to armpit. Turn over shoulder, rub outer side of arm downward to the back of left hand. Rub in this way for 10 times. Then change into left hand, and rub right arm in the same way for another 10 times.

Good for:

Improving flexibility of joints, preventing inflammation in the joints, clearing the main and collateral channels and preventing ache in arms.

(8) **Massaging Chest** (Fig. 105)

Fig. 105

Fig. 106

Put left hand at waist or at the root of thigh, press the upper part of right breast with right palm, thumb pointing upward and fingers pointing leftward, massage the chest clockwise in a circle for 20 times.

Good for:

Warming chest, strengthening the heart and easing stuffiness.

(9) **Massaging Abdomen** (Fig. 106)

Set left hand akimbo or at the root of thigh, press right palm on the lower part of right ribs with thumb pointing upward and other fingers pointing to the left. Massage the abdomen clockwise in a circle for 20 times.

Good for:

Nourishing intestine and stomach, strengthening digestion, improving appetite and removing intestine and stomach disorders.

(10) **Rubbing the Back of Waist** (Fig. 107)

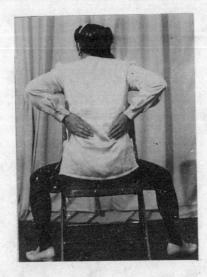

Fig. 107

Rub palms together till they are warm. Press them on the back of waist, rub with force downward to sacrum, and then upward as far as the arms can bend. This is taken as one cycle. Repeat the circle 40 times.

Good for:

Warming up the back of waist, enhancing the function of kidneys, clearing the Daimai (girdle channel). Constant practice of this exercise will keep one's back erect even at advanced age, and prevent backache. Sufferers with backache may repeat the rubbing hundreds of times till perspirating to produce curative effects.

(11) **Bathing Thighs** (Fig. 108)

144

Fig. 108

Fig. 109

First hold the root of one thigh with both hands. Rub downward with force to knee joint, and then upward to the thigh root. This is taken as one cycle, and repeat the cycle 10 times. Do the same with the other thigh.

Good for:

Strengthening the muscles of the thighs, removing soreness and pain, making the joints flexible and helping steady walking.

(12) **Rubbing the back of Legs** (Fig. 109)

Press hukou of left hand on right knee pit, rub the leg with force downward to heel and then upward. Repeat the rubbing 10 times. Do the same with the other leg for another 10 times.

Good for:

Loosening the muscles of legs, dispelling fatigue, making the tendons flexible and helping steady walking.

(13) **Rubbing Soles of Feet** (Fig. 110)

Fig. 110

Take a sitting posture, pull left toes outward to reveal the sole (Yongquan Point) of left foot. Massage the area with right palm for 20 times. Massage the right sole with left palm in the same way for another 20 times.

Good for:

Nourishing the Ying and reducing heat, easing liver and brightening eyes, and quieting the brain to have sound sleep. It will be more effective to do the exercise right after washing feet.

Points to remember for self-massage

1) Number of times for massage and force applied vary with

different people. It is good for you to feel comfortable and relaxed after massage. Force applied shouid be moderate, too little force produces no effect, too much force will injure the skin.

2) Always keep the skin clean, if there is sweat on hands or body, dry it with towel before the exercise.

3) When massaging, it will be more effective to be naked or wear thin clothes. Do not wash with cold water immediately after massage.

4) Stop doing massage if you have skin diseases or boils.

5) Self-massage combined with therapeutic breathing exercise according to one's physical condition will bring better effects.

(II) Self-Patting

(1) Sounding Heaven Drum (Fig. 111)

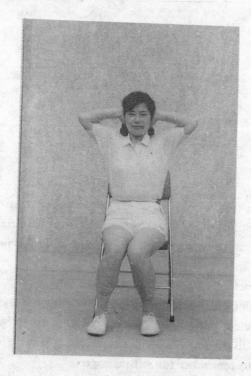

Fig. 111

Press palms on earholes with fingers tightly pressed on the occipital bone, and let loose all of a sudden, opening and closing in this way to sound the drum for 10 times.

Good for:

Refreshing the brain, dispelling tinitus, improving hearing ability, and preventing ear diseases.

(2) **patting Shoulders and Back** (Fig. 112 and 113)

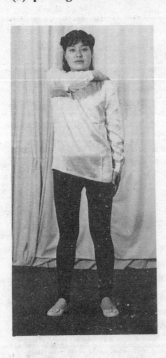

Fig. 112

Fig. 113

Pat shoulders and back with both hands, right palm patting left shoulder (at the back upperside of shoulder joint) and left hand patting the upper back (at the lower side of shoulder joint). Repeat the patting 20 times. And then pat right shoulder (at the back upperside of shoulder joint) with left palm and pat the upper back (at the lower side of shoulder joint) with right palm. Patting in this way 20 times.

Good for:

Loosening the shoulders and back and removing aches in shoulders and back.

(3) **Striking Abdomen** (Fig. 114)

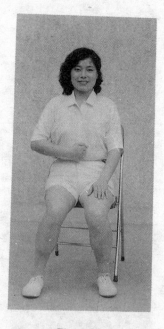 

Fig. 114   Fig. 115

Keep torso erect and gently clench hands with palms facing inward. Strike abdomen gently and slightly 20 times.

Good for:

Activating Qi and blood and strengthening intestine and spleen.

(4) **Striking the Lower Back and Buttocks** (Fig. 115)

Stand with torso bent slightly at an angle of about 80 degrees, clench hands gently and strike the lower back and buttocks 20 times with each of hollow fists alternately.

Good for:

Strengthening spleen and the lower back, and dispelling low back pain.

(5) **Striking Thighs** (Fig. 116)

Fig. 116

Sit naturally or sit back, clench hands gently into hollow fists, strike the front part of thighs alternately with each of the fist, left fist on left thigh and right fist on right thigh. Strike from the thigh roots to knees back and forth for 40 times.

Good for:

Relaxing muscles, smoothing Qi and blood and removing pain in the thighs.

86. How to Practise Limb Exercise?

Section 1 **Expanding Chest** (Fig. 117 and 118)

Fig. 117

Fig. 118

Stand naturally with hands half clenched and hukou facing inward. Bend elbows before chest and pull two arms to both sides (one pulling and retracting as one cycle), and return to in front of the chest with elbows bent. Repeat the pulling and retracting 20 times.

Good for:

Broadening chest, clearing lungs and strengthening heart.

Section 2 **Turning Shoulders** (Fig. 119 and 120)

Fig. 119

Fig. 120

152

Stand naturally with arms akimbo and hukou facing downward. Turn left shoulder forward and right shoulder backward. Then turn left shoulder backward and right shoulder forward. Turn alternately for 20 times.

Good for:

Strengthening the spleen and lessening depression, and clearing liver and regulating Qi.

Section 3 **Single Hand Holding the Sky** (Fig. 121)

Fig. 121   Fig. 122

Stand naturally with arms akimbo. Raise upward alternately with the hand, eyes looking at back of the hand. Raising the right hand and the left hand alternately for 20 times.

Good for:

Regulating spleen and stomach and enhancing digestion.

Section 4 **Turning Torso to Look At the Moon** (Fig. 122)

Stand naturally. Swing two arms left upward with torso turned leftward and eyes looking at the highest point of left hand. Then swing both arms right upward with torso turned rightward and eyes looking at the highest point of right hand. Swing right and left alternately for 20 times.

Good for:

Exercising muscles of the lower back, preventing neck disorders.

Section 5 **Double-Circling As Fetching Water** (Fig. 123 and 124)

Fig. 123

Fig. 124

Stand with one foot in the front and the other foot behind, torso sunk as starting to run. First the left foot steps forward, raise both hands forward as holding the handle of waterwheel, push the handles and then downward in the manner of circling. Circle in this way for 10 times, then do the same with right foot in front for another 10 times.

Good for:

Exercising muscles of chest and back and the joints, activating Qi.and blood, and dispelling aches.

Section 6   **Separating Heaven from Earth** (Fig. 125 and 126)

Fig. 125

Fig. 126

Set at a "bow" step with the front foot bent and back foot straightened. Swing both arms up and down and back and forth with fingers separated naturally. When at left bow step, swing right hand first, and when at right bow step, swing left hand first. Swing both hands alternately 20 times for each.

Good for:

Stimulating the functioning of channels and loosening muscles and joints to cause Qi and blood to flow downward.

Section 7 **Exercising the Hips** (Fig. 127)

Fig. 127

Stand with two feet in parallel a little wider than shoulder width, and set arms akimbo. Circle the hips from left forward to right forward and right backward to left backward continuously like turning a millstone for 20 times. Then do the circling in reverse direction for another 20 times.

Good for:

Exercising the lower back and hips, relaxing muscles and dispelling aches in these parts.

Section 8 **Twisting Knees** (Fig. 128)

Fig. 128

Bend knees in half squatting manner with both palms holding one knee, first turn the knee from left forward to right forward and then to right backward and finally to left backward for 20 times. Then turn in reverse direction for another 20 times.

Good for:

Exercising knee joints, strengthening strength and preventing pain of lower-limbs.

Finally, step in place for 20 times to finish the whole exercise.

87. How to Practise Ten-Section Joint Exercise?

Ten-Section Joint Exercise is especially effective for curing joint diseases. It may be taken as a preparatory exercise for doing Qigong.

Section 1

Stand erect with two feet apart by shoulder width, keep neck erect, eyes looking forward. Stretch two hands forward in parallel with palms facing downward. When 1 is given in word of command, bend knee-joints at an angle of about 140 degrees, the vertical line of knees not exceeding the tips of toes. Meanwhile, bend wrist joints, pointing downward. Then resume original standing posture at once. When 2 is given in command, repeat the above movements. Repeat 8-beats 4 times (Fig. 129 and 130).

Fig. 129

Fig. 130

Section 2

Resume standing posture, stretch out two arms with fingers of both hands pointing to each other and palms facing inward. When 1 is given in word of command, bend knee-joints, elbows and wrists simultaneously facing chest. Then resume original standing posture immediately. When 2 is given in command, repeat the above movements. Do 8-beats 4 times (Fig. 131 and 132).

Fig. 131

Fig. 132

Section 3

Resume standing posture, bend two arms before chest with fingers of both hands pointing to each other, and palms facing outward, back of hand about 10 centimetres from chest. When 1 is given in word of command, bend knee-joints, and stretch out elbows in parallel simultaneously, pushing palms forward. Then, resume original standing posture. When 2 is given in word of command, repeat the above movements. Do 8-beats 4 times (Fig. 133 and 134).

Fig. 133

Fig. 134

Section 4

Resume standing posture, bend two arms before chest with fingers pointing to each other and palms facing downward. When 1 is given in word of command, bend knee-joints, and wrists simultaneously in downward direction. Then, resume original standing posture at once. When giving 2 in word of command, repeat the movements. Do 8-beats 4 times (Fig. 135 and 136).

Fig. 135

Fig. 136

Section 5

Resume standing posture. Raise and stretch out two arms sideways with palms facing downward. When 1 is given in word of command, bend knee-joints and wrists simultaneously in downward direction. Then, resume original standing posture. When giving 2 in command, repeat the movements. Do 8-beats 4 times altogether (Fig. 137 and 138).

Fig. 137

Fig. 138

Section 6

Resume standing posture. Bend two arms before chest with fingers of both hands pointing to each other and palms facing upward. When 1 is given in word of command, bend knee-joints, straighten elbows and push palms upward simultaneously (like holding up a volley ball). Then, resume original standing posture. When 2 is given in word of command, repeat the movements. Do 8-beats 4 times (Fig. 139 and 140).

Fig. 139

Fig. 140

Section 7

Resume standing posture. Straighten two arms forward in parallel with palms facing downward. When 1 is given in word of command, bend knee-joints and wrist-joints simultaneously in downward direction. And then resume original standing posture. When 2 is given in word of command, do the same movements as command 1, with two palms moving leftward at an angle of 45 degrees. When giving 3 in word of command, maintain the movements as 1 and 2, with two palms moving leftward at an angle of 90 degrees. When giving 4 in word of command, maintain the movements of 1, 2, and 3 with two palms moving backward at an angle of about 135 degrees. Reverse the movements at the word command of 5, 6, 7 and 8, and resume original posture. And then, turn rightward and do another 8 beats. Altogether repeat 8-beats 8 times (Fig. 141 and 142).

Fig. 141

Fig. 142

Section 8

Resume standing posture. Straighten both arms forward in parallel with palms facing downward, and arm and chest at an angle of about 45 degrees. When giving 1 in word of command, bend knee-joints and simultaneously bend wrist-joints in forward and downward direction, and then resume original standing posture. When giving 2 in word of command, repeat the movements of command 1, and do 8-beats 4 times (Fig. 143 and 144).

Fig. 143

Fig. 144

Section 9

Step forward with left foot, toes pointing forward, right foot behind, forming a "T" shaped standing posture. Straighten two arms horizontally one in front and the other behind with palms facing downward. Set left hand in front in the direction of left toes. When giving 1 in word of command, bend knee-joint forming a "bow" step, and circle two wrist-joints simultaneously (i.e. turning them downward and inward), and resume original standing posture. When giving 2 in word of command, repeat the movements of command 1. Do 8-beats 4 times altogether (Fig. 145).

Fig. 145

Fig. 146

Section 10

Follow Section 9, turn torso and set right foot in front, toes pointing forward and forming a "T" shaped standing posture. Do all the movements of Section 9. Do 8-beats 4 times altogether (Fig. 146).

Finally, take easy walking and step in place at 8 beats for 4 times to finish the exercise. Then, you will feel warming up all over the body, or even perspire a little. This will prepare you for doing Qigong exercise. It is desirable to practise Ten-Section Joint Exercise especially in winter.

88. How to Practise Qigong Stick Exercise?

Qigong Stick Exercise is a combination of wooden stick exercise with Qigong regulation of breathing. It is simple in equipment and movement, easy to learn, and bringing good curative effects. It requires the exerciser to take correct postures, have strong sense of rhythm, and coordinate with breathing. This exercise is suitable for the weak and the sick to practise. Prepare a wooden or bamboo stick about 2 centimetres in diameter and 90 centimetres in length before doing the exercise.

Posture 1 **Raising Arms Upward** (Fig. 147 and 148)

Fig. 147

Fig. 148

Stand naturally with feet apart in parallel by shoulder width. Keep torso erect and relaxed. Two hands 60 — 70 centimetres apart, holding the stick in front of the chest.

Movements:

(1) Raise up the stick with both hands over headtop, and inhale at the same time.

(2) Lower the stick to original position and exhale at the same time.

Points to remember:

When raising upward, use internal force and move slowly, keep head erect. When lowering the stick, movement must be slow and coordinate with breathing. Inhale with nose and exhale with mouth. Repeat the cycle 20 times (one inhaling and exhaling as one cycle).

Posture 2 **Push Forward Horizontally Before Chest**
(Fig. 149 and 150)

Fig. 149

Fig. 150

168

Follow Posture 1.

(1) Push the stick forward horizontally with both arms and inhale.

(2) Retract the stick to the chest front horizontally and exhale.

Points to remember:

Stick is pushed forward and retracted backward horizontally in front of the chest. Use internal force. The movements should be coordinated with breathing.

Repeat the cycle 20 times (one inhaling and exhaling as one cycle).

Posture 3 **Turning Leftward and Rightward Horizontally** (Fig. 151 and 152)

Fig. 151

Fig. 152

Follow Posture 2.

(1) Inhale when pushing the stick forward horizontally with both arms.

(2) Turn torso leftward, arms holding up the stick horizontally and turning leftward as far as possible, and at the same time exhale.

(3) Resume the posture with the stick pushed forward horizontally and inhale at the same time.

(4) Retract the stick in front of the chest, and exhale at the same time. Then, turn rightward horizontally and do the same movements.

Points to remember:

When turning leftward or rightward, move the stick horizontally as far as possible.

Repeat the turning 20 times (turning leftward and rightward once as one time).

Posture 4 **Circling Round the Shoulder As Performing Dragon Dance** (Fig. 153, 154 and 155)

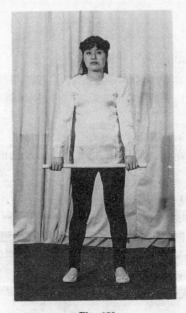

Fig. 153

Fig. 154, 155

Follow Posture 3.

(1) Swing up the stick left upward and inhale.

(2) Lower the stick naturally and make a circle before chest and exhale.

(3) Swing it up right upward and inhale.

(4) Lower the stick naturally and make a circle before chest and exhale.

Points to remember:

While turning around, arms are straightened. Movements should be done continuously with the stick raised to the highest point.

Repeat the swinging 20 times (Swinging leftward and rightward once as one time).

Posture 5 **Exercising Hipbones on Four Sides** (Fig. 156, 157, 158 and 159)

Fig. 156

Fig. 157

Fig. 158

Fig. 159

Follow Posture 4. Stand naturally upright with feet pointing forward in parallel by shoulder width. Hands holding the stick and placing it on the back of the neck horizontally.

(1) Inhale when bending the torso forward.

(2) Exhale when resuming standing posture.

(3) Inhale when leaning backward.

(4) Exhale when resuming standing posture.

(5) Inhale when bending leftward.

(6) Exhale when resuming standing posture.

(7) Inhale when bending rightward.

(8) Exhale when resuming standing posture.

Points to remember:

Bending of torso forward, backward, leftward and rightward should be done as far as possible with knee joints stretched and legs kept erect.

Repeat the bending 10 times (Bending forward and backward and leftward and rightward once as one time).

Posture 6 **Kicking Legs Leftward and Rightward** (Fig. 160 and 161)

Fig. 160, 161

Follow Posture 5.

(1) Raise the stick from the back of the neck, bring it to in front of the chest, and push it forward horizontally, and inhale at the same time.

(2) When kicking right upward with left foot, draw the stick backward to the left, and exhale at the same time.

(3) Return the stick to forward posture and inhale.

(4) When kicking left upward with right foot, draw the stick backward to the right, and exhale at the same time.

Points to remember:

While kicking legs, straighten the feet, and kick up as far as possible. Meanwhile, draw the stick with both hands backward as far as possible.

Repeat the kicking 20 times (Kicking leftward and rightward once as one time).

Posture 7 **Raising Up Overhead** (Fig. 162, 163 and 164)

Fig. 162

Fig. 163

Fig. 164

Follow Posture 6. Stand naturally with the stick held before thighs.

(1) Swing the stick upward with left foot stretching backward and inhale.

(2) Lower the stick and resume original standing posture and exhale.

(3) Swing the stick upward with right foot stretching backward and inhale.

(4) Lower the stick and resume original standing posture and exhale.

Points to remember:

Swinging up the stick should coordinate with legs stretching backward. This should be done as far as possible making the body fully stretched.

Repeat the stretching 20 times (Stretching back to the left and to the right once as one time).

Posture 8 **Bending the Waist and Knees** (Fig. 165, 166, 167 and 168)

Fig. 165

Fig. 166

176

Fig. 167

Fig. 168

Follow Posture 7.

(1) Raise the stick overhead and inhale.

(2) Press the stick downward in front of the body and bend the waist simyltaneously and exhale.

(3) Raise the stick forward horizontally and bend knees simultaneously and inhale.

(4) Place the stick before thighs and resume the original standing posture and exhale.

Points to remember:

When pressing down the stick, straighten the knees, and bend the waist as much as possible.

Repeat the bending 20 times (Bending the waist and knees once as one time).

Posture 9 **Rising and Falling with Knees Bent** (Fig. 169 and 170)

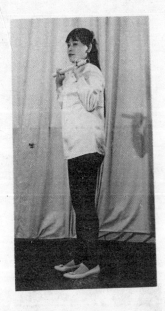

Fig. 169

Fig. 170

Follow Posture 8. Hold the stick naturally in front of the chest.

(1) Raise the stick horizontally overhead and bend knees simultaneously and inhale.

(2) Lower the stick naturally before chest, and resume the original standing posture and exhale.

Points to remember:

Bending knees and raising upward should be practised coordinately.

Repeat the movements 20 times (one bending and raising as one time).

Posture 10 **Straightening Chest and Stepping Forward** (Fig. 171 and 172)

Fig. 171

Fig. 172

Follow Posture 9. Take a half step forward with left foot.

(1) Raise the stick horizontally upward overhead, straighten chest, raise right heel and shift weight to left foot, and inhale at the same time.

(2) Lower the stick and place it before left thigh, and exhale.

Repeat the movements 20 times. Then take half a step forward with right foot, and repeat the same movements 20 times.

Points to remember:

When raising the stick horizontally upward, chest stretching and heel raising and lowering should be practised coordinately.

89. How to Perform Spontaneous Moving Exercise?

This is one of moving Qigong exercises. During the process, one can perform various movements spontaneously and involuntarily. For example, when a patient keeps on practising a certain exercise, he will involuntarily demonstrate various graceful movements of gymnastics, martial arts, or dance, or even movements one has never done before or very difficult movements one can never do in normal situation due to pathogenic troubles. These movements may be rigid or soft, quick or slow, or a sort of unconscious patting and massage along the main and collateral channels and acupuncture points related to the diseased area. For example, those who suffer from intestine and stomach troubles will unconsciously pat and massage such acupuncture points as Zhongwan, Guanyuan, Qihai, Weishu, Dachangshu, Mingmen, Zusanli, Sanyinjiao. This is a kind of self-curing of diseases more accurate than acupuncture therapy. During the exercise some people may have the feeling of "Internal Qi circulating", or of the Qi attacking the diseased part. It can exert better curative effects on diseases in nervous system, such as neurosis, insomnia, pain in joints, intestine and stomach troubles. Its curative function comes from tapping one's potentialities to activate main and collateral channels, harmonize vital energy and blood, and reinforce body resistance to eliminate pathogens, and thus cure diseases. Many people think, "spontaneous movement is the reflex of bioelectric wave circulating in the main and collateral channels. In modern medicine, it is called self-bioelectrotherapy." This opinion has some reasonable elements. Of course, in order to prove this point, it is necessary to do more scientific experiments to reveal the secret.

(I) Preparatory Work

Usually make preparation for 5 minutes before doing the exercise, mainly to calm down emotions, and keep in a state of tranquility. Choose a place where the light is not strong, with good ventilation, quiet, free from direct wind and free from loud noise. Undo tight clothes and belt, remove hard things such as watch and pen and the like, to avoid damaging the things or being hurt by them when moving during practising the exercise. Prepare a bed, a chair or a spot for standing (spacious enough for comfortable movement).

(II) Postures

(1) Supine posture

Lie flat on your back in a bed. Keep the neck naturally erect on a pillow of appropriate thickness. Close mouth and eyes gently, stretch the limbs naturally with two hands on the sides of your body.

(2) Sitting posture

Sit naturally upright on a stool of appropriate height, neck erect, shoulders sunk and elbows drooped, chest slightly drawn in and back erect, hands gently on the thighs, feet flat on the ground in parallel by shoulder width and pointing forward, torso and legs remain perpendicular to the thighs with 90-degree bend at the thighs and knees, mouth gently closed, eyelids naturally drooped. At the beginning you can sit with back supported if you are weak.

(3) Standing posture

Set two feet apart by shoulder width, toes in parallel pointing forward, torso naturally erect, chest slightly drawn in and shoulders sunk, hands naturally hanging on two sides of the body, head and neck erect, eyes gently closed.

(III) Way For Breathing

Natural breathing.

(IV) Method of Exercising

(1) Relax the whole body, concentrate the mind, take a proper posture, and gently close eyes.

(2) Press the navel slightly with the middle-finger of a hand (let go the finger after pressing, and resume the original posture).

(3) Imagine yourself mounting the clouds and riding the mist, like floating in the air.

(4) Imagine directing the Qi and blood flow slowly from the acupoint of Beihui at headtop down to the point of Yongquan at foot soles. Look inside with mind's eye at the acupoints and stay for a little while. Follow Qi and blood going through all the parts and you will sense pleasant feelings.

(5) Look inside at the acupoint of Zuqiao on the bridge of nose (leave it at once, you should not stay at it longer than necessary).

(6) Look inside at the acupoint of Dantian in navel (stay there for a little while).

(7) Imagine inhaling (gently) with the navel drawing back as if to stick to the acupoint of Mingmen at the vertebra, look inside with mind's eye at Mingmen (stay there for a little while).

(8) Imagine exhaling (gently) with the navel, the return it to original position.

(9) Concentrate the mind on Dantian inside the navel (the acupoint of Dantian is the locale about an inch inside the navel). You should keep "the four doors tightly closed". Concentrate your mind on Dantian all the time for 30 to 60 minutes. If no external movement occurs, you can bring the exercise to an end. If external movement should occur, let it go naturally before finishing the exercise.

(V) Method For Closing the Exercise

(1) Think of the Qi inside the navel, contract and relax the belly muscle with the mind. Imagine circling with the navel as centre from left to right, and turning in bigger and bigger circles. Turn 36 circles counter-clockwise (the largest circle not exceeding ribs above, and coccyx or pubis below), then reverse the circling and turning in smaller and smaller circles another 36 circles (with the female, the turning direction being the opposite). And then open your eyes.

(2) Take reverse breathing several times (slowly and gently). Inhale with nose and retract your belly at the same time, hands raised with elbows bent from two sides, palms facing upward and fingers pointing to each other, moving upward to the eye level. While raising hands, raise your heels gradually and soles touching the ground.

Exhale with mouth closed and relax the belly at the same time, hands dropped to the sides with palms facing downward, heels gradually touching the ground (while taking a lying posture, take reverse breathing only).

(3) Rub your palm and backs of hands till they are warm. Bathe your face and head and the back of the head 36 times.

(VI) Points to Remember

(1) When practising spontaneous moving exercise, never pursue the movements with effort. Let go naturally. Just go on practising and involuntary movements will come along naturally. Even no such movement occurs, it is only temporary and this can also keep the brain cortex in a state of protective inhibition, which helps to keep fit and achieve good results of practising stationary Qigong exercise.

(2) Try to avoid getting out-of-control. To practise spontaneous moving exercise, you should learn how to control yourself. Try to avoid moving violently at the very beginning and getting out-of-control later. The way to control yourself is to repeat the closing exercise, and you will stop moving naturally and resume the state of calmness and sobriety.

(3) If violent external movement such as jumping should occur, direct your attention downward and concentrate on the acupoint of Yongquan, press two palms downward and simultaneously exhale, saying "no jumping! no jumping!" in the mind, and thus you will stop jumping.

(4) If external moving of squatting down should occur, direct your attention upward, and concentrate on the acupoint of Baihui, raise palms upward, and simultaneously inhale, saying "stand up! stand up!"

in the mind, and then you will stand up gradually.

(5) For patients who suffer from dizziness, high blood pressure and coronary heart disease, it is better to take sitting posture and lying posture. This can prevent the internal Qi from gushing upward and causing a sudden fall when practising standing posture. If there is any internal Qi gushing upward, pay attention to the use of the method of pressing the Qi downward, leading the Qi downward from headtop to the acupoint of Yongquan at the soles, and simultaneously exhale so as to avoid Qi gushing upward.

(6) If the room is rather narrow with a lot of things around, you should open your eyes slightly or open your eyes slightly when you start moving involuntarily so that you can avoid bumping against something and hurting yourself.

(7) If you feel cold all over when you practise spontaneous moving exercise, it is better to do some sections of preparatory exercise, and get a little warmer before going on with the spontaneous moving exercise. This will bring better effects.

90. How to Practise the Exercise of Taking in Qi from the Sun for Tonification?

This is the exercise of taking in Qi from the sun and conducting it into Dantian with the mind after you have properly posed. The approach follows:

(I) Posture

Sitting posture:

Take the posture for Intrinsic-Nurishing Exercise and Relaxing Exercise.

Standing posture:

Take the posture for Keep-fit Exercise. Stand naturally in a state of relaxation, knees slightly bent. Weak persons may not have to bend knees.

(II) Breathing

Inhale fresh air through nose and exhale turbid air through mouth. Do the exhaling slowly with mouth slightly open, mind concentrated and calm.

(III) Mind-Intent

Look at the rising sun and imagine leading the Qi of the sun into your body. When you inhale, do it as if to inhale the Qi of the sun into Dantian.

(IV) Time and Place

When the sun is rising early in the morning, go to a quiet place where air is fresh and do the exercise facing the sun for 10 to 20 minutes. But take care not to look at the sun for its Qi when the light is very intense. Try to avoid hurting your eyes.

(V) Effect

It can enhance physique, prevent diseases, and bring good curative effects. It is good for sufferers with deficiency of Yang in particular.

Taking Qi from the sun can be taken as a supplementary exercise for Intrinsic-Nourishing Exercise and Keep-fit Exercise. Constant practice of taking Qi from the sun in the morning and from stars at night will help to keep fit and prolong life.

91. How to Practise the Exercise of Watching the Moon and Stars?

To do the exercise, you take a correct posture, watch the moon and stars and at the same time concentrate the mind on acupoint of Dantian while leading the Qi slowly into Dantian.

The method follows:

(I) Posture

Sitting posture:

Take the posture for Intrinsic-Nourishing Exercise and Relaxing Exercise.

Standing posture:

Take the posture for Keep-fit Exercise. Stand naturally in a state of complete relaxation, with knees slightly bent. Weak persons need not bend knees.

(II) Breathing

Concentrate your mind on Dantian, inhale fresh air through nose, and exhale turbid air through mouth. This is what people refer to as "getting rid of the stale and taking in the fresh." Breathe naturally and freely.

(III) Mind-Intent

Watch the moon or the stars with eyes half open, mind focused on Dantian. When your eyes grow tired, close them gently, but keep thinking of the moon and stars. If they vanish, open your eyes to see them again, and then close eyes. After doing the exercise in this way for 10 to 20 days, you don't have to see the moon and stars again but just imagine them at Dantian. Your mind is associated with the moon and stars, and merges with them into one. An old saying goes, "Take the essence of the moon to tonify man's spirit."

(IV) Time and Place

When the moon is rising at night, go to a quiet place with fresh air around, watch the moon and stars, and then have a leisure walk. Look up to see the stars or the North Star in a cheerful mood.

(V) Effect

Watching the moon and stars will make you quiet, broad-minded, and comfortable. To do some other exercises after watching the moon and stars will make you feel at ease and clear-minded. Constant practice will improve your eyesight, widen your outlook, quiet your mind and build up your brain.

92. How to Practise the Exercise of Attaining Xu and Jing (Nothingness and Tranquility)?

Clinical practice has proved this exercise is easy to learn and quick to produce effect. It is created in accordance with the requirements of Qigong therapy and the principles of combining recuperating with training.

The method follows:

(I) Posture

Take a natural and comfortable posture. You can take either lying, or sitting or standing posture in keeping with your habit.

(II) Breathing

Natural breathing.

(III) Mind-Intent

Do not focus your mind, but keep your body relaxed to the utmost extent. Maintain a state of relaxation and tranquility. The Chinese character "Xu" here means emptiness and nothingness, that is, forgetting any part of your body. "Jing" means complete calmness of the mind and freedom from distracting thoughts. This is the state in which you are sober-minded but not drowsy. Nothingness and tranquility imply soberness, while soberness is in nothingness and tranquility. Keeping sober-minded without attaining nothingness and tranquility results in dispersion of Qi; while keeping the state of nothingness and tranquility without a sober mind leads to drowsiness.

This exercise can be practised at any time and at any place. You do not have to pay attention to posture, breathing, or concentration of the mind on any point. Try to attain the state of nothingness and tranquility with a sober mind. It is a combination of recuperation with practice. Therefore, it can be taken as a supplementary exercise. It suits the aged, the weak and very sick patients.

93. How to Practise Yang-Cultivating Exercise?

The exercise is for tonifying Yang and strengthening kidneys. It is suitable for the aged and the weak to practise for strengthening kidneys and cultivating semen. This exercise requires concentration on Mingmen.

The method follows:

When you have entered into tranquility, focus your mind on Mingmen, conduct the Qi with the mind up from two kidneys (by the sides of Mingmen), through Dantian and directly to testis, and then from testis upward to penis right to its top. Change breaths and repeat the cycle for 36 times, and focus your mind on Mingmen. This exercise is effective to prevent and cure impotence.

For women this exercise helps regulate menstruation. In practice you lead the Qi from two kidneys through Dantian and directly down to uterus and vagina.

94. How to Practise Semen Preserving Exercise?

This is an exercise to prevent and cure emission and premature ejaculation. It is better to do the exercise before going to bed at night.

The method follows:

To lie in bed, head supported with pillow. First focus your mind on Dantian, palms facing downward, right fingers on the back of left hand, and left palm pressing the navel. Move hands in a circle from left to right (i.e., left upward — right upward — right downward — left downward — left upward) for 36 times. And then change hands and move them in reverse direction another 36 times. Then put the finger tips of both hands together, rub the abdomen up and down 36 times, with Dantian as the center, up to Jiantu and down to pubis below abdomen (rubbing up and down once as one time). When rubbing downward, use the force of thumbs only. And when rubbing upward, use the force of the small fingers only.

Then, you can go on practising according to the ancient classic, "Rub with both hands alternately, practise this exercise constantly and you can preserve Zhen Yang (semen)." The method follows: Push the testis with both hands near the spermatic duct in the scrotum, and rub its outer skin, first left and then right. This is taken as one cycle and repeat the cycle 81 times.

95. How to Practise Zhonggong Direct-Flowing Exercise?

It is a kind of breathing exercise for those who have had much Qigong training.

You can take either sitting or lying posture. Generally after you have opened up "Large Zhoutian" and "Small Zhoutian", you can lead the Qi with the mind from Dantian straight up to the acupoint of Baihui at the top of head, and again down to Dantian and Huiyin. That is to say, if you have mastered the art of Qigong, you can lead the Qi from Baihui directly down to Huiyin, which is thus called Zhonggong Direct Flowing Exercise. Details follow: While inhaling, conduct the Qi from Huiyin up through Dantian to Baihui; and while exhaling, conduct the Qi from Baihui down through Dantian to Huiyin. By inhaling and exhaling, you get the Qi flowing directly from the center on top of the body to the center at bottom. This exercise is effective for cultivating Yuan Qi (Zhen Qi), and building up Essence and Qi and Spirit.

96. How to Practise Qigong Eye Exercise?

Qigong Eye Exercise is an exercise of combining movements of eyeballs with breathing. It is effective for preventing and curing poor eyesight and failing eyesight, and far-sightedness of aged persons, nearsightedness and astigmatism of young people. Details follow:

Movement 1: **Looking Up and Down**

Close your eyes, turn eyeballs up and simultaneously inhale, turn forward and exhale. Then turn eyeballs downward and simultaneously inhale, turn forward and exhale. Repeat the movements 20 times (turning up and down once as one time).

Movement 2: **Looking Left and Right**

Close your eyes, turn eyeballs to the left and inhale, and back to the original position and inhale. Then turn eyeballs to the right and inhale, back to the original position and exhale. Practise the movements 20 times (Turning left and right once as one time).

Movement 3: **Looking Round Clockwise**

Close your eyes, move eyeballs in a circle clockwise, from left downward to left upward and inhale, and then from right upward to right downward and exhale. Practise the movements 20 times (Turning left and right in a circle once as one time).

Movement 4: **Looking Round Counter-clockwise**

Close your eyes, move eyeballs in a circle counter-clockwise from right downward to right upward and inhale, and from left upward to left downward and exhale. Practise the movements 20 times (Turning left and right in a circle once as one time).

Movement 5: **Looking Forward**

Open your eyes, look into the distance at an object (a peak, a house top, a tree trunk, a scenery, etc.) more than 100 meters away. Breathe naturally for 1 to 2 minutes.

It is preferable to take a sitting posture. Breathe softly and slowly, and move your eyeballs without much effort.

This eye exercise is simple and can be done wherever and whenever you choose. If you practise it in coordination with eye keeping-fit exercise, you can obtain better results.

97.   How to Practise Zhoutian Qigong Exercise?

It is a breathing exercise with the Qi flowing through Large Zhoutian and Small Zhoutian.

Take either a lying posture or a sitting posture. When internal Qi rises from Dantian, you will feel a warm stream there, follow it with your mind, down from Dantian to Huiyin and back through the point of Weilu along Dumai upward, and through the acupoints of Mingmen, Jiaji, Daizhui, Yuzhen and Baihui, and then downward through Shenting, Zuqiao, passing nose and mouth and throat, down to Tanzhong and then back to Dantian. This circle of "Zhoutian" through the channels of Renmai and Dumai is called "Small Zhoutian Qigong Exercise".

As for the Large Zhoutian Qigong Exercise, you take either a lying or a sitting posture. When internal Qi rises from Dantian, a warm stream starts flowing through the Twelve Regular Channels and the Eight Extra Channels over the whole body in keeping with ascending-and-descending, and opening and closing in circulation. This is called "Large Zhoutian Qigong Exercise."

This coordination of the mind with breathing to get the Qi circulate through Large and Small Zhoutians is called Zhoutian Qigong Exercise.

It can cultivate Yuan Qi (Vital Energy), increase Qing Qi (the purified principle) and decrease Zhuo Qi (the turbid principle). Therefore practice of Zhoutian Breathing Exercise will develop your primordial energy and make you extremely comfortable. It is effective for keeping-fit and preventing diseases.

However, this exercise is not suitable for beginners. Only when they have had considerable practice, and developed sufficient internal Qi can they practise this exercise. When the Qi (the vital energy) starts functioning you should let it go naturally. Never lead it with much effort nor use the mind too early, otherwise deviations will occur.

98.   How to Practise Circulating Round Dantian

Exercise?

This is an exercise of directing the Qi with mind to circulate around abdomen. Details follow:

When inhaling, lift your anus, direct Qi with your mind from Huiyin to Mingmen, and then up through Mingmen to Dantian. When exhaling, direct Qi with your mind down from Dantian to Huiyin. Proceed slowly, evenly, naturally and softly. This circulation of Qi will form a triangle line connecting Dantian and Huiyin and Mingmen, and these three acupoints will warm up. This exercise helps not only to activate the Qi but also to cultivate Jing Qi (the primordial energy) at Dantian. It is an effective measure to cure some diseases in urinary system and reproduction system, such as emission, impotence, menstrual irreqularities, infertility, and so on.

99. How to Practise Tranquilizing Exercise?

When you have entered a state of high tranquility in the process of Qigong exercise, you will see white light and various colors, which are a sort of "hallucination" and "illusion", representing a state of "forgetfulness", that is, a state of genuine tranquility. Thus it becomes an exercise of tranquilizing all thoughts.

This exercise suits those who suffer from deficiency of Yin or misuse of fire therapies, with such symptoms as fear of heat, insomnia, dreamfulness, restlessness, pale complexion, dizziness, etc. Details of method follow:

(I) Posture

Sit in a cross-legged posture. Having properly regulated your posture with attention on details, such as cross-legged sitting, keeping back erect, drawing chest slightly inward, drooping eyelids, holding hands, tongue-tip touching the hard palate, and so on, keep the entire body relaxed and natural, and maintain light-hearted and happy mood.

(II) Breathing

Having properly posed, breathe out 2 to 3 long breaths, but do not breathe in. Relax the internal organs and extend the diaphragm then you will enjoy the feeling of being tranquil and relaxed. After breathing out the long breaths, go on with natural breathing, without thinking whether the breath is long or short, thick or thin.

(III) Mind-Intent

Look lightly and naturally with mind's eye through an angle of 45 degrees at the point between the two crossed-legged knees with eyes slightly closed. That is, look with mind's eye at the point which is called "the place where an ox is sleeping" in Qigong. There is nothing there, but in the course of time, you will see with mind's eye various colors, blue, yellow, red, white and black. The common exercisers will first see misty white and glistening colors. If they go on practising, they can see the colors fading away except the misty white, changing gradually into bright moonlight. At this moment, the exerciser is coming near the "realm of tranquility", as if there were a bright clear moon hanging high in the sky, which gives cool and refreshing feeling all over the body, and keeps you free from all sorts of worries and anxieties.

When you see the white radiance, you should immerse your mind into it, thinking "The light is me, I am the light", "Light and I are one and the same thing" and "Light and I merge into one". As a result, the white light and your body will become integrated, and by and by you will feel your body bright and clean and non-existent. You only feel that you were a moon, peaceful and radiating, bright and clean, and absolutely still. That is the state of "forgetfulness", a state of "genuine tranquility". This is the best regulation of the nervous system and the nicest rest of the body. So, through this exercise, you will feel vigorous in spirit, healthy in body and mind, and strong in physique.

For beginners, 20 minutes' time or so will be sufficient for each session. Gradually you can increase the time to 30-40 minutes. Never pursue the white light if there is none. If colors should appear, let them go. You should not fear to see the light if there is any, and should not pursue it if there is no such thing. Let it proceed naturally and you will attain good results.

When you want to finish the exercise, just move your mind away from the light, and it will disappear, and your body will return to normal state.

Not everyone of the exercisers can attain the feelings of light and colors. That does not matter. By looking only at the required point with mind's eye, you will feel peaceful and quiet, which also brings good results.

100. How to Practise Zhen Qi Circulating Exercise?

Through constant exercise, internal Qi in the body develops. In other words, Zhen Qi grows so abundant that it can get through the two Channels — Renmai and Dumai. The measure to activate circulation of Qi through Renmai and Dumai is called Zhen Qi Circulating Exercise.

(I) Posture

There are four types of postures for this exercise: walking, standing, sitting and lying, of which sitting posture is most commonly adopted.

(II) Breathing

Breathing is the power to activate circulation of Zhen Qi, and thus, its regulation should be the first step to Zhen Qi Circulating Exercise. When you regulate breathing and cultivate Zhen Qi, you should mainly direct Zhen Qi into Dantian. Since physiological activities take place with Zhen Qi going down to Dantian along Renmai when exhaling, you have only to pay attention to exhaling during the regulation of breathing, and you will succeed in leading Zhen Qi into Dantian. With

194

inhaling, do it naturally with no need of attention. Some people inhale deeply with much effort for the purpose of "getting Qi into Dantian". This is not in conformity with physiology and is thus unacceptable.

(III) Mind-Intent

According to *Zhen Qi Circulating Exercise* developed by Li Shaobo, only five steps can lead you to the mastery of the exercise.

Step 1: **Take Care of the Heart When Breathing**

Having got everything ready for the exercise, minimize your field of vision, remove distractions, and concentrate your mind on the nose tip for a while, then close your eyes to look inward at the heart, and listen attentively to your exhaling. When exhaling, do not make any coarse noise. Follow the exhaling with the mind toward the heart. When inhaling, let it go naturally without the need of mind-intent.

Step 2: **Follow the Breathing With Mind Down Toward Dantian**

When the heart warming up with each exhaling during the 1st step, follow the breathing with the mind, and lead it down toward Dantian gradually, never do it in a hurry.

Step 3: **Regulate Breathing and Concentrate Mind on Dantian**

When you have done the 2nd step and feel something at Dantian, you can hold breath at Dantian somewhat intentionally. You don't have to inhale downward with much effort to prevent the point from getting too warm. Concentrate the mind on Dantian and nourish it with gentle warmth.

Step 4: **Go Through With Neither Neglect Nor Help**

Focus the mind on Dantian for about 40 days. When Zhen Qi has grown sufficient enough to flow upward along the spine, follow it with the mind (do not forget it). If it stays at a certain point, do not lead it up with effort (do not help it). The flowing speed of Zhen Qi depends upon the strength of Dantian. It will stop flowing when the strength is not sufficient, and go on flowing up when the strength is replenished. It is harmful to help it through a certain point and try to lead it upward with too much effort, which will probably result in the disconnection with the strength at Dantian. The ancient people had a vivid saying to describe this sort of situation. "Try to help the shoots grow by pulling them upward." Therefore, you must let things proceed naturally. The activity of Zhen Qi is independent of man's will. If Zhen Qi cannot pass through Yu Zhen Guan, look inward at the headtop, and it may get through the point.

Step 5: **Store Up Yuan Qi to Cultivate Vitality**

In principle you should return to concentrate the mind on Dantian, which is the area to be constantly thought of. After Zhen Qi has succeeded in flowing through all the channels, for example, you can feel something active at the acupoint of Baihui at the top of head, then you can focus the mind on this point. In short, you should be flexible in using your mind-intent. It is said, "Focus on the point when you sense comfort. Let go when you sense discomfort."

This can be regarded as the correct method to deal with the mind at different stages of the exercise.

The above-mentioned five steps should be followed in gradual progression. The previous step is the basis of the next step and the next step is the inevitable development of the previous step. The first three steps is the stage for regulating breathing and activating Zhen Qi, and gathering Zhen Qi of the body at Dantian. This stage is called "cultivating essence and transforming it into Qi." Step 4 is the stage for leading the Zhen Qi accumulated at Dantian to flow upward through Dumai and straight to the brain. This stage is called "cultivating Qi and transforming it into spirit." Step 5 is the stage in which one becomes proficient in the art and has attained the state of tranquility. His mind is as quiet as still water. This is the stage of "cultivating spirit and returning to void."

The above-mentioned five steps in three stages illustrates the process of exercising the circulation of Zhen Qi. As exercisers are different in physique and conditions, the effects they attain from this exercise are also different. Therefore, during practice go on with it naturally and be flexible, and never pursue the effects with too much effort. On the other hand, you should have patience and perseverance, and never let matters take their own course. This is the key to success.

101. How to Suit Exercises to Different Diseases?

To suit exercises to different diseases means to choose different exercising forms to treat different diseases in accordance with the state of five parenchymatous viscera and six hollow viscera and their channels and the collateral channels. Take six-character formulas for example. It is a method of "tonifying and purging through exhaling and inhaling". In accordance with six-character formulas of Yin-Yang and the five elements, it treats different diseases in five parenchymatous viscera, heart, liver, spleen, lungs, kidneys and the triple heater and their channels and the collateral channels by different ways of breathing, that is, by using the six Chinese characters "Xu", "He", "Hu", "Si", "Chui" and "Xi" to bring about tonification or purgation. Details follow:

Liver relates to wood, purge by breathing out "Xu", tonify by inhaling.

Heart relates to fire, purge by breathing out "He", tonify by inhaling.

Spleen relates to earth, purge by breathing out "Hu", tonify by inhaling.

Lungs relate to metal, purge by breathing out "Si", tonify by inhaling.

Kidneys relate to water, purge by breathing out "Chui", tonify by inhaling.

Triple heater relates to Qi, purge by breathing out "Xi", tonify by inhaling.

When you practise the exercise, first diagnose which of the viscera is diseased and decide which character is to be selected. Purging is for fever due to excess and tonifying is for cold due to deficiency. For example, for excessive cardiac fire, purging is prescribed by saying

"He", first exhaling and then inhaling. When exhaling, open mouth with tongue tip touching slightly on teeth root, and breathe out the character "He" (producing no sound) from Dantian. Exhale to the full with belly retracted and then inhale with nose to one third of the exhaling amount. One exhaling and inhaling is taken as one time, and say each word 6 times at most. For tonifying deficiency of heart-Yang, inhale with nose, first inhale and then exhale. While inhaling, close mouth and teeth with Dantian protruding out. Inhale to the full and then exhale with mouth, to one-third of the inhaling amount. Tonification is achieved through inhaling, 9 times at most. Purgation is achieved by breathing out the characters "Xu", "He", "Hu", "Si", "Chui" and "Xi" (producing no sound) according to different viscera, such as heart, liver, spleen, lungs, kidneys and the triple heater. If you practise the exercise by saying all the six characters (silently) it can also bring good health. But this should be done in the order of wood, fire, earth, metal and water, that is, "Xu", "He", "Hu", "Si", "Chui" and "Xi". You should not invert the order. You may take either sitting, or lying or standing posture in doing the exercise.

102. What Is Daoyin?

Daoyin is an ancient term for the present day Qigong. In *Zhuang Zi's: On Painstaking,* it is said, "Proper exhaling and inhaling, getting rid of the stale and taking in the fresh, imitating the walking movement of the bear and the stretch movement of the bird, are the secrets to longevity, in which those people who were practising Daoyin and nourishing the body, and long-lived Peng Zu were interested." From this we know, Daoyin includes posture, movement, breathing, massaging, and reposing. These are fundamentally similar to the present-day moving Qigong, stationary Qigong and combination of the two.

A silk painting of earlier Han period unearthed from the No.3 Han Tomb at Mawangdui, east of Changsha, contains more than forty figures in various exercising postures: sitting in repose with eyes closed, holding head with both hands, squatting down with belly contracted, bowing and bending waist, standing with head lifted up, pressing down with knees bent, all of them lively pictures.

The picture represents ancient Daoyin, which is of great importance to the present research of the source and development of Qigong.

103. What Is Chanxiu (Zen)?

Zen, or Chanxiu means sitting in meditation for self-cultivation. It is a sort of Qigong exercise adopted by Buddhists. According to what Master Ju Zan said, Chanxiu includes a wide range of exercising forms. Master Kui Ji mentioned in his writing that Chanxiu had been spoken of with seven different terms. The first one is "Shan Mo Si Dou" meaning "Preparation". When you have got free from dazedness and distraction which tend to affect Chanxiu, you are in a calm state ready for meditation. The second one is "Shan Mo Di" meaning "Waiting". You keep calm for everything to focus on one point. The third one is "Shan Mo Bo Di" meaning "Waiting to the end". Everything no matter whether intentional or unintentional is focused on one point. The fourth one is "Tuo Yan Na", which is generally meant as "Quiet Meditation", in fact its actual meaning should be termed as "Keep Quiet and Think". The fifth one is "Zhi Dao Yi Jia Ah Jie Luo Duo" meaning "With one mind". The sixth one is "She Mo Ta" meaning "Quiet and Still". The seventh one is "Xian Fa Le Zhu" which is the basis of the four kinds of "Quiet Meditation". In short, Chanxiu is one of the ways for Buddhists to cultivate themselves in "Quiet Meditation".

Chanxiu requires the doer to live a regular life in peaceful environment, to remove all personal considerations and focus attention on self-cultivation through continuous regulation of mind, the breath and the physical body.

Regulation of the body means to adjust postures in the process of Chanxiu exercise. The Buddhist is usually required to sit cross-legged, in neat and clean clothes, with torso erect, left hand being placed on the right one, eyes closed and tongue touching palate. He should keep his mind free from distracting thoughts.

Regulation of the breath means to breathe gently and softly and in a long-drawn-out way. In *Da An Ban Canon of Concentration* translated by An Shi-gao of Han Dynasty, it is said, "Breathing refers to four things: wind, air, breath and gasp. Wind is breathing with sound. Air is breathing without sound. Breath is the inhalation and exhalation. And Gasp means short breaths."

Regulation of the mind means to control wild thoughts, and focus attention permitting the brain to have sufficient rest. This is usually done in coordination with regulation of the breath. In the Fifth Volume of *Canon of Self-Cultivation* translated by Zhu Fa-hu of Western Jin Dynasty, it is said, "Counting breaths and concentrating the mind contains four things: First, counting breaths. Second, following. Third, staying and observing. Fourth, returning and quieting." These are the six forms of regulating the mind and the breath, which are later called "Six Knacks".

104. What Is Hua Tuo's "Five-Animal Play"?

Hua Tuo's "Five-Animal Play" is also called Hua Tuo's "Five-Animal Picture". Tradition has it that Hua Tuo of Later Han Dynasty, through assimilating the art of Daoyin exercise of a Taoist Jun Qian, worked out this series of exercises imitating the sportive and frolic movements of animals, including stretching waist, rolling up body and moving joints. Hua Tuo taught it to his disciples Wu Pu and Fan Ah. Wu Pu, who persevered in doing the "Five-Animal Play", had sharp hearing and sight, strong and firmly-rooted teeth in his nineties, enjoying good appetite as the young people. This shows that the exercise is one of health-building exercises.

Hua Tuo's Five-Animal Play includes:

The Tiger: another name being "Xian Men Tiger Style".

The Deer: another name being "She Cheng Qi Deer Style".

The Bear: another name being "Geng Sang Bear Style".

The Monkey: another name being "Fei Chang Fang Monkey Style."

The Bird: another name being "Kang Cang Zi Bird Style".

105. What Is Taiji 13-Exercises of Wudang School?

Taiji Exercise is a moving exercise invented by Zhang San-feng of Wudang School. It was later branched out into Yang Style Boxing, Chen Style Boxing and Wu Style Boxing, each with its own advantages. This kind of exercise enjoyed great popularity in the folks and many people practised it. It is a good exercise for promoting health, resisting diseases and prolonging life.

Taijiquan is one of moving exercises, varied in form and complicated in movement. There are numerous movements in Taijiquan, such as body turning, food stepping forward and backward, waist twisting leftward and rightward, hands and fingers bending, stretching, probing and scooping, chest and abdomen gulping down, throwing up, exhaling and inhaling, shoulders and back relaxing, shrugging, shaking and dragging, head and neck pushing and striking. However, Taiji 13-postures of Wudang School consists of relatively simple movements, similar to those of simplified Taijiquan. It requires one to take correct postures, relax the body, and direct Qi to Dantian. In short, it lays emphasis on internal exercise of activating Qi. This is called Taiji 13-postures of Wudang School.

106 What Is 12-Exercises of Dharma Yi Jin Jing of Shaolin School?

Yi Jin Jing (Canon of Changing Muscles) was created by the honored Buddhist Damo. It has become legendary that the honored

Bodhidharma came from India in the East and inhabited in Shaolin Temple, where he passed on Mahavana of Buddhist Chan Xiu and became the first ancestor of Zen Buddhism from East (according to the Indian conception he belonged to the 28th generation). He found the monks whom he taught were physically weak, so he worked out a series of exercises for them to practise to improve health. These exercises included stationary and moving exercises. Handed down from generation to generation, the stationary exercise lost its original features. The Zen Buddhists of later generations paid more attention to elucidation of Principles of Mahavana and kept only one form of the stationary exercise — Can Hua Tou. Many secrets to the exercises got lost in the folks.

The 12-Posture Moving Exercise kept to this day is something that Wang Zuyuan learnt at Shaolin Temple at the Song Mountain. It is somewhat different from the original *Picture of Stationary Exercise* and *Guide to the Art of Attack*. However, Wang's 12-Postures found to be concise through practice. It helps to enhance one's physical health. The main contents included are as follows:

Posture 1: Pithy Formula for Wei Tou Presenting Stick
Stand upright, arms bent horizontally at the chest front.
Stabilize the Qi and hold the spirit within;
Keep a clear head and you will appear serene.

Posture 2: Pithy Formula for Carrying Demon-subduing Stick Horizontal
Stand with toes touching the ground; arms parted horizontally at shoulder level.
Keep calm and no ruffling, stunned and speechless.

Posture 3: Pithy Formula for Holding the Sky
Raise hands with palms facing upward and eyes looking up, stand upright with toes touching the ground.
Keep torso erect, clench teeth and do not let loose.
Tongue tip touches palate and saliva increases, regulate breathing and you will feel at ease.

Draw back slowly two fists, hold them at the sides and eyes again looking forward.

Posture 4: Pithy Formula for Picking Stars

Hold the sky single-handed with palm over head, and eyes looking at the palm.

Inhale with nose and exhale with mouth, perform in this way alternately with both hands.

Posture 5: Pithy Formula for Dragging Ox By the Tail

Stand in a "bow step" with one leg bent in the front, and the other straightened behind, lead the Qi to abdomen.

Think only of the arms, look inside at two purples with the mind.

Posture 6: Pithy Formula for Putting out Paws and Spreading
Wings

Keep torso erect and open eyes wide, push the window open to look at the moon.

Topple the mountains to watch the nighttide, always follow the call of mind.

Posture 7: Pithy Formula for Ghost Drawing Sabre

Turn head and bend arms, hold head and press ears;

Open right armpit, and close the left;

Shake the right and retract the left;

Perform right and left alternately, and stretch the body to reach upward.

Posture 8: Pithy Formula for Dropping Shanpan to the Ground

Stick tongue tip to hard palate, open eyes and clench teeth;

Set two feet in a "horse step", and press two hands down;

Turn palms upward as if to hold a heavy weight;

Exhale with mouth and inhale with nose, squat down with torso erect.

Posture 9: Pithy Formula for Blue Dragon Putting Out Paws

Blue dragon moves its paws, left and right;

Swing left palm to search the way, and draw to the side;

Right paw rides the wind, and reveal the left at the Gate of Clouds.

Conduct the Qi around shoulders and back, twist waist and turn
abdomen;

Breathe gently to subdue the dragon and tame the tiger.

Posture 10: Pithy Formula for Tiger Seizing Its Prey

Squat down with torso leaning slightly, set a "bow step" with left
leg bent and right leg straightened, and alternate left and right;

Lift head up and throw chest out to move forward, and turn the
coccyx facing upward;

Breathe evenly and slowly, finger tips touching the ground for a
support;

Bend waist and back, and then resume the original posture and
stand upright.

Posture 11: Pithy Formula for Bending Down to Beat Drum

Hold the back of head with palms, and bend to the knees;

Drop head down to look for something under the hipbone, and close
mouth and clench teeth;

Touch tongue tip slightly to hard palate, and bend elbows horizontally.

Press palms on ears and strike the skull with fore-fingers like
sounding "heaven drum", with the effects of playing wind and
stringed instruments.

Posture 12: Pithy Formula for Turning Tail and Shaking Head

Straighten knees and stretch arms, push hands to touch ground;

Shake head with eyes wide open, and concentrate the mind;

Stand up and stamp foot, and stretch elbows and arms;

Perform leftward and rightward seven times, and come to the end of
the exercise;

Cure diseases and prolong life, and you will always feel happy.

107. What Is Fire Dragon Exercise of Sun School?

Sun School was a small section of Red Taoist School. It is known
in ancient legend that this small school was started by Princess Chang
of Emperor Chong Zhen, and some surviving followers of Ming

Dynasty, Gu Ting-lin and some others, for the purpose of fighting Qing Dynasty and reconstructing Ming Dynasty.

The exercise this school advocated most was called Fire Dragon Exercise. It is an effective measure to build up health and cure disease. What is more, you can learn it in a relatively short period of time. This exercise exerts effect only on the diseased area. The access to the mastery of this art is to have a good knowledge of the network of channels of human body, that is, the structure of the "Interior" in details. This exercise should be practised under instructor's guidance, and is not suitable for self-training.

Fire Dragon Exercise proceeds in the following manner:

First step: Take some "Golden Powder" — a sort of medicine for external use — (a mixture of refined pill and herb), put it in a cup and stir it with cold boiled water into a liquid as thick as rice water. Dip a writing brush into the liquid and let it soak to the full, draw a large circle on the skin with the brush along the prescribed channel starting from the Jing Point (one of the five Shu Points located at the tips of the fingers and toes) of the channel of Foot-Taiyin, upward along the channel route to the end of the channel of Hand Taiyin, then turn to the adjacent Jing point of the channel of Hand-Taiyang, downward along the channel route to the Jing point at the end of toes. This large circle is called "Kan Li Circle", which seems easy to draw but is difficult to do well because of the complexity of the network of channels of human body. Incorrect drawing affects free circulation of Qi and even causes its stagnation. To know the channels well and make the "Kan Li Circle" correct along the Yin-Yang route will bring curative effects.

When you draw the circle with the "Golden Powder" liquid, you will feel a cold stream of air penetrating into the bones and feel that the muscle and tendons comfortable and pleasant.

Second step: Having finished drawing of the circle, think of the "Image of the master", that is, close eyes and recall the voice and looks of one's master, demonstrating the reverence cherished by a disciple for his master and a patient for his doctor. This is an effective measure to "keep attention". Then, concentrate the mind on the "key point" — the Jing Point where the drawing starts — with body relaxed and eyes closed. You do not need to do exhaling and inhaling but focus the attention on the starting point of the circle. Repeat the process a few times each day, each time a few or a dozen minutes. Keep on doing in this way and in the course of time, a stream of warm air will rise from this point, circulate along the channel route of the large circle and return to the end point and finally vanish. With constant practice, this stream of warm air will condense into a fire ball as round as a bead, rolling along the circling route and giving you a comfortable feeling.

As a result of effective training, this fire ball circulating along the channel route under the skin can be seen or even felt with hand.

The "Golden Powder" used in Fire Dragon Exercise is golden in color. It is made up of the following components:

(1) Raw alum, 50 grams, ground fine, put in cooking vessel, heated dry with gentle fire and again ground into fine powder.

(2) Raw borax, 50 grams, ground fine, put into cooking vessel, heated with gentle fire until smoke dies, again ground into fine powder.

(3) Sodium sulfate, 50 grams, raw alum 25 grams, raw borax 25 grams, mixed and ground fine, put in cooking vessel, melted with gentle fire and stirred with mulberry stick, condensed slowly as thick as paste, the operation is called "baking foetus". Then turn the vessel upside down and bake it over gentle fire until it bubbles like steamed bread and turns white. Remove the fire, cool the vessel and take the content out. Grind it fine.

(4) Raw cattail pollen, 50 grams, ground fine.

(5) bone-penetrating herb (clematis intricata Bge.), 50 grams,

ground fine.

(6) Real plum borneol, 50 grams, ground fine.

Put the above mentioned six medicines into a pot to be ground into homogeneous mixture. Store it in a china container with sealing. When you need it, add in fresh water and stir it into a liquid as thick as rice water, ready for use.

(Note: bone-penetrating herb is a trailing herb, with stem like iron thread and somewhat square-shaped, leaves like coins with sawteeth-like edges. Through autumn frost, its stem turns pink and leaves turn into red ribs. The herb usually grows near water by fields. It is not the bone-penetrating herb sold in drugstore, nor is it garden balasm.)

108. What Is Jiao Hua Exercise?

This exercise was created by the ancient laboring people through experience of resistance against hunger and cold. Later it was adopted by the experts on health studies as a special exercise for training the intestines and stomach and resisting cold.

Generally speaking, Qigong exercise is not supposed to be practised when one is full or hungry. But JiaoHua Exercise can be practised after a meal since it is meant to enhance digestion. The exercise can help to resist cold if practised in cold weather. It is especially effective for curing diseases such as chronic indigestion, chronic ulcer, disorders in intestine and stomach nervous systems, constipation, hiccup, regurgitation and so on. The ancient people considered this exercise to be beneficial and harmless to one's health. Details follow:

(1) Find a flat and straight door plank or a smooth wall.

(2) Stand with the whole body relaxed, head, back, hips and legs straight against the plank or the wall, two feet apart by shoulder-width with heels at a distance of two-fists from the wall.

(3) Bend two legs and squat down slowly with torso still against the wall until buttocks touch heels and legs. Put two palms on knees,

middle fingers slightly pressed in the outer knee holes. While squatting say "Hay" in coordination with exhalation.

(4) Move the back and waist away from the wall, lift heels simultaneously and shift weight of the body onto toes. With the movement, push forward and move thighs forward until they are horizontal, back of head against the wall, but waist and buttocks and back away from it. Then throw out chest, waist and abdomen in a straight line, getting the intestines and stomach in motion. During the process, be sure to relax the whole body without any effort. At the same time say "Si" in coordination with inhalation.

(5) Resume the squatting posture, put down heels slowly, with shoulders, back, waist and buttocks clinging to the wall. At the same time, say "Hay" in coordination with exhalation.

Repeat the process 3 to 5 times, or 8 to 10 times depending on your own strength. When you want to stop, you may stand up slowly clinging to the wall. If you have had much practice, you may stand up with the movement of shoulders pressing against the wall, two palms enclosing before chest, and pushing forward.

Use reverse breathing. Say "Hey" when exhaling, with Zhen Qi going down to Dantian and abdomen expanded, and say "Si" when inhaling with Zhen Qi rising to Tanzhong and abdomen contracted.

(Note: "Hay" and "Si" are the sounds of breathing. When say "Hay", exhale with mouth open and tongue flat, producing guttural sound. When say "Si", inhale with lips slightly open and teeth chattering, producing sound through tongue and teeth.)

109. What Is Tiger-Step Exercise?

Tiger-Step Exercise is one of the six special exercises originated from E Mei School. It trains the back and legs externally and the kidneys and liver internally. It is a moving Qigong exercise especially effective for curing insufficiency of the kidney.

Insufficiency of the kidney refers to hypertension due to deficiency of Yin, backache resulting from deficiency of the kidney, legpain due to deficiency of the liver, and syndrome of upper excess and lower deficiency (congestion in the brain and weakness in legs) due to decificency of Yin. The aged persons usually suffer from diseases because of kidney insufficiency. This exercise is chiefly used to supplement other moving Qigong exercises. Experience over years has proved that this exercise is based on principles and brings good curative effects in practice. It is worth being popularized.

Details follow:

1st Movement:

Stand naturally. Droop two arms with hands slightly touching the sides of thighs. Look forward, appearing calm and at ease. Set two feet apart by shoulder-width.

2nd Movement:

Raise two hands slowly, set them akimbo with thumbs in rear pressing the acupoint of Yaoyan (at the hollow of the small of the back) and four fingers closing together in front, index finger tips touching the acupoint of Zangmen (at the end of the last rib).

3rd Movement:

Raise left thigh with knee slightly bent, tip of big toe touching the ground with body weight shifted on right leg which squats down slowly at the same time, eyes looking forward. This is the exercise of alternating the leg to carry the body weight.

4th Movement:

Straighten left leg with toes pointing downward and ankle stretching to form a straight line. Kick out gently and slowly with sole 5 to 6 inches from the ground. At the same time bend right foot slightly to support body weight. This is called "Searching Crotch".

5th Movement:

With left leg kicking out, slant toes up and stretch heel with an effort in the former direction. This is called "Holding Up Scissors". Then turn toe tips down a little and heel retracts to resume the posture with instep and tibia in a straight line. This is called "Phoenix Nodding Its Head". And then, circle the sole inward, and again circle it outward, in coordination with ankle movement. This is called "Clockwise and Counter-Clockwise Taiji Circle". With foot slanting up and heel stretching, get ready for the next movement.

6th Movement:

With the previous movement, bring the heel down to touch the ground, bend knee slowly, move thigh forward, flatten the whole sole to form a "bow step". At the same time straighten the right leg to form an "arrow step". Say "Hay" in coordination with reverse breathing to lead the Qi down to Dantian.

7th Movement:

The bow and arrow step cannot be set wider than half a step. Move forward and backward with lower back following the movement of the legs. Simultaneously thumbs press the sides of the waist when moving forward, and get loosened when moving backward. Concentrate your mind on the pressing and loosening of thumbs at the sides of the waist in coordination with forward and backward movements. Carefully feel the opening and closing of kidneys. People with much practice of the exercise can feel the inner movements of kidneys and the mechanism of Qi through "looking inside".

8th Movement:

Stretch the right leg in "arrow step" and lean forward a bit with the movement. Then retract right leg to set in parallel with left leg, toes touching the ground as the 3rd movement. Right foot becomes insubstantial and left foot substantial. At the same time, the bow step of left foot changes into the stance of the 3rd movement to support the body weight.

9th Movement:

Straighten right leg as the 4th movement and go on with the movements 5, 6 and 7. Practise alternately left and right and move forward step by step as taking a walk. You can turn about and go on practising in the same manner. Duration for a session of practice must vary with different situation of different people. If you feel pain in the leg, you may bring the exercise to an end.

10th Movement:

When coming to a stop, first retract the foot in rear from a bow and arrow step to resume standing posture, drop down two hands and let loose the Qi at Dantian.

110. What Is 12-Exercises of E Mei Origin?

The school of E Mei is famous in the circle of Qigong because it has taken in the advantages of Buddhist and Taoist schools in both moving and stationary exercises, and worked out a series of exercises which are comparatively comprehensive. Theoretically, they lay emphasis on both "color (outer expression)" and "heart (inner movement)", that is, on both moving and stationary exercises. In other word, they have combined Taoist moving exercise with Buddhist meditation exercise, resulting in the 12 postures of E Mei Origin. They are:

(1) Posture of "Tian (sky)"

(2) Posture of "Di (earth)"

(3) Posture of "Zhi (zigzag)"

(4) Posture of "Xin (heart)"

(5) Posture of "Long (dragon)"

(6) Posture of "He (crane)"

(7) Posture of "Feng (wind)"

(8) Posture of "Yun (cloud)"

(9) Posture of "Da (big)"

(10) Posture of "Xiao (small)"

(11) Posture of "You (quiet)"

(12) Posture of "Ming (bright)"

Six stationary exercises for self-cultivation are as follows:

(1) Tiger Step Exercise

(2) Heavy Thumping Exercise

(3) Huddling Up on the Ground Exercise

(4) Bag Hanging Exercise

(5) Acupoint Pointing Exercise

(6) Nirvana Exercise

For details of these exercises, refer to treatises concerned.

111. What Is Yoga?

Yoga is a word of Sanskrit tranliteration, meaning to fasten a horse to the shaft. In Old Chinese translation it was turned into "agreement", meaning to seek harmony between body and mind.

A foreigner once said, "Yoga means that all mental activities come to a stop, 'small self' and 'large self' merge into one, that is, Heaven and Man merge into one. It can bring success and happiness. This tranquility, wisdom and loving each other can bring about harmony between body and mind, and that between man and his outer surroundings. This is called Yoga."

Yoga Exercise has a history of thousands of years in India. It was brought to the region of the Himalayas along the Ganges River by the Buddhists and their desciples, and was passed on from generation to generation in the long course of time. To this day, it has changed much including in it many connotations and exercising forms.

Yoga coming into China was closely connected with Buddhism. It was first used as a means to illustrate and express the philosophic ideas of Buddhism. Recently, it has drawn world-wide attention for its effects of regulating body and mind and has been passed around rapidly. Yoga Exercises have been shown on TV in the United States and Britain, and included in the curriculum of some schools in the United States, Britain, France, Japan, Switzerland and other countries. In New York City alone there are more than eighty schools teaching Yoga exercises. Even astronauts are required to take Yoga exercises as a special training course. By making use of Chinese Qigong and Indian Yoga, medical scientists of many countries have created biofeedback and the like therapies.

112. What Is Hard Qigong? How to Practise It?

Hard Qigong is also called Martial Qigong. The term was formally accepted at a National Qigong Meeting in 1978, and has since become known throughout the country. In the past, it was referred to as "Sword and spear cannot pierce," "Golden bell-cover," "Iron garment", "Iron sand palm", etc. They are all aimed at training muscles and bones and skins externally (i.e., training the exterior of the body through patting and striking) and the Qi internally (i.e., mustering up the Qi to a certain point of the body), so that one can stand great force and tolerate the piercing of things that have sharp points. This is called Hard Qigong.

It should be noticed that Hard Qigong is mainly aimed at enhancing one's physical health. One must not use it to bully others or cheat folks by showing it off here and there or by selling false medicine at the same time.

Different schools have different ways of practising Hard Qigong. You may practise the exercise single-handed or in pairs. You may practise the basic items or special items: squatting in 'horse step', patting and striking, finger and palm exerting strength, and heavy weight withstanding. Hard Qigong is practised by the following steps:

Step 1

Practise the basic items such as standing in 'horse step' and 'bow step', kicking legs, bending waist, pressing ligaments, etc. to train the essential qualities of the body.

Step 2

Train the finger and palm exerting strength under the guidance of mind. Practise thrusting fingers and palms into heaps of mungbeans, sand grains or iron sand to train finger strength and palm strength.

Step 3

With the mind leading, pat and strike any part of the body with palm, fist, stick or club to train muscles, bones and skin to make them firm enough to stand strikes.

Step 4

Bump against a trunk or wooden pole with palm, arm, Dantian, foot, etc, to train these parts to withstand great force.

Step 5

Pat and strike suspending big sandbags or large stones with palm, fist, or any part of the body you wish to train or with Dantian. You should coordinate training of the outer parts with inner Qi to form them into a coherent whole. Constant effort yields sure success.

Step 6

More effort should be made on those parts (head, neck, chest, abdomen or limbs) which require special training. In the course of time, those parts can stand great pressure and sharp-pointed piercing. As a result you will acquire the skills of resisting "sword and spear" and withstanding heavy weight.

The Eighteen Arhats Hard Qigong introduced by Sun Bin includes three aspects: lifting Qi, spurting Qi, and swallowing Qi. They are correlated and coordinated with one another. Details follow:

Tie a belt (about 6 feet long and 2 inches wide) around the waist, at the level of the navel, with a tightness admitting two small fingers inserting in.

(I) Lifting Qi

The method to practise:

(1) Stand upright with feet apart by shoulder-width. Set left hand akimbo, and right hand hanging naturally. Put tongue tip against upper palate.

(2) Inhale gently, slowly, deeply and in a long-drawn manner. Throw out chest naturally.

(3) Gather your whole strength to right hand and left arm. Press right hand on right waist with palm facing leftward and fingers pointing forward. Push the hand to lower abdomen with fingers pointing

upward, and move it upward along the middle line of abdomen to the middle of two eyes and go up to the headtop. When pushing the hand upward, move head from side to side gently.

Points to remember:

(1) Lifting Qi is mainly to lead the Qi of the whole body up to the acupoint of Baihui at headtop.

(2) Highly concentrate your mind and keep thinking of the headtop in the process.

(3) Keep torso and head erect, and draw the chins inward slightly.

(4) At the beginning you will feel head depressed, face bloated and red. These symptoms are normal and will disappear after half a month practice. Concentration of the mind on Baihui should be done under teacher's guidance.

(II) Spurting Qi

The method to practise:

(1) Stand with feet apart to form the shape of "/\". Squat half way to form a 'horse step'. Two hands hang naturally, and put tongue tip against upper palate.

(2) When inhaling, retract lower abdomen, protrude chest, and separate two arms to both sides by shoulder level with fingers close together and palms facing upward.

(3) Two arms move inward and forward in a curve and chop down at the chest front (two palms chopping down to the place about two inches below the mid-point of the line of two breasts).

(4) When two palms chop down to chest front, spurt Qi through nose and protrude lower abdomen.

Points to remember:

(1) Spurting Qi is the key link of this exercise. It causes muscles of the whole body to move and retract violently, the thoracic cavity to expand and fill with Qi and blood.

(2) Exert your strength at two arms and two palms.

(3) Draw chest slightly inward and keep back erect. Do not

protrude chest and abdomen.

(4) For a beginner, do not use too much force when doing palm chopping. Increase force gradually and steadily, otherwise you will feel pain in the chest.

(5) In the process of the exercise, you will occasionally experience tinnitus, or tears welling up at inner eye corners. That is normal phenomenon and you don't have to worry about it.

(III) Swallowing Qi

The method to practise:

(1) Separate two feet by shoulder width, slightly press two palms on two sides of chest, and put tongue tip gently against upper palate.

(2) Inhale. When inhaling, do it slowly and evenly with abdomen naturally protruded; and push two hands toward abdomen.

(3) When two hands reach the abdomen, swallow the Qi just like swallowing food in coordination with movements of the mouth and throat.

Points to remember:

(1) Relax head and chest, lead the Qi down to Dantian to cause Qi and blood to go downward.

(2) Take care to use only your mind and not to use any effort. Completely relax the muscles of whole body, slightly close two eyes and concentrate the mind on Dantian.

(3) In the process of exercising, you will sometimes hiccup, break wind, or hear sounds in intestines. These are normal reactions of circulation of the Qi.

In short, when practising lifting Qi and spurting Qi, you should exert force, but when practising swallowing Qi, you should use only the mind without any effort.

113. What Is Iron Sand Palm? How to Practise It?

Iron Sand Palm is for the Qigong exercisers to train palms. They train their palms by means of iron sand. In the course of time, their arms and palms become as hard as iron that can break up bricks and stones, and chop up steel rod. This is called Iron Sand Palm.

To practise Iron Sand Palm, first prepare a square bag made of two to three layers of canvas, filled with iron sand and tied up. Put it on a stool or hold it with one hand, and then strike the sand bag repeatedly with four parts of the other hand: the palm, the dorsal part of the hand, hand back, inner side and outer side. Exhale when striking down, lead the Qi to the palm with mind. Inhale when retracting the hand, and change legs into 'horse step' or 'bow-and-arrow-step'. Each time strike 20 times with each of the four parts of each hand, alternate left and right repeatedly. For beginners do not use too much force to avoid hurting muscles and bones. Increase force gradually. Constant effort yields sure success. If your hand is cut or broken through repeated striking, sterilize it with medicinal liquid.

You may also use mung beans mixed with Cayenne pepper instead of iron sand. Use more mung beans than Cayenne pepper in the mixture, for the former is harder. Both of them have detoxifying effect, so it is simpler to rub hands with them instead of using medicinal liquid. If the beans have been struck into powder, change another bag. If neither iron sand nor mung beans can be found, sand grains as big as mung beans can also be used. Only through constant practice with determination can you gain success in the course of time.

114. What Is Cinnabar Palm? How to Practise It?

Cinnabar Palm is a Qigong exercise for one to learn to lead inner Qi to circulate through both hands. In the course of practice, one's strength of the hand will be greatly enhanced. It is said that anybody who receives a slap of the cinnabar palm feels no pain at the moment, but will have a red palm print coming out at the spot several days later.

That is why it is called Cinnabar Palm.

This exercise can strengthen one's muscles and bones, help the Qi and blood circulate, and improve the function of viscera, so that one will feel full of vitality, and is able to cure diseases and prolong life. Those who have had much practice of the exercise can emit Qi out of the hands.

According to what Yang Yong illustrated, this exercise requires: Keep torso erect; separate two feet by shoulder width in parallel with toes in a line. Keep head and neck erect, eyes looking forward and the whole body relaxed. Tongue tip touches upper palate with mouth slightly closed. Breathe with nose. Concentrate the mind and expel distracting thoughts. It is better to practise it in the woods every morning facing east and taking in fresh air.

There are five movements for the beginners to follow:

1st movement

Droop two hands with palms facing downward and ten fingers pointing forward. Inhale air into Dantian. When exhaling ten toes keep fast to the ground. Retract anus and protrude abdomen and clench teeth. Lead the Qi from Dantian to palms with mind and press palms downward. It is appropriate to repeat the movement 49 times.

2nd movement

Raise two-arms forward to shoulder level; stand palms up at wrists, palms in parallel with the body, ten fingers pointing upward. Inhale air into Dantian. When exhaling, ten toes keep fast to the ground. Retract anus and protrude abdomen and clench teeth. Lead and Qi from Dantian to palms with mind, push palms forward. Repeat the movement 49 times.

3rd movement

Raise two arms straight up, palms facing upward and fingers pointing backward. Inhale air into Dantian and exhale with ten toes keeping fast to the ground. Retract anus and protrude abdomen and clench teeth. Lead the Qi from Dantian to palms and push palms upward. Repeat the movement 49 times.

4th movement

Raise two arms on both sides to shoulder level, palms stand upright and facing outward, fingers pointing upward. Inhale air into Dantian and exhale with ten toes keep fast to the ground. Retract anus and protrude abdomen and clench teeth. Lead the Qi from Dantian to palms and push palms out leftward and rightward. Repeat the movement 49 times.

5th movement

Droop two arms, turn body to the left with waist as the core and feet unmoved. At the same time, two hands cross inward and curve upward. Inhale air into Dantian. When turning torso to the left, two hands curve from inside and lower position upward and cross above the head. Then two hands curve outward and push out on two sides, palms facing outward, ten fingers pointing up. Lead the Qi from Dantian to two palms and push palms outward. Retract anus and protrude abdomen and clench teeth. Move downward and upward slowly and resume original posture. Then turn to the right and do the same movement. Go on alternating left and right for 49 times.

The important thing is perseverance in practising the exercise. Fits and starts can only lead to dispersion of Qi and decline of one's strength.

115. What Is Light-bodied Exercise? How to Practise It?

Constant practice of this exercise can make one as light as a swallow and as nimble as a goat. One can even feel as if the body were floating up when sitting in quiescence. This exercise varies greatly in form. Here is a brief introduction of the forms of "Wall Running" and "Wall Creeping" according to what Zhang Yu-geng described as Shaolin martial art handed down in a direct line from the master.

Wall Running is known as Horizontal Eight Steps. The exerciser is asked to fasten two bags, which are made of coarse cloth and filled with iron sand that is soaked through in pig blood, to two fore arms respectively, tie some lead tiles to both legs, and begin to practise running across a wall. You stand some distance away from a wall and run to it; left foot steps on it first and right foot follows up quickly, and with this force, begin running on the wall horizontally. When you feel your strength exhausted, right foot drops first and stands the body upright. This is left running. Then alternate left and right. If you can manage to run eight steps (about 16 feet) horizontally, you score well on the first step. If you can run eight steps in a slanting direction upward, you score well on the second step. When you manage to reach the top of the wall, swing down the arm near the wall and swing up the arm on the outer side, and with this movement, you can stand upright on the top of the wall.

Wall Creeping is known as Gecko Creeping or Snake Crawling. The exerciser is asked to lie on his back on the ground, prop up the body with both elbows and heels on the ground and move the body forward and backward by using the strength of elbows and heels. When you become skillful in the movements after much practice, tie some lead on your body and begin to practise moving on an uneven wall upward and downward, leftward and rightward. Increase the load of lead and creep on a smoother wall. With more practice, remove the load of lead, and you are able to move up and down at will on a smooth wall with your body kept close to it.

116. What Are the Basic Methods for Practising Release of Outer Qi?

The basic methods for practising release of outer Qi are varied in form but serve the same purpose. They require the exerciser to perservere in practice over a long period of time so that his internal Qi is developed and stored in the body, and can be emitted through certain acupoints of the body in case of need. This is the release of "Outer Qi". Here is a brief introduction of one of the basic methods.

(I) Preparation

(1)   First do the Joint Exercise (See the section of Joint Exercise).

(2) Squat down in "Horse Step" and thrust out the fist 100 — 200 times (Squat low and thrust fast and with force).

(II) Posture

(1) **Keep firm to the ground** (squat down with hands pressing down. See Fig. 173).

Fig. 173

Stand with feet apart by shoulder width and parallel to each other; keep torso and head and neck erect, eyes looking forward, lips and teeth closed; draw chest in and keep back erect; sink shoulders and droop arms; hold head naturally erect as if there is a thing on top; relax the whole body with hips down; bend both knees (at an angle of 90 degrees between the thigh and leg) with knees in vertical line with toes.

(2) **Flying sword in the air** (See Fig. 174)

Fig. 174

Follow the previous movement, clench left hand into fist and put it by the waist, palm facing upward and the part between thumb and index finger facing outward. Stretch right arm forward to shoulder level, with index finger and middle finger closing together and pointing forward, ring finger and small finger bending slightly, and thumb pointing forward and upward, palm facing inward. Keep shoulder, upper arm, forearm, index finger and middle finger in a line.

(3) **Hawk taking steps** (See Fig. 175)

Fig. 175

Stand naturally and straighten two arms, palm facing upward, raise palms to chest front, left palm at a higher position and right palm facing downward. Left foot takes a step forward, with knee straightened, instep stretched tight and toe tips touching the ground. Right knee bends at an angle of 120 degrees or so. Keep torso erect and weight on right foot. At the same time, draw right hand downward and put it by the waist, palm facing downward and fingers separated and pointing forward and pressing down like hawk claw. Left arm stretches forward with elbow bending slightly, the part between index finger and thumb at the level of the eyes, palm facing rightward and fingers separated and pointing upward like hawk claw. Look forward. Shift weight to left foot and take a step forward with right foot, with knee straightened and instep stretched tight and toe tips touching the ground. Left knee bends at an angle of 120 degrees or so. Keep torso erect. At the same time, draw left hand down and put it by the waist, palm facing downward and fingers separated and pointing forward and pressing down like hawk claw. Right arm stretches forward and upward with elbow bending slightly, the part between index finger and thumb at the level of the eyes, palm facing leftward, fingers separated and pointing upward like hawk claw. Take steps forward in the same manner by alternating left and right.

(III)　Breathing

Use natural breathing.

(IV)　Mind-Intent

Concentrate the mind on fine and pleasant things.

(V)　Time Schedule

Do the exercise once or twice everyday, usually in the afternoon or at night, 20 — 60 minutes each time.

(VI)　Points for Attention

(1) Take correct postures, persevere in practice and always keep the body relaxed.

(2) When you have taken the correct posture, you are allowed to talk, or listen to light music, but do not move the body at will.

(3) In the process of the exercise, breathe naturally and think only of pleasant things. Do not swear at others or get angry.

(4) Have a warm drink before doing the exercise. You should not do the exercise when feeling hungry or full in the stomach.

(5) Before taking the exercise, do some physical activities. First practise the movements of "Keeping Firm to the Ground", about an hour each time for a year. Then go on practising the movements of "Flying Sword in the Air" for another year before proceeding to practise the movements of "Hawk Taking Steps".

(6) Take natural posture and do not pursue the feelings intentionally.

(7) It is a good sign to feel the palms warming up or even the whole body warming up and sweating a little in the process of the exercise. If you feel cold, perform the closing movement and come to a stop. Go on practising the next day.

(8) For beginners, it is advisable to arrange one's time properly and to avoid fatigue. It is normal for one to feel soreness and pain in the knees after the exercise. Too much practice will produce bad effects.

(9) Follow a schedule of gradual progression in practice. Spend less time practising the exercise at the beginning and increase time and effort gradually.

(10) If the exercise makes you sweat, have a hot bath and some hot drink after the exercise. If there is no hot water, take a short rest after the exercise before going to wash and drink so as to avoid catching cold.

QIGONG EXERCISE FOR COMMON DISEASES

117. How to Practise Qigong for Hypertension?

Hypertension means that arterial pressure is higher than normal limits. Blood pressure of an adult is within the range of 110 — 120/ 70 — 80 (systolic pressure/diastolic pressure) mm Hg. If the systolic pressure of a man in the prime of life should be over 140 mm Hg., it is called hypertension. Blood pressure goes up with age. The systolic pressure of an ordinary man over fifty is over 150 mm Hg. Generally, it is not regarded as hypertension for a man over fifty to be below 160 mm Hg., and for a man over sixty to be below 170 mm Hg. However, no matter what the age is, if one's diastolic pressure surpasses 90 mm Hg., it is taken as hypertension.

There are two kinds of hypertension: one is primary hypertension, of which the cause is still not known. Perhaps it is the result of overtension, disorder of the nervous system, or a result of heredity. The other kind is secondary hypertension (or symptomatic hypertension) which results from some other diseases, such as kidney diseases (acute or chronic nephritis), endocrine diseases (pheochromocytoma), increase of pressure in cranial cavity, and so on.

What we generally mean by hypertension refers to the primary one.

Hypertension over a long-time affects some vital organs, such as heart, brain, kidneys, and eyes. Without proper and prompt treatment it will cause hypertrophy of the left atrium, resulting in hypertension heart disease; it will cause the arteriosclerosis of coronary arteries, resulting in insufficient blood supply to cardiac muscle, or even myocardial infarction; it will cause the hardening of cerebral vessels, resluting in cerebral haemorrhage (commonly called as stroke); it will cause the hardening of renal arteries, resulting in blood insufficiency in kidneys, insufficiency of renal function and even uraemia; it will cause the hardening of the retina arteries, and break of blood vessels resulting in haemorrhage and oedema and oozing of retina which will affect eyesight or even make one go blind. All these symptoms mentioned above come out only when the disease becomes serious. Therefore, if Qigong therapy is prescribed in time and is practised in coordination with other treatments, one can avoid going from bad to worse.

Qigong exercise therapy for hypertension:

(I) Qigong Practice

(1) Lying or sitting exercise: 1) Take Relaxing Qigong Exercise part by part or along three-lines, about 20 to 30 minutes. 2) Concentrate the mind at Dantian or Yongquan, about 20 to 30 minutes. 3) Lead the Qi from Dantian to Yongquan, that is, to keep the mind at Dantian when inhaling and at Yongquan when exhaling, about 10 to 20 minutes.

(2) Standing Qigong Exercise to lead the Qi:

Pressing hands down at a high position. Relax the whole body with mind-intent. Supposing that you were right under water tap with warm water flowing slowly down from neck to chest to abdomen to thighs to legs and to soles. Repeatedly lead the Qi from the head down to soles for about 15 minutes.

(3) Ascending-descending and opening-closing exercise in standing posture:

Ascending-descending exercise is the breathing-regulation of the commencing form of Taiji Qigong. Opening-closing exercise is: When inhaling, separate two palms from the front of abdomen to two sides, palms facing inward and legs stretching straight. When exhaling, draw two palms from two sides to the front of abdomen, palms still facing inward and legs bending slightly. The movements should be practised slowly and gently for 50 to 100 times continuously with one ascending-descending exercise and one opening-closing exercise as one time.

(4) Practise the movements of Separating Heaven From Earth (See Section 6 of Limb Exercise) about 100 times (swing leftward and rightward as one time), swinging with the range of motion increasing

gradually.

(II) Self-Massage

(1) Rub the pressure-reducing point:

Clench two hands into half fists, with index-finger in front of the ear and thumb in its rear (the pressure-reducing point is at one third of the helix), and massage the point 100 times.

(2) Press Taiyang point:

Press the Taiyang points with thumbs or index-fingers of both hands for 2 minutes. (Taiyang point is at about an inch from the part between the tip of the brow and the outside corner of the eye.)

(3) Knead Fengchi point:

Knead the two Fengchi points with thumbs and index-fingers of both hands for two minutes. (Fengchi point is at the hollow by the hair fringe beside the big tendon on the back of the neck.)

(4) Press Quchi point:

Left elbow bends in front of chest, with palm facing downward, right hand presses left Quchi point tightly for 2 minutes in coordination with shaking and soft kneading. (Quchi point is at the elbow joint.)

118. How to Practise Qigong for Heart Disease?

Heart is the vital organ of human body and the centre of circulating system. Pathological changes in the heart will affect its normal functioning. Common heart diseases include: rheumatic heart disease, hypertension heart disease, pulmonary heart disease, coronary heart disease and congenital heart disease.

For a long time in the past people used to consider taking medicine to be the only way to cure heart disease, and strictly restricting patients' activities and physical work, and making them lie in bed to be the right way to reduce symptoms of heart disease. However, a large amount of practice and long-term clinical observation have proved that only those whose heart disease is serious should lie in bed, while to ordinary

227

patients doing some exercises will dó them more good than harm. Exercise helps increase oxygen supply for heart muscles, adapt heart muscles to certain amount of activity, and remove various symptoms of heart disease.

Generally speaking, patients with heart disease are not supposed to do vigorous physical exercise, but it is appropriate for them to have some physical exercise and Qigong training, which is beneficial to enhancing the function of heart muscles. It will be more effective to combine Qigong exercise with medical treatment.

(I) Qigong Exercise

(1) Qigong Exercise in lying or sitting posture. For Mind-intent you can practise relaxing, saying words in the mind and concentrating the mind at Dantian.

(2) Eighteen-Form Taiji Qigong Exercise.

(3) Shiduanjin Exercise on bed.

(4) Walking Exercise by 200 steps, and the increase of distance should be gradual according to physical conditions.

(II) Self-Massage

(1) Rub chest

Movement: Press tightly on left breast with right hand, massage from upper part to lower part or massage chest clockwise for 200 times.

Effect: Relieve of chest distress and chest pain.

Points to remember: Dress thinly when doing massage so as not to affect the results.

(2) Pat heart

Movement: Pat the front area of the heart 200 times with right palm (or half-clenched fist).

Effect: Relieve of chest distress and chest pain.

Points to remember: Pat gently first and increase force gradually if you feel comfortable.

(3) Press or rub the point of Neiguan

Movement: 1) Sit naturally upright with left palm facing upward on abdomen. Press hard the point of Neiguan on the left forearm with the tip of right thumb (the location of Neiguan point is between the two tendons on the wrist two-finger-width above stria). First press down, then press centripetally without changing its location. In the same way press the Neiguan point on right hand with left hand.

2) Take a sitting posture with left palm facing upward and placed naturally on thigh, press the Neiguan point on the left hand with right index and middle fingers, and then massage up and down 200 times along the arm.

Effect: Improve arrhythmia, tachycardia, bradycardia and the like symptoms.

Points to remember: Those who suffer from arrhythmia should be massaged evenly. Those who suffer from tachycardia should be massaged gently and with gradually increased force in coordination with quivering and gentle rubbing. Those who suffer from bradycardia should be treated with strong stimulation.

119. How to Practise Qigong for Diabetes?

Diabetes is a common disease in metabolism, with symptoms of polyuria, polydipsia, over-eating, hyperglycemia and glucosuria. If diabetes is not properly treated or strictly controlled, it will cause complications, such as ketonic acidosis arteriosclerosis, cataract and suppurative infection, or even lead to septicaemia when becoming serious.

Diabetes is a chronic disease. It is most proper for the sufferer to have some physical exercise and Qigong exercise in coordination with medical treatment. Physical exercise and Qigong exercise as well as control of diet are the fundamental methods to cure diabetes. To those fat persons and mental workers, doing physical exercise will bring great benefit, because it will increase the body's cell sensitivity to insulin, especially increase the combination of insulin and the receptor of insulin in muscle cells involved in exercise. It will also enhance the metabolic reaction after the combination. Therefore, the glucose taken in by the muscle cells will be multiplied resulting in the decrease in blood sugar. But after practising exercise, dosages of both antidiabetic medicine or insulin taken by mouth should be decreased. In sugar metabolism, practising exercise is found helpful for improvement of patient's glucose tolerance. For those obese patients with light diabetes, physical exercise should not be neglected, for it can reduce the patient's weight, restore insulin receptors on the fatty cell membrane to normal. The declining combination of insulin with the receptors on fatty cell membrane will also return to normal.

If the patient practises exercise after taking medicine, he should properly control the time for exercise and try to avoid the time when the insulin is producing the strongest effect. The patient who takes insulin should not practise exercise around 11 a.m., because it is the time when insulin functions most actively. The patient suffering from serious diabetes or with acute complication should stop the exercise, otherwise, physical activity will cause ketonic acidosis or even a coma.

Methods for practice follow:

(I) Qigong Exercise

(1) Qigong Exercise in lying posture (supine or lying sideway). For mind-intent, you can do relaxing Qigong exercise, concentrating the mind at Dantian, Guan Qi Exercise (shifting attention between Tanzhong and Yongquan).

(2) Standing Qigong Exercise at high position.

(3) Eighteen-Form Taiji Qigong Exercise.

(4) Shiduanjin Exercise on bed or taking a standing posture..

(5) Walking Exercise by 200 steps.

(II) Self-Massage

(1) Rub Kidney Points

Set two hands akimbo with hukou facing downward, rub the acupoints of kidney up and down 200 times.

(2) Knead the acupoint of Zusanli

Press at Zusanli point with thumb and knead 200 times. Knead the points on both feet alternately (Zusanli point is at the area three fingers width downward from the bumping part of shin bone and the one finger width from the outer part of shin bone).

(3) Press the acupoint of Sanyinjiao

Press the Sanyinjiao point at the inner side of right leg 2 minutes with right thumb, the feeling of soreness, numbness and distension will bring better results. Then press the Sanyinjiao point at the inner side of left leg with left thumb (Sanyinjiao point is at the area four horizontal fingers width right above inner ankle and hind edge of shin bone).

120.   How to Practise Qigong for Tuberculosis?

Tuberculosis is also called "pulmonary consumption", which is a lung infection caused by tubercle bacillus getting into lungs through respiratory tract. Sufferers with mild tuberculosis may have no distinct symptoms when the disease is not serious. But when it becomes serious, he has distinctive symptoms, such as fever (usually in the afternoon and in the evening), night-sweating (sweating unconsciously), cough or even hemoptysis. Prolonged illness will cause asthenia, listlessness, dyspepsia, emaciation, and eventual death.

Tuberculosis is a chronic disease. Taking medicine and taking an active part in therapeutic physical exercise and Qigong exercise will produce better results.

Methods for practice follow:

(I)   Qigong Exercise

(1) Qigong Exercise in lying posture (supine). Use the method of concentrating the mind at Dantian and abdominal breathing, 20 to 30 minutes each time.

(2) Standing Qigong Exercise at a high position for 3 to 5 minutes.

(3) Eighteen-Form Taiji Qigong Exercise. Chiefly perform the movements of Expanding Chest, Pigeon Spreading Wings, and Wild Goose In Flight. Practise 100 times for each movement.

(4) Shiduanjin Exercise on bed or at standing posture.

(5) Six-Character Formula. Say the word "Si" (method of tonifying the lungs) for 3 minutes.

(6) Walking Exercise. Take 300 steps and increase the distance gradually according to one's physical conditions.

(II) Self-Massage

(1) Rub chest

Set left hand akimbo or at the end of thigh. Press the upper area of right breast with right hand, thumb pointing upward and four fingers facing leftward. Massage in a clockwise circle on the chest for 100 times.

(2) Press the point of Neiguan

Press the point of Neiguan at the left forearm with right thumb, or press the point of Neiguan at the right forearm for two minutes with left thumb.

(3) Rub the point of Yanglingquan

First press the point of Yanglingquan with index and middle fingers, and then massage up and down 200 times. Massage the point of Yanglingquan in two legs alternately (The point of Yanglingquan is located at the hollow place about one inch below the protruding round bone at the outer side of knee joint).

(4) Pat the shoulder back

Pat the shoulder backs alternately right and left with two hands. Pat left shoulder (at the back upper part of shoulder joint) with right palm, and pat the back (at the lower part of shoulder joint) with left palm, and then pat right shoulder (at the back upper part of shoulder joint) with left palm, and pat the back (at the lower part of shoulder joint) with right palm. In this way, pat the shoulder backs alternately 100 times for each shoulder back.

232

121. How to Practise Qigong for Nephritis?

Nephritis is known as kidney disease, which is a kind of pathological change of non-suppurative inflammation in the kidney. The most serious portion of the pathological change is in glomerulus, sometimes affecting renal tubule. Nephritis may either be acute or chronic. Sufferer of acute nephritis is likely to be found among children and teenagers, while sufferer of chronic nephritis is most likely among youngsters and adults. The main symptoms are edema, rise of blood pressure, haematuria and albuminuria. If treatment is delayed, complications will occur, such as heart failure, hypertension brain disease and acute renal failure. Therefore, while having medical treatment, it is necessary for the patient to have some physical and Qigong exercises.

Methods of exercise for nephritis follow:

(I) Qigong Exercise

(1) Qigong Exercise in lying supine posture. Practise Guan Qi Exercise (shifting attention between Dantian and Yongquan) 20 to 30 minutes.

(2) Sitting Qigong Exercise. Keep mind at Dantian and use abdominal breathing for 20 to 30 minutes.

(3) Eighteen-Form Taiji Qigong Exercise. Practise the movements of Commencing Form and Regulating Breathing, Waving Like Rainbow, and Dredging From the Sea and Looking at the Sky. Practise each movement 100 times.

(4) Standing Qigong Exercise at high position for 3 to 5 minutes.

(5) Practise Six-Character Formula, say the word "Chui" (kidney-tonifying exercise) for 3 minutes.

(6) Practise Walking Exercise by 200 meters each day, increase the distance gradually according to one's physical conditions.

(II) Self-Massage

(1) Rub kidney points 200 times.

(2) Press or massage the point of Sanyinjiao. Press the point of Sanyinjiao at the inner side of right leg with right thumb, and massage up and down 200 times. And then change to left side, use left hand to press the point of Sanyinjiao at left leg. Massage right leg and left leg alternately.

122. How to Practise Qigong for Peptic Ulcer?

Ulcer includes gastric ulcer and duodenal ulcer. It is a common disease of the digestive tract. The main symptom of ulcer is pain in the upper abdomen. The disease usually lasts for a long time, and the patient has to suffer from repeated attacks of pain. If the case is serious, massive haemorrhage or acute gastric perforation may result, and gastric ulcer may even deteriorate into gastric carcinoma. Therefore, we must treat it seriously.

Ulcer is a chronic disease. Of course, measure should first be taken to stop sour liquid and remove local spasm. What is more important for the patient is to be optimistic live a regular life and to be on a diet at fixed hours. While being treated with Chinese and Western medicines, the patient should take an active part in physical and Qigong exercises, which have proved most effective for healing of ulcer.

Methods for practice follow:

(I) Qigong Exercise

(1) Qigong Exercise in lying posture (lying supine or lying sideway). Keep mind at Dantian and take abdominal breathing. Each time practise 20 to 30 minutes.

(2) Sitting Qigong posture (sitting upright or sitting with support). Keep mind at Dantian and take abdominal breathing. Each time practise 10 to 20 minutes.

(3) Taiji Qigong Exercise. Practise the movements of Waving Arms As Separating Clouds, Fix Step and Whirl Arms on Both Sides

234

and Turning Torse to Look at the Moon. Practise each movement 100 times.

(4) Practise Six-Character Formula, say the word "Xi" in the mind to tonify stomach and Sanjiao (the triple heater). Each time practise 3 minutes.

(II) Self-Massage

(1) Massage abdomen 200 times.

(2) Press the point of Zhongwan. Each time practise 1 to 3 minutes (The point of Zhongwan is located at the mid point of the line from the lower end of heart-protecting rib to navel).

(3) Press and massage the point of Zusanli 1 to 3 minutes.

123. How to Practise Qigong for Asthma?

Asthma includes asthmatic bronchitis, which is caused by infection of the bronchial tube, and bronchial asthma, a kind of allergic disease. It is the latter that people usually speak of as asthma.

The attack of asthma has something to do with one's allergic constitution and hypersensitivity to certain factors, such as touching paint or animal hair, breathing in pollen or dust, eating shrimp, crab, fish, egg and the like. The symptoms are, when the attack begins, coughing, itchiness in the throat, watery nasal discharge, chest distention, and shortness of breath. Then, in serious cases, there come panting, lengthening of exhalation, shortening of inhalation, accompanied with wheezy rhonchi. The patient will sweat all over in agony.

Measures taken to treat asthma are first of all to control infection and then relieve the patient of asthma symptoms. Generally, on the basis of controlling the infection, prescribe medicines to induce expectoration, stop coughing, resist allergy, and to calm the nerves. Besides, advise the patient to give up smoking and drinking, to keep warm, and take an active part in physical exercise so as to enhance

~resistance to diseases.

Methods for practice follow:

(I) Qigong Exercise

(1) Take a lying or sitting posture and keep the mind at the point for curing asthma (The point is at the bone edge between the seventh cervical vertebra and the two sides of the first thoracic vertebra) for 20 to 30 minutes.

Breathing: Abdominal breathing.

(2) Taiji Qigong Exercise. Practise the following movements: Waving Arms As Separating Clouds, Waving Hands Like Clouds In Horse Step, Churning Up Waves and Billows, Marking Time and Bouncing A Ball. Practise each movement 100 times.

(3) Standing Qigong Exercise at high position or at medium position. Practise 3 to 5 minutes.

(4) Six-Character Formula. Say the word "Si" in the mind to tonify lungs for 3 minutes.

(II) Self-Massage

Massage the point of Tiantu (It is at the upper edge of breastbone, the hollow place right at the center of throat), or the point of Neiguan. The disease can be controlled if the sufferer takes part in physical exercise, take appropriate measures of prevention and treatment. Attention should be paid to two points in prevention and treatment: One is to give timely treatment when the first-stage symptoms are found, and the other is to take the right medicines and never use too much antibiotic.

124. How to Practise Qigong for Virus Hepatitis?

Virus hepatitis is an infectious disease, mainly affecting the liver. At present there is said to be two kinds of viruses: type A and type B. People who have in contact with virus or have transfusion of blood

236

or blood product with hepatitis virus may incur hepatitis. Type A
hepatitis is commonly found among youngsters and children, and Type
B hepatitis among adults throughout all four seasons of the year. In
accordance with the development of the disease, there are acute hepatitis
and chronic hepatitis; acute jaundice hepatitis, and acute non-jaundice
hepatitis if there is any jaundice; and serious hepatitis, transient
hepatitis, chronic hepatitis and long-termed jaundice heaptitis, etc.

Main symptoms are lassitude, loss of appetite, anorexia and
aversion to fatty food, hepatomegaly with pain when pressed,
accompanied with fever, nausea, vomiting, abdominal distension,
diarrhea and constipation. Jaundice hepatitis has symptoms of
yellowish pigmentation of the skin and sclera of the eye. Serious
hepatitis has symptoms of rapid atrophy of liver, subcutaneous
hemorrhage, and blood in the feces, and sufferer will soon fall into
coma.

At present there are no specific drugs to cure hepatitis, but timely
and reasonable treatments are effective to most sufferers. The patient
of acute hepatitis should have good rest and appropriate nourishment
besides treatment with Chinese and Western medicines. The patient of
transient hepatitis or chronic hepatitis should take physical exercise
therapy besides a proper balance between work and rest.

Methods for practice follow:

(I) Qigong Exercise

(1) Take a lying or sitting posture. Practise Relaxing Qigong
Exercise (Relaxing the Body Along Three Lines or part by part) 20
minutes. Keep the mind at Dantian or Tanzhong 20 minutes. Practise
Guan Qi Exercise, shifting attention between Dantian and Yongquan
15 minutes. Practise Spontaneous Moving Qigong Exercise in sitting
posture 30 minutes.

(2) Practise Standing Qigong Exercise With Hands Pressing
Downward at high position 10 to 15 minutes.

(3) Taiji Qigong Exercise.

(II) Self-Massage

(1) Massage chest and abdomen 100 times for each.

(2) Massage the point of Zusanli or the point of Dannang 100 times.

125. How to Practise Qigong for Neurasthenia?

Neurasthenia is a kind of functional disease resulting from imbalance of cerebral excitation and inhibition.

Symptoms of neurasthenia are various, involving different systems. Of nervous system: insomnia and dreamfulness, low spirit, fatigue and sleepiness, dizziness, absent-mindedness, failing memory, restlessness etc. Of the gastrointestinal system: indigestion, distention and fullness of stomach, constipation and diarrhea, etc. Of reproductive symptoms: emission, impotence, premature ejaculation, and menstrual irregularities, etc. Of cardiovascular system: palpitation, nervousness, erythema of the skin, cold limbs, etc.

The sufferer of neurasthenia should first of all have confidence in getting over the disease, live a regular life, and take part in some activities beneficial to health, such as Qigong exercise, Taiji Boxing, self-massage and walking. Besides, he may take some medicine as supplementary treatment according to doctor's instructions. Thus, many sufferers can restore to health soon.

Methods for Practice follow:

(I) Qigong Exercise

(1) Practise Standing Qigong Exercise With Hands Pressing Downward at mid and high position 10 to 20 minutes until you feel hot and sweat slightly. Practise 2 times each day.

(2) Eighteen-Form Taiji Qigong Exercise.

(3) Walking Exercise. 100 to 200 meters.

(4) Qigong Stick Exercise.

(5) Spontaneous Moving Qigong Exercise. 30 minutes.

(II) Self-Massage

Before going to sleep, massage the point of Yongquan 100 times. And then wash hands and feet with warm water, which can help you fall into sleep.

126. How to Practise Qigong for Cerebrovascular Accident?

Cerebrovascular Accident is an acute disease mainly found among people above middle-aged and mostly related to arteriosclerosis. Its clinical symptoms are sudden disturbance of consciousness and limb paralysis. Although the rate of sufferers of this disease and its death rate in China are lower than those in the Western countries, yet it is still one of the main causes for death of the aged persons. Therefore, it is an important job to prevent and cure cerebrovasular accident.

Cerebrovascular accident includes two kinds: haemorrhage and ischemia. The former refers to cerebral haemorrhage and haemorrhage at subarachnoid space; the latter refers to formation of cerebral thrombus and cerebral embolism. When cerebrovascular accident occurs, the patient will lose consciousness for some time and have limb defect. After treatment, he will come to consciousness, his muscle tension of the injured limb will be improved and its function recovered gradually. However, the serious patient will usually suffer from limb paralysis and speech defect to varying degrees, or even death.

No matter whether the accident is caused by cerebral haemorrhage, haemorrhage at lower chamber of cobweb membrane, cerebral thrombus or cerebral embolism, the patient should be treated with both Chinese and Western medicines during the acute period, and have Qigong practice and functional physical exercises during the recovering period in order to regain health.

Methods for Practice follow:

(I) Qigong Exercise

(1) Take a lying or sitting posture. Practise Relaxing Qigong Exercise, Relaxation Along Three Lines. Keep the mind at Laogong point of the stiff hand and at Yongquan point of the foot. Each time practise 20 to 30 minutes.

(2) Shiduanjin Exercise on bed.

(3) Practise Spontaneous Moving Qigong Exercise in a lying or sitting posture. Each time practise 30 minutes.

(4) Practise Walking Qigong Exercise constantly 300 to 500 steps each day.

(II) Massage-Pat Exercise

For the unmovable parts of the body, it is advisable to massage and pat them to bring curative effect.

127. How to Practise Qigong for Obesity?

Obesity is caused by improper diet, which is most commonly seen, or endocrine functional defect. When one has had more food energy than needed by the organism over a long period of time, the surplus energy is transformed into fat and stored up in the body, resulting in obesity.

Only a few cases of obesity are caused by endocrine disturbance or other diseases. Most cases belong to simple obesity, that is, they eat too much and consume too little, which leads to gradual accumulation of fat in the body and causes the body weight to surpass the normal standard (the standard weight should be: stature (cm) — 100 = weight (kg). If a person's stature is 150cm, his standard weight should be 150 — 100 = 50 (kg). It is regarded as normal that the actual weight is 10% more or less than the standard weight). The superfluous fat, which generally accumulates beneath the skin, in the abdominal cavity, or in the viscera such as heart, blood vessels, liver and so on, is likely to cause diseases like coronary disease, hypertension, diabetes, and fatty liver. This does great harm to one's health or even shortens his lifetime.

How to prevent obesity? How can an obese person reduce fat? Recently both Chinese and overseas experts regard proper diet and exercises as the most effective means to prevent obesity and reduce fat. There is an institution, in which 45 obese persons were treated with physical exercise therapy. After three months' practice, their average weight was reduced by 4.87 kg, the thickness of the abdominal fat reduced by 1.43 cm. As a result, both their abdominal measurements and chest measurements turned out at least 3 cm less on the average. Physical exercise can reduce fat simply because it consumes a lot of energy. The exercises with large amount of movement consume three times more energy than ordinary activities. Because of the increase in energy consumption, the stored fat has to be used as a supply. Constant physical exercise will continuously consume the superfluous fat beneath the skin and cure obesity.

Physical exercises for the obese persons should be prescribed according to their physique, constitution, age and state of disease. Generally they are included into two groups, one for the strong, and the other for the weak. Those who are physically stronger without any pathological changes in angiocardic organs may take part in the group for the strong. And those who are weak with coronary disease or hypertension may take part in the group for the weak. The strong group may take exercises, such as swimming, gymnastics, running, playing ball, climbing and so on. Statistics has proved that swimming for 45 minutes on end will reduce one's weight by 350 grams. If an obese person with a weight 15 to 20 kg over the normal standard insists on swimming exercise for over a half year, his weight will come down to normal standard. Running is a more effective exercise. A Japanese medical man once observed five obese women doing physical exercises. They were required to run 20 minutes a day at the speed of 125 meters per minute, and perform 15-minute gymnastic exercise.

Three months later their weights were reduced by 3 to 9 kg, and a half year later, up to 4 to 10 kg. With constant practice for two years their weights were reduced 8 to 11 kg. The group for the weak persons may do some exercises, requiring less amount of movement.

Methods for Practice for the weak:

(I) Qigong Exercise

(1) Practise Standing Qigong Exercise With Hands Pressing Downward at middle position 5 to 20 minutes.

(2) Eighteen-Form Taiji Qigong Exercise.

(3) Shiduanjin Exercise at standing posture.

(4) Walking Qigong Exercise. 200 meters.

(5) Practise Spontaneous Moving Qigong Exercise 30 minutes.

(II) Exercise for Abdominal Muscle

(1) Practise abdominal muscle exercise in supine lying posture, such as raising two straightened legs upward, moving the straightened legs up and down like lapping water, doing sit-ups, etc. Practise each movement 20 to 50 times each day.

(2) Practise lower back muscle and musculus glutaeus exercise in lying-on-abdomen posture, such as raising two straightened legs backward and upward, and at the same time raising head and shoulders to form a "bridge" shape. Practise the movements 20 to 50 times each day.

(III) Dumbbell Exercise

Raise the dumbbell, heavy or light, to reduce the fat at the chest and shoulders.

(IV) Squatting-Down Exercise

Stand with two feet apart by shoulder width in parallel. While squatting down, exhale, and while standing up, inhale. Practise squatting down 20 to 40 times each day.

(V) Single Foot Hopping

Practise hopping exercise with left foot and right foot alternately 20 to 40 times.

(VI) Reducing-Fat Exercise

Namely the Joint Exercise.

128. How to Practise Qigong for Cold?

Cold is an illness which is commonly seen and frequently occurring in all four seasons, especially in winter and spring, or when the weather suddenly changes.

Cold includes common Cold and influenza. Common cold is caused by common cold virus, while influenza by influenza virus. Although the two kinds of virus are entirely different, they live on the secretion of the patient's mouth and nose and are spread through sneezing, coughing, and saliva spurting when people are speaking. Besides, one can be infected through touching the towel, the handkerchief, the food container, and the like. One may also catch cold because of sudden change of weather, sweating, taking off clothes, sleeping in a draught, being caught in the rain, etc. The symptoms are: nasal obstruction, nasal discharge, sorethroat, sneezing, coughing, headache, and fever. Attacks of influenza come very quickly with serious poisoning symptoms all over the body: high fever, severe headache, and body aching. If the case is serious, there will occur loss of consciousness, arrhythmia and decrease of blood pressure.

The patient should have medical treatment and physical exercise as well for better curative effect.

Methods for practice follow:

(I) Qigong Exercise

Practise Standing Qigong Exercise with hands pressing downward at low position or mid position 5 to 20 minutes until sweating a little.

(II)   Self-Massage

(1) Bathe face and rub the sides of nose, 200 times for each movement until feeling hot on the face and sweating a little at the forehead.

(2) Press the points of Fengchi and Taiyang with thumbs and index fingers, 10 minutes for each movement.

(III)   Taking Hot Bath

Take a bath in hot water for half an hour until sweating.

(IV)   Running

If physical condition permits, you can practise long-distance running until you begin sweating.

129.   How to Practise Qigong for Shoulder Periarthritis?

Shoulder Periarthritis is often found among persons over the age of 40. Generally it is degeneration in the local tissues, accompanied by pathogenic wind and cold or trauma, that causes adhesion and inflammation in the shoulder joints and results in functional obstacle and pain. The functional movements of the injured part, such as raising, stretching outward, retracting, or bending are restricted. If serious, the patient will have difficulty in daily activities.

Taking an active part in Shoulder Joint Exercise will help improve blood circulation at the shoulder and back and upper limbs, actuate main and collateral channels, lessen myospasm, and remove pains. It can further strengthen one's muscles of the shoulder, back and upper limbs, and recover the muscle's normal elasticity and retracting function. One should begin the exercise with gentle movements, and, after several weeks' practice, goes on with more strenuous movements gradually if he feels less painful.

Methods for practice follow:

(I) Qigong Exercise

(1) Taiji Qigong Exercise. Practise the following movements: Commencing Form and Regulating Breathing, Broadening the Chest, Waving Like Rainbow, Waving Arms as Separating Clouds, Rowing Boat in Lake Centre, Turning Waist and Pushing Palms, Straightening Arms and Pounding Fist, and Revolving Like Flyingwheel. Practise 20 times for each movement.

(2) Shiduanjin Exercise on bed. Practise the following movements: Turning Over Palms and Expanding Chest, Holding Up Heavy Weight With Both Palms, Turning Head and Aiming At Vulture, Holding Head and Bending Waist, and Turning A Millstone With Both Hands. Practise 20 times for each movement.

(3) Shiduanjin Exercise at standing posture. Practise the following movements: A Gigantic Stature With Head Pointing to the Sky and Feet Onto the Ground, Picking Fruit and Pulling Downward, Holding Head and Bending Sideways, and Horizontal Raising and Half-Squatting. Practise 20 times for each movement.

(4) Spontaneous Moving Qigong Exercise. Practise 30 minutes.

(II) Relaxing Exercise

(Suitable for the disease in acute period)

(1) Bend waist forward at 60 to 80 degrees with two upper limbs naturally drooped down. Then swing two straightened arms forward and backward alternately 100 to 200 times.

(2) Stand upright. First use the palm of a healthy arm to pat the diseased shoulder back 50 times. Then use the palm of the diseased arm to pat the healthy side of the shoulder back 50 times.

(III) Self-Supporting Movement

(1) Stand upright. Clench two hands before the body. Raise the diseased arm with the healthy arm to train the shoulder joint.

(2) Stand upright. Clench two hands at the headtop. Draw the diseased limb with the healthy hand to the healthy side, and help practise stretching outward movement to train the shoulder joints.

(3) Stand upright. Clench two hands at the back. Draw the diseased limb with healthy hand to the healthy side, and help practise the turning inward and retracting inward movements to train the shoulder joint.

(IV) Active Rising Movement

(1) Stand upright facing the wall. Let the hand of the diseased limb move along the wall from a lower place upward gradually.

(2) Stand with the side of the diseased shoulder against the wall. Let the hand of the diseased limb move along the wall from a lower place upward gradually to stretch the diseased shoulder joint outward with the body leaning toward the wall gradually.

(V) Stick Exercise

Prepare a wooden stick about one meter long.

(1) Stand upright. Hold the stick with both hands before the body, with two hands apart by shoulder-width. Raise forward and upward to move the shoulder joint with the aid of the healthy upper limb.

(2) Stand upright. Hold both ends of the stick with two hands. Push the diseased hand with the aid of the healthy one, stretch the shoulder joint of the diseased limb outward as far as possible.

(3) Stand upright. Hold the stick with both hands at the back with two hands apart by shoulder width. Stretch the shoulder joint of the diseased limb backward with the aid of the healthy upper limb.

(4) Stand upright. Hold the stick vertically close to the back with the hand of diseased limb holding the lower end, and the hand of healthy limb holding the upper end. Draw the stick upward with the

healthy hand, practise turning inward and retracting inward movements to train the shoulder joint.

(VI) Passive Exercise

(Suitable for sufferer of hinderance at shoulder joint)

The patient should relax the muscles completely. Let someone else press the diseased shoulder joint with one hand and hold the forearm of the diseased limb with the other hand. Then help to practise the movements of raising forward and upward, stretching outward, stretching backward, retracting inward, and turning round so as to train the shoulder joint. Increase the range of movement gradually. And practise combing hair activity with the diseased limb.

(VII) Exercise for Strengthening Muscle Force

(1) Practise Clenching Fist and Bending Elbow Exercise with the diseased limb.

(2) Practise Striking Fist Exercise at all sides with the diseased limb.

(3) Practise Shrugging Shoulder Exercise with the diseased limb.

The sufferer should begin the exercises once a day, 3 to 4 items of the exercises each time. Repeat every movement 20 times. A week later practise 2 to 3 times a day, more than 5 items of the exercises each time. Repeat every movement 25 times. Use thermotherapy or massage, if possible, in coordination with the exercises. This is more effective.

130. How to Practise Qigong for Low Back Pain and Leg Pain?

Low back and leg pain is a common disease, which is caused by many factors such as injury and infection of soft tissue in the low back, or pathological changes in the vertebra. Low back pain and leg pain may either be acute waist strain or chronic waist strain. Acute waist strain usually occurs suddenly at sacrum or sacroiliac joint. Sacrum is the bridge which connects the body with the lower limbs, and has to bear great weight and a lot of movements. So this portion is more likely to suffer from the body's impact and external injury. Sprain is mostly caused by incorrect waist posture when one is raising heavy weight, which can lacerate the sacrum muscles, tendons or ligaments. Clinical examination will find cramp and tenderness at the two sides of ligamentun scarospinosum; and lumbar spine movements of bowing forward, facing upward or turning around to be restricted.

In the case of an acute sprain on the low back, let the patient lie on his back on a hard plank bed, support the waist with a small pillow to get the muscle and ligament relaxed. Then measures of osteopathy and tendon massage may be taken to deal with the injured portion in coordination with treatment such as plaster. Besides, the patient should take physical exercise therapy. Methods for practice are the same as those for chronic low back pain and leg pain. Chronic low back pain and leg pain is slow in the processes of occurrence and development. It is usually caused by improper use of force when doing physical labour, engaging in work with the body in a forward bending position over a long period of time, or an acute low back sprain being delayed in treatment, or being improperly treated. Causes of the disease can also be traced to other diseases of the spine, urinary system and gynecologic conditions, such as rheumatoid spondylitis, osteosarcoma, pyelonephritis, sciatica, nephroptosis, pelvic inflammation, and so on.

For chronic low back pain and leg pain, first find out its causes. When the disease is being treated, do not let the patient lie in bed all the time, but ask him to take appropriate exercises to resist the disease. Only by so doing can better curative effects result.

Methods for practice follow:

(I) Qigong Exercise

(1) Qigong Exercise in lying or sitting posture. Keep the mind at the

point of Yaoyangguan (The point of Yaoyangguan is between the fourth and fifth lumbar vertebrae). Practise 15 to 20 minutes each time.

(2) Eighteen-Form Taiji Qigong Exercise.

(3) Shiduanjin Exercise in standing posture.

(4) Qigong Stick Exercise.

(5) Practise Spontaneous Moving Exercise 30 minutes.

(II) Massage and Limb Exercise

(1) Rub the Kidney Points 200 times.

(2) and hip exercise. Set both hands akimbo, turn the lumbar spine forward, backward, leftward, rightward and turn round, altogether 50 times.

131. How to Practise Qigong for Arthritis?

Arthritis is a kind of inflammation in joints and its causes are various. The chief clinical manifestations are pains in joints and functional obstacles of varying degrees. Rheumatic arthritis, rheumatoid arthritis and osteoarthritis are the commonly seen arthritis.

Rheumatic arthritis is often found among youngsters. Before its occurrence there is often infection of the upper respiratory tract. Typical rheumatic arthritis has wandering pain, involving the main joints such as knee, ankle, shoulder, wrist and hip. There are local pain, red and swollen area and fever, which can sometimes disappear, or show its effect repeatedly. After acute symptoms are removed, there is usually no pathological changes left in the diseased joint. However, some sufferers have pathological changes in the heart. Rheumatoid arthritis is often found among the young and middle-aged people of 20 to 40 years of age. Joint lesion is often symmetrical, involving minor joints of fingers and toes as well as vertebra joints causing eventual joint deformity. Ostearthritis is mostly found among the middle-aged people over 40. Joint lesion mostly occurs at the joint bearing heavy weight or much movement, such as lumbar vertebrae, hip, knee and fingers.

This disease usually occurs without one's being conscious of it. One will feel the soreness and pain at the joints growing more serious, and sometimes even hear frictional sound at the bones during exercise. There is no swelling of the diseased joint.

Arthritis of all kinds usually become more serious due to sudden change of weather and cold stimulus.

(I) Qigong Exercise

(1) Qigong Exercise in lying or sitting posture. Keep your mind at the point of Dantian. Practise 20 to 30 minutes each time.

(2) Standing Qigong Exercise. Stand with knees bending at mid position with hands pressing downward. Practise 3 to 20 minutes each time.

(3) Shiduanjin Exercise in standing posture.

(4) Spontaneous Moving Exercise. Practise 30 minutes.

(II) Limb Exercise and Massage

(1) Ten Sections of Joint Exercise.

(2) Eight Sections of Limb Exercise.

(3) Massaging and Patting Exercises. Especially massage the diseased joints.

132. How to Practise Qigong for Herniated Lumbar Disk?

Herniated Disk is a disease at the lower back caused by external factors, such as waist clashing into things or spraining. The break of annuli fibrosi which forms the disk at the lumbar vertebrae, and elastic nucleus pulposus in the disk protruding out will press nerve roots or spinal cords, resulting in backache and sciatica. The disease is mostly found between the fourth-and-fifth lumbar vertebrae and the fifth lumbar vertebrae and the first sacral vertebrae. Main symptoms are backache, sciatica, and obstacle in lumbar spine movement. Most patients suffer from scoliosis or flat back, or pelvis tilting to one side, and thus have difficulty in walking. If the illness lasts a relatively long period, the patient will feel numb or blunt at the area of outer side of leg back, instep, heel, and so on.

Herniated disk should first be treated by means of traction and pushing-and-pulling maneuver to be restored to its original position. Then the patient must lie on a bed of hard plank for a week or so in order to restore the local ligament tissue and prevent the disk from protruding out again. And then, when the patient gets better or feels only slight pain, he can practise some functional exercises to strengthen the muscles on the lower back and improve the elasticity of ligaments.

(I) Walking with Arms Akimbo

Set two arms akimbo, and walk 5 to 10 minutes.

(II) Stretch Legs Backward Alternately

Hold the bed frame or chair back or table edge with both hands, keep torso upright, stretch legs backward alternately, at the same time raise head and throw out chest. Increase the range of movement gradually. Practise 1 to 2 times each day, and 2 to 5 minutes each time.

(III) Hands Suspending

Let hands hold a horizontal bar or the upper part of door frame with palms facing backward, feet leaving the ground, and the back and the lower limbs swinging forward and backward. Hold on until the strength of two arms nearly get exhausted. Practise 1 to 2 times each day.

(IV) Exercising the Lumbar Spine and the Hip Joint

Stand upright with two feet apart in parallel. Set both arms akimbo. Bend torso forward, backward, leftward and rightward; or turn round gently. Practise 1 to 2 minutes each time.

(V) Squatting Low with Arms Akimbo

Stand upright with two feet apart in parallel. Set two arms akimbo. Practise low squatting exercise, 1 to 2 minutes each time.

(VI) Qigong Exercise

(1) Taiji Qigong Exercise. Specially practise the following movements: Turning Torso to Look at the Moon, Dredging From the Sea and Looking at the Sky, Churning Up Waves and Billows. Practise each movement 20 to 30 times.

(2) Qigong Exercise in supine posture. Keep the mind at the point of Yaoyangguan 15 to 20 minutes.

133. How to Practise Qigong for Varicosis?

Varicosis refers to expansion, twisting and elongation of the vein; and obstacle of blood back-flow in the vein. There are great saphenous vein and small saphenous vein in the superficial veins of the lower limbs, where the disease of lower-limb varicosis occurs most often.

The lower-limb vein serves as a passage for blood to flow back from the soles to the heart. Therefore, standing on one's feet will cause the pressure of lower-limb vein to grow higher. There are 12 to 18 pairs of valvula venosa on the inner wall of the big saphenae vein, which can prevent blood from flowing back to the soles, and cause blood to flow in the direction leading to the heart. If the wall of the lower-limb vein become weak and thin, or the valvula venosa has not well developed, or the valvula venosa has been injured due to phlebitis. Varicosis in the lower limb is likely to occur. Besides, long distance walk with heavy load, standing too long, or repeated pregnancies can also be the causes of varicosis in the lower limb.

The main symptoms are: expanding and swelling of shallow veins or twisting like earthworm at the inner sides of legs resulting from long-standing; and sense of heaviness in legs, or getting tired easily and sometimes with vague pain, resulting from walking and standing for a long time. At the advanced stage of the disease, there will be atrophy, hardening and desquamating of the leg skin due to block of backflow in the vein over long period of time. What's more, there will occur rupture of the vein and haemorrhage, thrombosis in the vein, and chronic leg ulcer.

Serious varicosis is usually treated by means of operation, such as high position ligature of the big saphenae vein and removal of the whole length of the diseased vein. Light varicosis needs no operation, and can be prescribed medicines and physical exercises.

Methods for practice follow:

(I) Qigong Exercise

(1) Qigong Exercise in lying posture. The patient can do Relaxing Exercise part by part or along three-lines. Guan Qi Exercise (shifting attention between Dantian and Yongquan), and keep mind at Yongquan.

(2) Shiduanjin Exercise on bed.

(II) Self-Massage

Practise Massage and Patting Exercise. Especially rub thighs and massage the calf of the leg, 100 times for each movement.

Bandaging: Raise the diseased leg, and tie up the portion from feet to knees with elastic bandages to lessen the varicosis and reduce the swelling gradually.

134. How to Practise Qigong for Traumatic Paraplegia?

Traumatic Paraplegia is mostly the result of a sudden accident, such as violent impact on the brain, cervical vertebra, thoracic vertebra, lumbar vertebra, and sacral vertebra, resulting in injury of certain section of the spinal cord, and interruption of nervous path. Nerves thus are not able to innervate muscles, causing paralysis of limbs, and urine and fecal incontinence. Sufferers can neither walk nor deal with daily needs but lie in bed.

According to extent of injury at different section of the spinal cord, clinical manifestations are basically grouped into paraplegia due to higher spinal cord injury and paraplegia due to lower spinal cord injury. The former includes injuries from the first cervical vertebra to the second thoracic vertebra with the symptoms: loss of feeling below the level of the injured part, spastic or flaccid paralysis of the lower limbs and urine and fecal incontinence. The latter includes injuries from the third thoracic vertebra to the fifth sacral vertebra with the following symptoms: loss of feeling below the level of the injured part, urine and fecal incontinence, lower-limb spastic or flaccid paralysis.

The sufferer should have timely treatment. In the acute period or at an early stage of the disease, methods of Chinese and Western medicines or operation should be used in accordance with specific conditions. If the sufferer is in a later stage or recovering stage of the disease, it is important for him to have some functional training and Qigong exercise according to his physical conditions.

Besides medical treatment, paralytic sufferer must have some functional training and Qigong exercise to prevent muscular atrophy, joint stiffness, bedsore and infection in urinary system; and to train one's will, enhance one's physical constitution, improve the function of all the tissues and organs, and restore the paralysed limbs to normal functioning. One can follow the procedure of exercises prescribed by departments of surgery and orthopaedics either on bed or away from bed. Here we introduce only Qigong exercises.

(1) Qigong exercise in lying posture. Supine posture is suitable for paralytic sufferer unable to get up.

(2) Qigong exercise in sitting posture. On the basis of the original posture, the paralytic sufferer may take a sitting posture with or without support.

Practise Relaxing Exercise, keep the mind at Dantian or Yongquan, and practise the Guan Qi Exercise shifting attention between Dantian and Yongquan.

Breathing: Use deep breathing and abdominal breathing.

(3) Shiduanjin Exercise on bed.

(4) Spontaneous Moving Qigong Exercise in lying posture and sitting posture.

(5) Massage and Patting Exercise.

135. How to Practise Qigong for Tumor?

Tumor is a commonly-seen disease. It is an unusual hyperplasia, or called neoplasm, in certain tissue of the body, which does not suit the need of human organism. Tumor can be grouped into benign tumor and malignant tumor in accordance with its nature.

Benign tumor develops slowly, and stays unchanged over a long period of time. There is some integument around the tumor which does not transfer to other parts of the body. It can be removed altogether by means of operation and usually will not recur. Common benign tumors include lipoma, fibroid tumor, angioma, leiomyoma, and so on.

Malignant tumor develops rapidly. It often injures adjacent tissues and organs, and is easy to transfer to other parts. It cannot be removed thoroughly by operation and is likely to recur. So the disease is extremely hazardous to human life.

Of course, whether a tumor is benign or malignant cannot be fixed absolutely. If a benign tumor should occur at a vital organ or area, such as the brain, it is also a threat to human health. Some benign tumors can change into malignant ones. For instance, the polyposis (turmorous polyposis), which occurs frequently in the large intestine, is benign tumor, but can easily turn into malignant tumor. Therefore, special attention should be paid to prevention and cure of tumor. In recent years, medical workers in China have used both Chinese and Western medicines to treat the malignant tumor, and have achieved considerable success. Besides operation, radioactive therapy, chemical therapy and medicines, it is of great significance for the patient to practise exercises, so as to enhance physical constitution and build up resistance to disease. In the course of using Qigong Exercise to cure liver cancer, stomach cancer, intestine cancer and lung cancer, we have found that Qigong exercise does bring good effects in enhancing one's constitution, inhibiting the growth of cancer cells and prolonging the sufferer's life.

Methods of practice for cancer sufferers follow:

(1) Relaxing Qigong Exercise in lying or sitting posture. For the mind, use method of thinking of pleasant things. For breathing, use natural breathing or deep breathing method.

(2) Standing Qigong Exercise with hands pressing downward at high position. Practise 5 to 20 minutes.

(3) Walking Exercise. 500 meters, or a distance which suits one's physical conditions. Practise Walking Exercise worked out by Guo Lin.

(4) Taiji Qigong Exercise.

(5) Shiduanjin Exercise on bed or in standing posture.

(6) Massage and Patting Exercise.

CLINICAL PRACTICE

136. What Physiological Changes Do Qigong Exercises Cause in the Respiratory System?

Qigong exercises produce obvious effect on the respiratory system, especially on the respiratory function of the lungs, the range of diaphragmatic contraction, the respiratory rate, the pulmonary alveoli, the composition of the air exhaled and the metabolism of air and energy consumption, etc.

Experiments on the respiratory function: In treating pulmonary TB, Shanghai No. 2 Tuberculosis Hospital has once divided some patients of pulmonary TB into two groups and kept them under observation. These patients were in the similar state of illness, with one group practising Qigong Exercises Group (that is, mainly treated with the Intrinsic-Nourishing Exercise when under comprehensive treatment), and the other control group (that is, patients were not treated with Qigong exercises when undergoing comprehensive treatment). After they had been treated for some time, the patients in the Qigong Exercises Group were found a remarkable improvement in respiratory function of the lungs. But there was not much change in the control group. Besides, it has also been noticed that with patients who had had thoracic operations there were fewer cases of failing lung function in the Qigong Exercises Group than in the control group in terms of percentage. Such results have proved that Qigong exercises have the good effect of enhancing lung function and that they are not only fit for recuperating patients belonging to the department of internal medicine but it is also of even greater significance to patients after surgical operations in helping them to regain and improve their lung function.

Experiments on the range of disphragmatic movement: 27 cases of pulmonary emphysema were kept under treatment with Qigong exercises for two months. Before being treated, their average range of the diaphragmatic movement (deep breathing) was 2.8 centimeters. In two months, there was an increase in the range of the diaphragmatic movement to some extent. The average range of the diaphragmatic movement became 4.4 centimeters. And after a year's treatment with Qigong exercises, it became 4.9 centimeters (P < 0.01). The change is remarkable. Besides, in reexamining the patients after two months' treatment, doctors found that the average breathing rate of these patients was reduced by 2.7 times per minute (P < 0.01); follow-up on these patients after a year, it was found that the breathing rate of 16 patients who kept on doing Qigong exercises was reduced by 5 times per minute (P < 0.01) and that their vital capacity was increased by 8.1% (D < 0.01). It can be inferred that Qigong exercises are of some significance to patients in helping them to regain the physiological function of the lungs.

Experiments on the change in breathing rate: The average breathing rate of healthy adults is 16.5 times per minute before they pick up Qigong exercise. When they are doing the exercise in a lying posture, their average breathing rate is reduced to 6.9 times per minute. The breathing rate of 42.8 per cent of these people is reduced to 5 times per minutes. Some people who have practised Qigong exercises for over 30 years have a breathing rate of 6 times per minute on an average when they are at rest; when they are doing Qigong exercises, their breathing rate is reduced to 4 times per minute. The curve in the diaphragms of the respiration of the people who can fall into tranquility when doing Qigong exercises can display a regular and soft quality and such people can maintain slow breathing for over 30 minutes. Those people who do not do Qigong exercises very well can only maintain slow breathing for 10 minutes and the curves in the diagrams of respiration of such people present rather great fluctuation. The ability to maintain slow breathing for a quite long a period of time results from a long-term practice of Qigong exercises.

Experiments on air metabolism and energy consumption: It has been found that people's gas metabolism is reduced to different degrees when they practise Qigong exercises. The more deeply one falls into the state of tranquility, the more obviously gas metabolism is reduced. Moreover, the rate of air metabolism within the half an hour after one stops doing Qigong exercises is still lower than the rate he had before he began to do the exercises. Meanwhile, the amount of energy consumed in per unit time is also reduced correspondingly. When one is doing Qigong exercises in the lying posture, the amount of energy consumed is the minimum, averagely 30 per cent less than that before exercises.

The Xingcheng Worker's Convalescent Hospital in Liaoning Province treated 22 cases of bronchial asthma with the Intrinsic-Nourishing Exercise in a sitting posture. They examined the patients' blood and sputum and made an X-ray examination and measured their vital capacity, chest girth, respiration and pulse both before and after the treatment. Results show the following things: the range of diaphragmatic movement is increased by 1 — 2.5 centimeters; the vital capacity is enlarged remarkably; the rhythm and frequency of breathing is lowered; the eosinophils in the blood and the acidophils in the sputum are both reduced or restored to normal values. According to statistics, patients no longer had the symptoms and signs after they had been treated and they were able to go back to work again. 10 of the patients suffered fewer fits of bronchial asthma and their symptoms and signs diminished remarkably. Their health was improved. 18 of the patients gainěd weight and their appetite was in general enlarged by 1 — 2 times after practising Qigong exercise for about 10 days.

137. What Physiological Changes Do Qigong Exercises Cause in the Circulatory System?

The Teaching and Research Group of Physiology in Shanghai No. 1 Medical College has once made observation of the function of the mental power of the people who do Qigong exercises in controlling the circulatory system. Their findings are:

Measurement of the blood pressure of the humeral arteries in the upper arm: A man who does Qigong exercises can control his own systolic pressure and make it rise from 132 mm Hg to 180 mm Hg and the diastolic pressure rises in the meantime. The blood pressure is rather slow to fall down and it takes about 5 — 10 minutes. After one has repeated this action for several times, the extent to which the blood pressure rises becomes less great. But after an hour's rest, he can control his own blood pressure and make it rise again. While the blood pressure is rising, the arm muscles of the person who does Qigong exercises are also becoming tense. But at that time, he is still speaking naturally and all the other muscles of his body are in a relaxed state.

Measurement of pulse: Pulse changes in two ways, one is that pulse quickens and it throbs more forcefully when the blood pressure is rising; the other is that pulse slows down instead of speeding up, but it throbs more forcefully when the blood pressure is rising and when it begins to fall down pulse slows down and also throbs less forcefully.

Record of blood volume in the lower limbs: The man who is doing Qigong exercises is in a state of long-term exhalation and short-term inhalation. When he exhales the volume of the blood vessels decreases and the blood vessels expand when he inhales; when the blood pressure is rising, the volume of the blood vessels decreases, however, the blood vessels will expand when he inhales.

The above-mentioned facts indicate the following two points: (1) People can control the functions of their viscera with their own mental power through doing Qigong exercises. For instance, they can control the functions of the heart and the blood vessels. (2) The relation between the respiratory cycle and the mechanism for adjusting the tension of the blood vessels of a person who does Qigong exercises is different from that of an ordinary person. That is, when one does Qigong exercises, his blood vessels contract when he exhales, but they do not contract when he inhales.

Measurement of the patency of the blood vessels: The Isotope Lab of Suzhou Medical College once used P⁸² in measuring the effect of Qigong exercises on the patency of the blood vessels. Results show that Qigong exercises can improve the blood flow and initial results drawn from observation also show that RBC and hemoglobin increase when one is doing Qigong exercises. The measurement of the RBC and hemoglobin of a person one hour before and after he does Qigong exercises and three months before and after he does Qigong exercises shows us these facts: in three months, the maximum increase in RBC is 750,000 and the average increase is 267,000; the maximum increase in hemoglobin is 1 gram and the average is 0.725 gram; in three months, the maximum increase in RBC is 2,320,000 and the average is 690,000, while the maximum increase in RBC in hamoglobin is 7 grams and the average is 1.03 gram. Besides, it has also been noticed that eosinophils are inclined to increase after one has done Qigong exercises. The more skillful one masters the Qigong exercises, the greater the increase is.

Measurement of skin temperature: Skin temperature is determined by the conditions of blood vessels in and under the skin and by the amount of blood flow in them. When one is doing Qigong exercises, the skin temperature at the acupuncture point Hegu and at various points on the middle finger is generally raised by 2 — 3°C and at some particular points it is even raised by 6 — 7°C. It is only 20 — 60 minutes after one has stopped doing Qigong exercises that the skin temperature will gradually fall down to the level before one begins to do Qigong exercises.

Measurement of heart rate and the output of the heart: When one is doing Qigong exercises, the output of the heart is related to the respiratory cycle. When inhalation takes longer time than exhalation does, the output of the heart per minute is increased. When exhalation takes longer time than inhalation does, the output of the heart is decreased. This is because of the effect which the respiratory center has on the vagal center and the heart beat. Whether the Intrinsic Nourishing Exercise which demands long exhalation and short inhalation or the Relaxtion-Tranquility Qigong Exercise which demands smooth breathing is practiced, there is always a decrease in the heart rate. Experiments with animals also show that when their peripheral blood vessels expand, their blood pressure falls down and their heart rate decreases.

Measurement of blood pressure: Qigong exercises have the effect of lowering the blood pressure of patients of hypertension. If a patient with pulmonary tuberculosis does Qigong exercises for 15 minutes before an operation, his pulmonary arteries pressure will fall down. After doing Qigong exercises, the amplitude of the temporal artery pulse wave will decrease and the amplitude of radial artery pulse wave will expand. This shows that Qigong exercises have the effect of adjusting the functions of the blood circulation. The reaction to negative stimulus of coldness is less obvious after Qigong exercise than before it. This shows that Qigong exercise can improve the ability of the organism to resist coldness. The level of the blood pressure is determined by the output of the heart and the resistance in the peripheral vessels. When one is doing Qigong exercises, his or her vessels in and under the skin will expand and the resistance in them will necessarily decrease. The change in blood pressure corresponds to the change in the area one keeps his mind on. It has been found among the people who did Qigong exercises that if he keeps his mind on Dantian, blood pressure will fall down; if he keeps his mind on the nose, blood pressure will rise. These facts lead us to the idea that Qigong exercises can be used as "the method of bio-feedback" or the method of self-adjustment in the prophylaxis and treatment of diseases.

Examination of blood: Experiments show that both red blood cells and hemoglobin increase after Qigong exercises and that the change in them is more obvious in the hour before and after Qigong exercises. This kind of phenomenon is perhaps due to the fact that the abdominal breathing in Qigong exercises has a soothing effect on the liver and the spleen and it makes the comparatively thicker blood fluid join in the blood circulation in the whole body. After Qigong exercises, there is an increase in the number of eosinophils and in the phagocytosis of white blood cells. The experiments on the phagocytosis by using the staphyloccus aureus and brucella as the opsonin of the species of bacteria have proved that there is an increase in both the phagocytic index and phagocytic ability in most of the patients after they have done Qigong exercises. Shanghai No.2 Tuberculosis Hospital adopted Qigong exercises therapy whereby they restored the ESR (erythrocyte sedimentation rate) of 87% of the TB patients to the normal range.

138. What Physiological Changes Do Qigong Exercises Cause in the Digestive System?

Qigong exercises emphasize the training or the adjustment of breath, therefore the range of the diaphragmatic movement widens as Qigong exercises go on. Experiments show that every time the excursion of the diaphragm after Qigong exercises is greater by 6.5 centimeters than that before Qigong exercises and the average difference is 5 centimeters. With people who do not do Qigong exercises, the difference between the excursions of diaphragm in deep breathing and calm breathing is not great. The average difference is 1.7 centimeters. The observation of the kymograms of gastric peristalsis under X-ray before and after Qigong exercises has revealed that, after Qigong exercises, the amplitude of gastric peristalsis is increased. Besides, it has also been found that the range within which the lowest part of the stomach moves has been increased by 3 — 4 times and that the range of the movement of the upper most part of the stomach is also increased when one does Qigong exercises. The gastric peristalsis is increased and the tension of the stomach is enhanced. Therefore, the position of the stomach is raised and the time needed for the stomach to evacuate is shortened. Comparisons between the standing, sitting and lying postures adopted for Qigong exercises show that there is no great difference between the effects produced by Qigong exercises in these three different postures. This shows that the postures adopted for Qigong exercises can bring about similar effects. Barium-meal fluroscopic examination of the stomach before and after Qigong exercises shows that the rate of gastric peristalsis is heightened and the wave of gastric peristalsis lasts for a longer time. The above-cited results are consistent with the following effects produced By Qigong exercises: the peristaltic sound becomes louder; the appetite is improved; the digestive function of the stomach is better; and the state of nourishment is improved.

Measurement of gastric peristalsis: The rate of gastric peristalsis of a healthy man is 3 times per minute. But the rate of gastric peristalsis is higher and the wave of gastric peristalsis lasts for a shorter time when doing Qigong exercise than before the session. The rate of gastric peristalsis and the duration of the wave of gastric peristalsis are related with the progress of Qigong exercises. For instance, the level of development in the rate of gastric peristalsis and duration of the wave of gastric peristalsis when Qigong exercises are done for five minutes is higher than that in fifteen minutes. The number of the waves of gastric peristalsis during Qigong exercises is greater than that at the time of rest and meanwhile the evacuation of the stomach is quicker. The range in which the lowest part of the stomach moves is the greatest when one is doing Qigong exercises in the lying posture and that during Qigong exercises in the sitting posture is less great while that during Qigong exercises in the standing posture is the least great. With the progress of Qigong exercises, the position and the tension of the stomach are generally raised. It has been found among some patients of gastric ulcer that those who do not display the movement of the stomach before Qigong exercises will display a rhythmic gastric peristalsis when they are practising the Breath-regulation exercise. Those who already displayed an obvious gastric peristalsis before Qigong exercises will have a weakened gastric movement when doing Qigong exercises. This reveals that Qigong exercises can serve to adjust gastric functions. Qigong exercises can also produce a remarkable effect of raising the position of the stomach. For instance, a patient who had suffered from gastroptosis for 18 years benefited a lot from 3 months of Qigong exercises. The lowest part of his stomach was raised to the point 3 centimeters below the line between the iliac crests from the point 9 centimeters below the line.

Examination of gastric juice: When one is doing Qigong exercises, there is an increase in the amount of gastric juice secreted. Therefore, the absolute value of free acid is bound to increase correspondingly. Among some of the patients of gastric ulcer who had been treated with Qigong exercises therapy it has been found that their basal gastric juice, total acidity and free acid all tend to increase. The observation of some patients also show that the amount of gastric juice secreted, the concentration of the gastric juice and the amount of pepsin were increased after these patients had done Qigong exercises. Meanwhile, Qigong exercises can also supress the hyperactivity of gastric function; hence the hyperactivity of pepsin is restricted.

Examination of saliva: The secretion of saliva is controlled by the bulbar secretive center. Stimulating the efferent fibre of parasympathetic nerves can cause parotic and sub-maxillary secretion. A man who does Qigong exercises will feel that saliva is increased because, as a reflex, the parasympathetic nervous system is stimulated by the movement of the tongue and the effect of breathing, and thereby saliva secretion is increased. But the state of tranquility during Qigong exercises reduces the excitation of the bulbar secretive nerve center whereby saliva is prevented from being discharged immediately. When Qigong exercises is stopped, the cerebral cortex and bulb are relieved of suppression and saliva is discharged in large amount. The content of amylase in the saliva of a pulmonary tuberculosis patient is generally smaller than that of a healthy man, but it will be increased after Qigong exercises. The increase can even be seen after one has done the exercise just for once.

139. What Physiological Changes Do Qigong Exercises Cause in the Nervous System?

Central nervous system: According to the tests done by the department concerned, there is change in the electroencephalogram (ECG) during Qigong exercises. The change in the ECG is a reflex of the change in the state in which central nervous system functions. But the ECG during Qigong exercises is different from that on a man who is in the state of clear consciousness, rest with the eyes closed or sleep. It has its own special properties. That is, its alpha wave is lengthened; its amplitude is heightened and the frequency of the wave is shortened; the theta wave appears and spreads out. When the theta wave appears, the alpha wave is still present.

The change in the frequency and the amplitude of the brain wave is quite closely related to the change in the mood of a person, especially a patient with neurasthenia. When the patient is excited or worried, brain wave of low amplitude and high frequency often appears; when the patient is in low spirits, brain wave of low frequency often appears. When Qigong exercises are practised, the amplitude of the brain wave is heightened and the rhythm is slowed down. This shows that the process of inhibition is strengthened. Under the protection of the strengthened process of inhibition, the cells of the cerebral cortex are restored to a normal state of function from disorder caused by overexcitement. This helps one to recover one's health. The occurrence of slow brain wave during Qigong exercises is related with the fact that the man who is doing Qigong exercises is out of an anxious state of mind temporarily or for a while. If the average amplitude of the alpha wave does reflect the state of metabolism of the nerve cells of the cerebral cortex, the level of metabolism of the brain cells fluctuates rather greatly in the different stages of the sleep. However, absence of the fall in the amplitude of the alpha wave shows that the metabolism of brain cells does not fluctuate greatly.

The subordinate chronaxie of muscular movement and the vestibular chronaxie: People generally think that the subordinate chronaxie of muscular movement is closely related with the functional state of cerebral cortex. The development of excitative process causes the subordinate chronaxie of muscular movement to shorten. But the development of the inhibition process causes the subordinate chronaxie of muscular movement to lengthen. Whether patients with hypertension and patients with pulmonary tuberculosis practice the Relaxation-tranquility Exercise in a lying posture or the Intrinsic-Nourishing Exercise in a sitting posture, their subordinate chronaxie is lengthened and their vestibular chronaxie is also lengthened when they fall deeper into the state of tranquility. The vestibular chronaxie of a man who has done Qigong exercises for 30 minutes is longer than that of a man who has a rest for 30 minutes. Meanwhile, the vestibular chronaxie of those who have mastered the skills of Qigong exercises sooner is longer than that of those who mastered them later. The average vestibular chronaxie of 5 milliseconds of a hypertension patient before Qigong exercises is lengthened to 9 milliseconds after the exercises. Judging from the change in the vestibular chronaxie and the reaction capacity of the vestibule of a hypertension patient, Qigong exercises can lengthen the vestibular chronaxie and reduce the excitement of autonomic nerves, whereby it shows that the balance between sympathetic nerves and parasympathetic nerves can be readjusted by doing Qigong exercises.

The electric potential of the skin: When patients of asthma are doing Qigong exercises, the electric potential at the acupuncture points of left and right Feishu and Zusanli will fall down in general. But the electric potential at places where there are no acupuncture point will not change significantly. When the whole body is relaxed, the electric potential will fall down. When one begins to keep his mind on Dantian, Dazhui or Yongquan, the electric potential at these places will rise to a certain degree, but at other places where one does not keep his mind on the electric potential will still fall down. The change in the electric potential at the acupuncture point of a sleeping man who does Qigong exercises is greater than that at the same point of a sleeping man who does not do Qigong exercises. The electric potential at the acupuncture point of a man who masters Qigong exercises skills falls down to a greater extent and it fluctuated less greatly. Therefore, the change of the electric potential at the acupuncture point can be taken as an indicator of the progress in doing Qigong exercises.

The change in electric potential is mainly adjusted by central nerves and is also related with visceral functions to some extent. When Qigong exercises are carried on to a certain extent, the spontaneously rhythmic activity of the bioelectricity in a human body will be synchronized with the activity of breathing. This shows that the function of the central nervous system is improved.

Wink reflex and the sensitivity of the acoustic analyzer: Wink reflex not only reflects the degree of excitement of the optic nerve center of the cerebral cortex but also serves as a standard to judge the organic sensitivity. Those patients whose eyes wink automatically before and after Qigong exercises will have a lowered degree of automatic wink and wink reflex during Qigong exercises. To most people, five minutes after they have stopped Qigong exercises their wink reflex is still weaker than before the exercises. Whether or not wink reflex becomes weaker depends on whether one can fall into the state of tranquility or not. Patients with hypertension who display a remarkable increase in the value of high-frequency and low-frequency acoustic thresholds before Qigong exercises will have an obviously improved value of low-frequency acoustic threshold after Qigong exercises. But there will be no great change in the value of high-frequency acoustic threshold.

140. What Physiological Changes Do Qigong Exercises Cause in the Endocrine System?

According to a certain Journal of Traditional Chinese Medicine, the physiological changes in the endocrine system caused by Qigong exercises manifest themselves mainly in the following aspects:

Glucose tolerance: The process of doing Qigong exercises is also the process of improving the function of adjusting glucose. This is perhaps the result of the speeding up of the synthesization of liver glycogen and the reduction of the decomposition of liver glycogen.

Qigong exercises can perhaps excite vagus-insulin system but it can perhaps also inhibit sympathetic-adrenal gland system and pituitary-adrenal gland system.

The 17 — KS in urine: The 17 — KS (ketosteroid) in the urine of pulmonary patients does not change obviously before and after Qigong exercises. But it has been found among patients with bronchial asthma that their 17 — KS which was originally decreasing will increase after Qigong exercises. Ten patients of severe deficiency of kidney-yin did Qigong exercises for two weeks and then there was an obvious increase in the 17 — KS in their urine. But once the exercises were stopped, the 17 — KS would fall remarkably. Therefore, it can be inferred that Qigong exercises are directly related to the change in the value of 17 — KS in the urine. The mechanism of Qigong exercises perhaps is closely related with suprarenal cortex. Qigong exercises increase the blood flow in the suprarenal cortex, and in particular, the state of tranquility in Qigong exercises cuts off the pathological relationship between cerebral cortex and the nerve center under it. Therefore, the nervous center under the cerebral cortex of patients with bronchial asthma has a better control and coordination of the reaction system of pituitary-adrenal cortex.

141. What Influence and Effects Do Qigong Exercises Have in Conditions of Gynaecology and Obstetrics?

Observation has revealed that Qigong exercises have certain effects on the embryo heart and the date of labour. The concerned medical institutions examined the embryo hearts in 196 pregnant women before and after Qigong exercises. It was found that the heart rate of the fetuses was slowed down or quickened, the congestion in the mother's chest alleviated and the blood vessels in the mother's limbs dilated. The increase in the amplitude was found in the examination of both the ballistocardiogram and the arterial waves. This tells us that the force of the heart beat becomes greater after doing Qigong exercises.

Qigong exercises also contribute to natural labour. No case of premature labour or difficult labour was found among 21 lying-in women who had practised Intrinsic-Nourishing Exercise before they gave birth. This is because abdominal respiration makes the diaphragm move up the down in a greater range and the abdominal muscles rise and fall in a greater extent, thus forming a squeezing and massaging effect on the abdominal viscera , speeding up the blood circulation in the visceras and improving the functions of the stomach and intestines. The increase in the abdominal pressure and the contractive ability of the abdominal muscles help to bring about a natural labour.

142. What Influence and Effects Do Qigong Exercises Have in Diseases of the Eyes?

The Teaching and Research Group of Ophthalmology and the Department of Ophthalmology of Shanghai No.1 People's Hospital have done clinical observation and experiments on physiological indicators based on this to see the curative effect Qigong exercises have in treating glaucoma.

The influence Qigong exercises have on the central nervous system of patients with primary glaucoma: Results obtained in testing the speed of response show that the latent period between the positive signal and motion reaction of patients (115 cases) of glaucoma is longer than that of healthy people (40 people tested). The change in the latent period is even greater when the signal changed. When the signal changes from the positive to the negative, the average number of mistakes is greater. Most of the 20 patients who were treated with Qigong exercises were improved (the latent period is shortened; the change in the latent period is smaller; the number of mistakes is decreased to the average value of healthy people). This means that the function of the higher nervous center has been improved.

The result of tracing the volume of blood vessels in the limbs of

34 patients of primary glaucoma shows that among 21 patients of simple type of primary glaucoma, 10 patients's base lines are smooth and curves fluctuate rather greatly; when patients of these two types were examined to see how many of them show a weak response to a cold stimulation, it was found that out of 21 patients of the simple type 13 patients did so, and out of 19 patients of the congestive type 13 patients did the same. But after Qigong exercises, they displayed a change in the fluctuation of both the base lines and the curves, and their responses to the cold stimulation were all weakened. This proves that Qigong exercises can cause the sympathetic nerve center to be rather stablized.

The influence of Qigong exercises upon the intra-occular pressure: Qigong exercises do not have obvious influence on the intra-occular pressure of normal eyes (19 eyes were observed), but it can cause the intra-occular pressure of patients of glaucoma (130 eyes were observed) to rise or fall and as to the degree of the rise and fall, it has something to do with how much progress one has made in mastering the Qigong exercises and the baseline of the intra-occular pressure. The intra-occular pressure of most of the patients who have mastered Qigong quite well and whose intra-occular pressure was rather high before Qigong exercises will fall down; but on the contrary, the intra-occular pressure of those patients whose intra-occular pressure was rather low will rise. 48 patients were examined with electrotonometer. It has been found that most of them display a normal intra-occular pressure after Qigong exercises. How long can the pressure-lowering effect of Qigong last? According to the measurement of the intra-occular pressure of 25 patients of glaucoma carried out 30, 60 and 90 minutes after Qigong exercises, the effect of Qigong can last 1 hour after Qigong exercises are done for one time. Testing of patients who have done Qigong exercises for one month to half a year shows that the percentage of patients whose intra-occular pressure has fallen has increased. The results of these tests prove that Qigong can decrease the amplitude of the fluctuation of intra-occular pressure and lower the base line and make it gradually come nearer and nearer to the normal level.

The influence of Qigong treatment upon the value of the visual threshold of patients of primary glaucoma: Testing of the value of visual threshold with condenser chronomyometer shows that the value of the visual threshold of patients of glaucoma is one time greater than that of healthy people. This means that the excitation of the visual analyzer of those patients is decreased. But tests carried out before and after Qigong exercises show that the value of visual threshold of 60 eyes of healthy people is a little bit reduced after the exercises while that of 9 out of 61 eyes of patients of glaucoma rises and 2 of them falls down. This means that the excitation of visual analyzer has been remarkably improved. Besides, observation of patients in different stages of illness shows that the more advanced the stage is, the more remarkably the value of visual threshold is reduced and the more remarkably it is improved after Qigong exercises.

The observation of the above-mentioned physiological indicators shows that the principles of Qigong exercises in curing glaucoma are perhaps: (1) Qigong exercises improve the process of the activities of the central nervous system, adjust the functional disturbances, stablize the process of activities of the central nervous system and keep the functions of the central nervous system in good coordination; (2) Qigong exercises coordinate the central nerves whereby the secretion of chamber liquid is reduced, intra-occular pressure is reduced and the amplitude of fluctuation of the pressure is decreased; (3) Qigong exercises heighten the excitation of the visual analyzer.

143. How Well Do Qigong Exercises Cure Pulmonary Tuberculosis?

Shanghai No.2 Tuberculosis Hospital made a preliminary observation on the anti-bacterial and immunity effect of the blood of the patients of pulmonary tuberculosis. They found that after Qigong exercises the ability of the white blood cells to phagocytose bacteria has been promoted. This shows that Qigong therapy has certain effect of strengthening the defence mechanism of the human organism. The analysis of 296 cases shows that 225 of them have an improved focal lesion (76%), 69 of them do not display any change in the focal lesion (23%) and 2 of them display a worse focal lesion. 158 patients who originally had pulmonary cavities were treated with Qigong exercises. Among them 102 patients' cavities closed or became smaller (64%). 180 patients whose bacteria in sputum were positive were treated with Qigong exercises and then the bacteria in the sputum of 110 patients (61%) became negative.

144. How Well Do Qigong Exercises Cure Pulmonary Emphysema?

Shanghai Research Institute of the Health and Occupational Diseases of Workers and the other institutions asked 60 patients of pulmonary emphysema to do Qigong exercises and the curative effect was achieved on every one of the patients. The average excursion of the diaphragm of the patients before Qigong exercises was 2.8 centimeters. After two months of treatment with Qigong exercises, progress was seen with an average excursion of 4.4 centimeters. In one year, it became 4.9 centimeters (P < 0.01) and the breathing rate was remarkably slowed down. It was reduced by 2.7 times per minute (P < 0.01). The tidal volume was increased by 101.2 ml (P < 0.01). The vital capacity was increased by 8.1 per cent (P < 0.01). Among all the symptoms, pleuralgia was most remarkably diminished. The short-term curative effect was very good.

145. How Well Do Qigong Exercises Cure Bronchial Asthma?

The pathogenesis of bronchial asthma is accompanied by the diseases of metabolic disorder besides obvious phenomenon of disturbance of autonomic nervous system and allergic reaction. In terms of the cause of the disease, it is due to the patients' hypersensitivity and reflex to external factors, the patients' internal focal lesion and the imbalance of metabolism. These types of stimulation have left a sustained excitative focus on the cerebral cortex. This cuts off the relation between the activities of the higher nervours system and the autonomic nervous system and causes the spasm of the smooth muscle of the bronchus. Qigong therapy is the treatment taking the patient's organism as a whole. It can provide the nerves of the cerebral cortex with sufficient rest, thus enabling them to resume a normal function, establishing a new normal relation between the cerebral cortex and the viscera and relieving the spasm of the smooth muscle. Therefore, curative effect can be achieved by doing Qigong exercises. Using comprehensive therapy with Qigong exercises as the chief method in it, Shanghai No.6 People's Hospital achieved good curative effect in curing bronchial asthma. Out of 129 patients, 83 (64%) persons were remarkably improved, 42 (33%) took a turn for the better and it proved in effective only in 4 cases (3%). Examinations of respiration, skin temperature and electric potential of the skin were made before and after Qigong exercises. Besides, comparisons were also made before and after the exercises between the results of blood examinations, sputum examinations and X-ray examinations as well as vital capacity chest measurement and pulse measurement after respiration. It has been proved that after Qigong exercises, the amplitude of diaphragmatic movement is increased by 1 — 2.5 centimeters, the vital capacity is remarkably increased, the rhythm and breathing rate are slowed down, both the eosinophils in the blood and the acidophils in the sputum are either reduced or restored to a normal value.

146. How Well Do Qigong Exercises Cure Gastric Ulcer and Ulcer of the Duodenal Bulb?

The cause of ulcer is a long-term tension of cerebral cortex.

Overwork of the cerebral cortex causes its functional disorder and the functional disturbance of the autonomic nerves. The result is the spasm of gastric wall and blood vessels, the functional disorder of nutition in the human organism, the decrease in the resistance of mucosa. Then, ulcer disease is formed. Qigong therapy is a treatment of the human organism as a whole. It adjusts the functional disorder of the cerebral cortex. Therefore, it can recuperate the brain and enable it to fully exercise its function of coordinating the viscera . Hence, a balance between the positive and the negative is reached, achieving curative effects. The Physiology Department of the Institute of Experimental Medicine of the Chinese Medical College, and some other institutions made an analysis of 1,385 patients of gastric ulcer and ulcer of duodenal bulb who were treated with Qigong. According to their report. 77.4% of the patients were cured, 20.9% of the patients took a turn for the better and it was ineffective only in 1.7% of the patients. The method of the experiment is as follows: the doctors examined the patients' conditioned reflex of defensive wink to see the state of the function of the patients' higher nervous system, they also examined the patients' unconditioned reflex of the volume of blood vessels and the reflex of the eye ball to see the state of the function of their autonomic nervous center. Meanwhile, they also made X-ray examination of the patients' stomachs and intestines and other clinical examinations. They took the results of these examinations as parameters by which they judged whether the patients had taken a turn for the better or recovered. In the examination of conditioned reflex of wink, they found that before being treated, there were only 3.3% of the patients had a balance between the process of excitation and inhibition. After being treated, the percentage rose to 38.6%. Before being treated, those who had a weakened process of inhibition and those who had a weakened process of excitation made up 49.3% and 37.4% of the total number of patients respectively. After the treatment with Qigong exercises, the percentage of former group of patients was reduced to 29.3% and that of the latter to 32.1%. This shows that the functional state of the higher nervous system of the patients with ulcer has been improved and has almost reached the level of that of healthy people. 44.8% of the patients who had had an abnormal reflex of the blood vessels before treatment regained a normal reflex of the blood vessels after their disease of ulcer was cured. Those patients whose abnormality was lessened after having been cured of the disease of ulcer amounted to 12.8%. Those patients whose reflex of the blood vessels did not improve or even became worse after having been cured accounted for 11.6%. Patients who had had an abnormal reflex of the eye ball before being treated amounted to 64% and those who had had a normal reflex accounted for 37.5%. After they had recovered, the percentage of those who had an abnormal reflex was reduced to 45.2% and the percentage of those who had a normal one was raised to 54.8%. It has almost become the same as the situation with healthy people. Meanwhile, it has also been discovered that after Qigong exercises, the time needed for the patients' stomachs to be evacuated is shortened and the diaphragmatic excursion is increased. Therefore, the peristaltic function of the stomach and the intestines is improved and the clinical symptoms take a turn for the better, disappeared or wholly recovered.

147. How Well Do Qigong Exercises Cure Gastroptosis?

The reason why Qigong can cure gastroptosis is that it can inhibit the sympathetic nervous system and improve the function of the parasympathetic nervous system. Therefore, the peristalsis of the stomach and the intestines is strengthened during the process of Qigong exercises. This helps to create the tension of the stomach and to restore the stomach to its normal position. Besides, Qigong exercises heighten the pressure in the abdominal cavity (abdominal pressure) which helps the circulation of blood and lymph in the abdominal cavity and helps to improve the blood circulation in the abdominal cavity. The digestive function of the stomach and intestines and the function of respiration are also improved. The abdominal muscles are strengthened and the tension of the gastric wall is increased through Qigong exercises. This helps to restore the prolapsing stomach to its normal position. According to the report of Longhua Hospital affiliated to Shanghai College of Traditional Chinese Medicine which made clinical observation of 50 gastroptosis patients who received Qigong treatment, after a thirty-day course of treatment, eleven of the 50 patients recovered, 14 were remarkably improved and 9 took a turn for the better. These 34 patients accounted for 68% of the total number of patients. Only 15 patients did not show any change for the better and only one patient's health deteriorated. According to X-ray examination with barium meal, 11 patients' stomachs were raised to the normal position. The highest rise in the position of the stomach is 9 centimeters. The average rise is 3.03 centimeters. The fall in the position of the stomachs of nine patients was on an average 1.91 centimeters. Clinical observation shows that the curative effect is in direct proportion to the patients' original constitution, the mood they were in during the process of treatment and their degree of earnestness towards Qigong exercises when they were doing Qigong exercises.

148. How Well Do Qigong Exercises Cure Hepatitis?

Tianjin No.1 Worker's Convalescent Hospital once made an observation on 41 patients with non-iteric infectious hepatitis. These patients all had a poor appetite and were both mentally and physically worn-out. The onset of the disease was usually slow. Most of the patients' pulse was thready and sunken. Their tongues were pale and without coating. There was hepatomegaly to different degrees. And 27 patients' livers were tender. Four patients had splenomegaly. Jaundice was discovered in none of them. After a month's Qigong exercises, they gained weight and had a better appetite. Their hepatomegaly and splenomegaly were decreased to different degrees. Among 28 of the patients the enlargement of the liver and spleen was undetectable with palpation or could just be detected. After being discharged from hospital, 34 patients resumed full-time work, 5 patients began to do part time work and only 2 patients were unable to resume work.

149. How Well Do Qigong Exercises Cure Constipation?

Using Qigong exercises to treat patients with constipation means that the patients treat themselves for the illness. It can effect a permanent cure. Because of the abdominal breathing, the movement of the diaphragm and the abdominal muscles are strengthened. This is turn gives a strengthened pushing and massaging effect on the stomach and the intestines. Therefore, the tension and the peristalsis of the smooth muscles of the stomach and intestines were increased and defecation becomes on time. Qigong exercises are better than enema and taking cathartic in that it will not cause the mechanical stimulation brought about by the former and the harmful effect produced by the latter. Tangshan Convalescent Hospital of Qigong Exercises has made clinical observation of 126 patients of constipation. One of the patients did not defecate for as long as ten days. All the patients did Intrinsic-Nourishing Exercise and did not take cathartic and purgative on the whole. Most patients got rid of constipation after having done Qigong exercises for a week and the exercises turned out to be ineffective only in one patient with constipation of a colonic spasm type.

150. What Is the Curative Effect of Qigong Exercises for Allergic Colitis Like?

Nanjing College of Chinese Traditional Medicine made an analysis of the curative effect of Qigong exercises on 9 patients of chronic allergic colitis. The report tells us the following things: 8 of the patients of allergic colitis are female and only one is male. The youngest of them is 22 years old and the oldest is fifty; the longest course of disease is thirty years and the shortest is two months; they defecate 2 — 4 times a day or even 5 — 6 times a day. The diarrhea of most of these patients is related with what they eat and with the climate; if they eat uncooked, cold or greasy food, their disease will take a turn for the worse. Most of them have the symptoms such as abdominal pain, abdominal distension, anorexia and pain in the lower back and upper back; among these nine patients, 7 are found to be suffering from hepatomegaly of a width of 1 — 2 fingers; examination shows that they have a normal liver function; X-ray examination with barium meal of the stomach and intestines shows that 6 of the patients are normal in this respect, two of the patients are suffering from duodenal ulcer and another one is suffering from gastroptosis; sigmoidoscopy shows that four of the patients are normal; hatching stool and the culture of bacteria shows that findings are negative in all nine patients; these patients have been treated with both Chinese and western medicines before, but no curative effect has been achieved. Later on, they were treated with Qigong therapy. During the process of Qigong exercises, no other therapies were adopted. After 1 — 2 months' of Qigong exercises, 7 of the patients were cured and 2 took an obvious turn for the better. It was found in a month or two that those who recovered could eat uncooked, cold or greasy food without suffering from the disease again.

151. What Is the Curative Effect of Qigong Exercises for Neurasthenia Like?

The Teaching and Research Group of Neurology and the Research Group of the Prevention and Cure of Neurasthenia in Shanghai No.1 Medical College adopted a comprehensive therapy with Qigong exercises as the major means in treating patients with neurasthenia. Among the 973 patients who underwent such a treatment for about 30 days, it proved to be effective in 870 patients (89.5% of the total number of patients) and in effective for 103 patients (10.5%). They continued to use Qigong exercises as a major means to treat 64 patients for whom it had proved to be not highly effective. After from three months' to a year's exercises, it was found that 20 patients took a turn for the better, 23 did not undergo any change and 21 took a turn for the worse when their condition then was compared with that at the time when the comprehensive therapy was stopped for the first time after the 30-day course of treatment. If the patient had a correct understanding of his own illness, accepted various measures of medical treatment and coorperated with their doctors actively, the curative effect would be better. They tested 16 patients' eye ball reflex, sitting-lying reflex and their blood vessels to find that the curative effect and the change in the tension and reflexive ability of the patients' sympathetic and parasympathetic nerves had much to do with their motivation and initiative and that the tension and the reflexive ability of their autonomic nerves are closely related with the improvement in the flexibility and the adjustment in the balance of the activity of the sympathetic nerves.

152. What Is the Curative Effect of Qigong Exercises for Schizophrenia Like?

The Chenghai People's Hospital in Guangdong Province once treated 200 patients of various types of schizophrenia with Qigong therapy. After half a year's of Qigong exercises, 93% of the patients recovered. They think that all human activities, including their behavious and mental activities and the movement of their visceras, are carried out under the directions from their nervous systems and the coordination between the nervous systems. Qigong exercises can bring about the state of tranquility and gradually produce the balance between the excitation and the inhibition of the nerves. Hence, the adjusting ability of the nervous system is improved, vitality of the human organism is strengthened and the physical as well as the mental health is achieved.

153. What Is the Curative Effect of Qigong Exercises for Slipped Lumbar Disk?

Nanjing College of Traditional Chinese Medicine made an observation of 10 patients of slipped lumbar disk while treating them. 9 of the patients are male while one is female. The longest course of the disease is more than two years and the shortest is 3 months. Five of the patients have had traumatic experience while the other half of them have not. Before being treated, all of them have restrictions in lumbar movement. The greatest degree of anteflexion is 40^{0} and the smallest is 20^{0}. In bradgard test of the sick leg shows that the greatest degree is 40^{0} and the smallest is 20^{0}. Laseque test shows that the greatest degree is 35^{0} and the smallest is 15^{0}. The examination of the frontal and lateral X-ray films shows that there are no other organic pathological changes in lumbar vertebra and lumbar joints. These patients have all undergone conservative treatments such as acupuncture-and-moxibustion-therapy, physical therapy, the blockade therapy, lying on the hard bed and fixation by wearing the plaster of Paris jacket and with medication, etc. But none of them is effective. After the treatment with Qigong exercises (the smallest number of times of treatment is 10 and the greatest one is 20 times. The average number is 15 times), 7 patients recovered and 3 took a remarkable turn for the better.

154. What Is the Curative Effect of Qigong Exercises for Hypertension Like?

Shanghai Research Institute of Hypertension once treated 100 patients of hypertension with a comprehensive therapy with Qigong exercises as the major means (50 of them are in-patients, a quarter of them are out-patients and another quarter of them are patients in the worker's convalescent hospitals). Through the comprehensive therapy, curative effect was achieved in 93% of the patients. The shorter the course of the disease, the greater the curative effect. Out of 9 patients who had suffered from the disease for over ten years, 8 people took a turn for the better and only one patient did not do so. They made an observation of these 100 patients while they were doing Qigong exercises and they found that 5 minutes after Qigong exercises their blood pressure began to fall down and 20 minutes after the exercises the effect was the same as that seen 3 hours after amytal test. Therefore, it can be said that Qigong exercises have an obvious effect upon lowering the blood pressure. The study of electro-encephalogram and the value of the electric potential of the skin shows that when the patient falls into the state of tranquility during Qigong exercises, the cerebral cortex is in a state of active inhibition and not only the blood pressure can be lowered but the imbalance of the higher nervous system can be removed as well. Qigong exercises have the effect upon lowering the blood pressure and consolidating the curative effects. If antihypertensive drugs are used during the process of treatment with Qigong exercises, they will add to the curative effect and the effect will be more obvious.

155. What Is the Curative Effect of Qigong Exercises for Heart Diseases Like?

Shanghai Hospital of Chest Surgery once made an observation of 53 patients with cardiopathy to see the curative effect of Qigong exercises. They found that Qigong exercises have a curative effect of different degrees on all types of cardiopathy. After Qigong exercises, every patient will feel himself to be in a quiet and calm state of the mind; their vital energy and blood are regulated and the circulation of the vital energy and blood is improved. During Qigong exercises the rate of the basal metabolism of the whole body is obviously reduced and the organism's consumption of energy is obviously reduced, too. Hence, the burden on the heart is lightened, the function of the heart is improved and the heart disease is prevented from becoming worse. They think that Qigong exercises can be taken as the major means in comprehensive therapy of various types of organic heart diseases. Besides, Qigong therapy can also be employed as a means to help prepare the patients for an operation. It can kill the pain after the operation and help the patients to regain and strengthen the functions of their lungs and their hearts.

156. What Is the Curative Effect of Qigong Exercises for Tachycardia Like?

Shanghai Hospital of Chest Surgery once treated 9 patients with tachycardia with Qigong exercises. After a period of exercises, all of the 9 patients took a turn for the better. The attack of paroxysmal supraventricular tachycardia was stopped immediately. The heart-rate fell from 180 — 200 times to 70 — 80 times per minutes. Sinus tachycardia was prevented and the rate of heartbeat gradually became normal. Palpitation, precordial discomfort, shortness of breath, the feeling of oppression in the chest, dizziness, weariness and symptoms like these diminished or disappeared. They also noticed that Qigong exercises have some curative effect for sinus tachycardia and supraventricular tachycardia. But it only has some subsidiary effect for curing the tachcardia caused by serious disease, such as rheumatic fever, bacterial endocarditis and so on.

157. What Is the Curative Effect of Qigong Exercises for Glaucoma Like?

The Teaching and Research Group of Ophthalmology of Shanghai No.1 Medical College made a study of the curative effect and mechanism of Qigong exercises for curing primary glaucoma. The clinical observation of 115 patients shows that Qigong can produce some curative effect for curing some patients with glaucoma whose ocular pressure could not be controlled by other therapies. It has been found that the exercises are effective among 60% of the patients. But it takes a rather long period of exercises (1 — 3 months) for the effect to be achieved, the patient should master a particular skill of Qigong exercises which is fit for himself. He needs to keep on doing the exercises in order to consolidate the curative effect. Qigong exercises produce greater effect on young patients in the early stage of the illness.

The Ophthalmology Department of Shanghai No.1 People's Hospital divided 230 patients of glaucoma into 3 groups and made comparisons between them during treatment. The first group consisting of 104 patients (80 of them suffering from the congestive type of glaucoma and 24 from a simple type of glaucoma) was treated only with therapies of western medicine. The second group consisting of 72 patients (52 were of the congestive type and 20 of the simple type) was treated with western medicine and the therapies on the basis of the differentiation of symptoms and signs. The third group consisting of 54 patients (36 were of the congestive type and 20 of the simple type) was treated in the same way as those in the second group except that they did Qigong exercises. The result is as follows: The number of patients in the third group who needed an operation was reduced greatly and only 5 (it made up 15.2% of the total number of patients in this group) needed the operation; but the numbers of those who needed an operation in the first and the second groups were 34 (32.7%) and 11 (15.2%) respectively. In the third group, the number of patients who needed to take only miotic and did not need to take Diamox in order to maintain a normal ocular pressure was enlarged, being 34 (62.9%). While the number of such patients in the first and the second groups were 28 (26.9%) and 34 (47.2%) respectively.

While making a clinical observation of patients with various types of glaucoma in different stages of illness who underwent a comprehensive therapy with Qigong exercises as the major means, some hospitals found that the curative effects of Qigong exercises were mainly as follows: (1) it can reduce the ocular pressure; (2) it can improve the visual functions (sight and the field of vision); (3) it can remove the chief complaints; and (4) it can reduce the number of attacks of the disease and diminish the fluctuation in the ocular pressure.

Practice has shown that it is still necessary to base the selection of treatment on the differentiation of symptoms and signs even if we adopt the comprehensive therapy including Qigong exercises to treat primary glaucoma. The curative effect can only be made greater and consolidated by applying different ways of doing Qigong exercises to different patients in the light of the difference in the types of the disease, the difference in the stages of illness, the difference in the symptoms, etc. On the whole, acute glaucoma of a congestive type usually displays the excess syndrome of excessive heart-fire and liver-fire (these patients belong to the type of excess in the upper part). According to the principle that excess syndrome should be treated by purgation, the patient should adopt such Qigong exercise as focusing the mind on the lower part of the body, long-exhalation and short-inhalation which belongs to the purgative method. On the contrary. glaucoma in the advanced stage or of a chronic and simple type usually displays the symptoms such as deficiency of both vital energy and blood and deficiency syndrome of asthenia in both the upper and lower parts of the body. According to the principle that deficiency syndrome should be treated with the therapy of invigoration, patients should adopt such Qigong exercise as focusing the mind at Dantian, storing the Qi by holding the breath, swallowing the saliva and lifting up the anus, which belong to invigorative method.

THE DIRECTING-QI THERAPY

158. What Is the Directing-Qi Therapy of Qigong?

The directing-Qi therapy is one of the precious gems in the treasure trove of Chinese traditional medicine. It is a school of Qigong therapies. The doctor practises Qigong exercises and directs his Qi through keeping his mind on a part of his own body and then he sends out his internal Qi through a particular acupuncture point (it is also called emitting "external Qi"). The doctor does not touch the patient's body. Instead, the "external Qi" is received by the patient through some particular acupuncture point and then it turns into the "internal Qi" of the patient who will have the sensations of aching, numbness, fullness, cold, hot or heaviness, etc. Such sensations are similar to those a man has when he receives acupuncture treatment. It is called the "normal sensation of receiving Qi" in Qigong. A very small number of patients will display the response of perspiration and muscular contraction. In this way, the curative effect is achieved. Such a therapy is called the directing-Qi therapy of Qigong.

159. What Experiments Have Been Carried Out on Animals and Bacteria by Using the Directing-Qi Therapy?

Experiments on animals: Several people from Shanghai Research Institute of Qigong, among whom are Doctor Lin Ya-gu and Doctor Zheng Rong-rong, have made tests on the "external Qi" emitted by Qigong Master, Mr. Lin Hou-sheng, author of this book, from his acupuncture point Laogong. The "external Qi" was emitted at a place 10 centimeters away from a certain acupuncture point on the body of a rabbit. The cell electrophoresis changed remarkably and the temperature on the tip of the nose of the rabbit rises by 3°C after the rabbit has received the "external Qi".

Experiments on bacteria: The Institute of Microbiology of Chinese Academy of Sciences has tested the "external Qi" emitted by Mr. Lin Hou-sheng, author of this book, from his acupuncture point Laogong. The "external Qi" was emitted at a place 15 centimeters away from some fluoresent bacteria. It exerted influence on the bacteria and immediately increased their illumination by 68%.

160. What Physical Experiments Have Been Done by Using the Directing-Qi Therapy?

Experiments on liquid crystals: People from the Institute of Biophysics of Chinese Academy of Sciences, such as Mr. Zhang Fa-jie and Mr. Ye Zhi-shuan, have tested the "external Qi" emitted by Mr. Lin Hou-sheng, author of this book. The "external Qi" emitted by him 0.333 meter away from the plate of liquid crystal can turn the black liquid crystal into blue.

Experiments with thermograph: Mr. Wang Chong-xing and some other people from Shanghai Ruijing Hospital tested the "external Qi" emitted by Mr. Lin Hou-sheng, author of this book, from his acupuncture point Laogong. They used the thermograph developed by the Shanghai Institute of Technical Physics. The "external Qi" was emitted one meter away from the thermograph. The photographs taken with this system show that the skin temperature around Mr. Lin Hou-sheng's acupuncture point Laogong rose by 2.8°C and there is an obvious ring of light around his Laogong acupuncture point.

161. What Physiological Experiments Have Been Done on the Directing-Qi Therapy?

Examination of blood pressure: Nanjing College of Traditional Chinese Medicine adopted the directing-Qi therapy to cure hypertension. They observed 33 patients of this disease and found that it produced the effect of reducing the blood pressure in every one of the cases. 2 patients' blood pressure (systolic) was reduced by more than 20 mm Hg. Another one's blood pressure was reduced by 24 mm Hg. Such a fall in the blood pressure took place within half an hour when the patient was lying in bed. It should be said that the fall is significant. Another patient was treated with this therapy for 8 times. Comparisons were made between the results of blood examination before and after the treatment. It was found that there was a fall in the blood pressure each time after the treatment. His blood pressure once fell from 190/100 to 166/104 mm Hg. and this was the most remarkable fall ever seen in this patient. It proves that the directing-Qi therapy does have certain effect on the blood pressure.

Experiments to see the change in hemogram (including the absolute value of eosinophiles): The experiments done by Nanjing College of Traditional Chinese Medicine show that the total number of white blood cell increase in all patients who were treated with the directing-Qi therapy, the lymphocytes in it increase proportionally and the neutrophils decrease accordingly. The number of eosinophiles is closely related with the functional state of the cerebral cortex. When a man is sleeping, the number of his eosinophiles increases and when the cerebral cortex is in tension, it decreases. However, the fluctuation in the number of the patient's eosinophiles changes remarkably when he is being treated with the directing-Qi therapy. This signifies that this therapy has some influence upon the number of eosinophiles.

Experiments for observing gastric peristalsis: Nanjing College of Traditional Chinese Medicine observed the influence of the directing-Qi therapy upon two patients' gastric peristalsis under X-ray. One of the patients had suffered from gastroptosis for over ten years. The number of his gastric peristalsis increased and its speed quickened after having been treated with the directing-Qi therapy. The other patient suffered from allergic colitis. There was also a rise in the number and the speed of his gastric peristalsis after he had been treated in the same way. Besides, it could be seen that the stomach contracted obviously and its lowest part had moved up.

162. In How Many Ways Has the Directing-Qi Therapy Been Applied to Clinical Practice?

According to incomplete statistics, curative effect has been achieved by applying this therapy to the treatment of the intervertebral disk of lumbar, hypertension and paraplegia, etc.

ANESTHESIA WITH EXTERNAL QI

163. What Is Qigong Anesthesia?

Qigong anesthesia is another bold attempt which followed the attempt of acupuncture anesthesia. The doctor first directs his own Qi to a particular part of his own body and then he sends out the "external Qi" through a certain part on his own body and the "external Qi" enters the patient's body through an acupuncture point on the patient's body though the doctor does not touch the patient. Thus the patient will not suffer from pain during a surgical operation and the anesthetic effect and the effect of killing pain are achieved without using any narcotic or acupuncture anesthesia.

164. What Is the Theoretical Basis for Qigong Anesthesia?

We worked together with some scientific research institutes concerned in testing with some apparatus the "external Qi" emitted by doctors. These tests have proved that some infrared signals under the control of the rise and fall in the low frequency have been discharged. We also carried out other experiments such as the experiments on animals, crystals, fluorescent bacteria and the experiments with the thermograph. It has been proved by these tests that the "external Qi" emitted in a place away from the living beings and inanimate objects can cause in these things some change in varying degrees. Moreover, the "external Qi", emitted by the doctor acting upon a certain acupuncture point on the patient's body without touching him, can make the patient have the sensations of aching, numbness, distending pain, cold and heaviness, etc. These sensations are similar to the normal sensations felt by the patient during acupuncture treatment. Patients with neurosis of szhiophrenia who had been in a hot temper will calm down immediately when Qigong anesthesia is applied. It also has some effect on patients who are suffering from pain caused by cancer or dysmenorrhea. All these things provide more direct basis for the "external Qi" anesthesia, sedation and pain-killing.

We have accomplished 22 excellent operations in which the "external Qi" anesthesia was applied in the light of the above-mentioned basis provided by experimentation.

165. How Well Does Qigong Anesthesia Work in Surgery?

On the morning of May 9, 1980, an operation in which Qigong anesthesia was applied was performed successfully on a patient for the extirpation of thyroid tumour in Shanghai No.8 People's Hospital. The success achieved in the first operation in which Qigong anesthesia was applied has added to doctor's confidence in the application of Qigong anesthesia to future surgical operations and has laid down a good foundation for future operations.

Shanghai Research Institute of Traditional Chinese Medicine, Shanghai No.8 People's Hospital, Shanghai Shuguang Hospital and Zhuhai People's Hospital in Guangdong Province, etc. worked together and made successful use of the "external Qi" emitted by Mr. Lin Hou-sheng, author of this book, for anesthesia in the surgical operations for the extirpation of tumour on the coat of the tongue and the removal of a large part of the stomach. During the operation, the patient remained fully conscious and was able to speak. After the operation, there was no side-effect and the patients recovered rather quickly. Both the patients and the doctors felt satisfied.

166. What Are the Prospects for Qigong Anesthesia Like?

It has not been long since Qigong anesthesia was put into practice. Therefore, there has not been sufficient time to carry out experiments for scientific research. It is still necessary for us to accumulate more cases in order to sum up the laws governing Qigong anesthesia. What is the principle on which Qigong produces anesthesia? What is the mechanism of Qigong anesthesia? Such questions are still waiting to be answered. Not many hospitals have adopted Qigong anesthesia. Therefore, we intend to adopt the techniques of bionics and replace the doctor with apparatus which send out imitation "external Qi" similar to that emitted by the doctor to achieve the effect of anesthesia. Thus, Qigong anesthesia can be popularized and its value in clinical practice can also be enhanced. If a suitable apparatus can be developed to imitate the "external Qi" and if its functions remain at a satisfactory level, the effect of Qigong anesthesia will be more satisfactory. We hope that those who have an interest in the research work will join their efforts and coordinate with one another in their research work on biological phenomena and achieve greater success.

TECHNIQUES OF BIONICS

167. What Are the Meanings of Information and Qigong-Information Therapy?

What's information? To use a common expression, it is signals and messages. In other words, it is the mode of existence and the state of matter, the characteristics, signals and messages of movement. In human societies, there is social information and in the world of nature, there is natural information. For non-living matters, there is inanimate information and for living beings, there is animate information.

It is said that the term "information" first appeared in the book entitled "On Cybernetics" written by the American mathematician Norbert Wiener. It is said in the book that information is the name for what is being exchanged between human beings and the outside world when human beings try to adapt themselves to the outside world and make the adaptation react on the outside world. Therefore, information is closely related with matter and its motion (energy). To put it in a simple language, information is the objective reflexion of certain properties of the motion of matter. Information exists in every field of sciences. A comprehensive frontier science has been established, based on the study of information. It is called the "information theory" or the "science of information".

The information therapy was developed a few years ago, based on the emission of the external Qi in Qigong exercises. Therefore, this new therapy belongs to the category of Qigong therapy. According to the results of tests done by using apparatus, the external Qi emitted by the doctor is such information as infrared electromagnetic waves, magnetism and static electricity. The Qigong-information therapy makes use of the external Qi emitted by the doctor to cure diseases. Such external Qi emitted by the doctor may well be considered a kind of information.

168. What Progress Has Been Made in Our Country in the Study and Application of Qigong Information Based on the Theory of Bionics?

The imitation of Qigong information on a bionic basis refers to the use of the apparatus which can imitate the infrared information sent out by the doctor for the purpose of curing diseases. Such an apparatus is developed on the principles of bionics and the imitation of the external Qi (such as the infrared electromagnetic waves which are under the control of the rise and fall of the low frequency). The function of such an apparatus is similar to that of the external Qi emitted by the doctor. This kind of method of imitation is called the bionic means for producing Qigong information. This apparatus is also called the "infrared-information-medical-apparatus" because most of the material carriers sent out by the apparatus are the infrared radiation.

The first Qigong-information-medical-apparatus was developed by Mr. He Qing-nian of the Beijing Research Institute of Traditional Chinese Medicine and Mr. Zhang Hui-ming of Beijing Research Institute of Medical Apparatus. They were inspired by the directing-Qi therapy in Qigong therapies and developed the far-infrared-information-medical-apparatus by imitating the far-infrared information sent out by Doctor Zhao Guang of the Xiyuan Hospital in Beijing.

They used this apparatus to cure over 200 patients with various diseases and achieved rather good curative effects which were similar to those produced by the treatment with the external Qi emitted by the doctor himself. Later on, the Qingdao City Hospital of Traditional Chinese Medicine and the Shanghai Research Institute of Nuclear Science managed to develop the QX-4 type of Qigong Infrared Information Medical Apparatus, based on the principles of the transformation between light and electricity and the imitation of one of the materials in the "external Qi" emitted by Mr. Lin Hou-sheng, author of this book. This material is the infrared electromagnetic waves under the control of the rise and fall of the low frequency. This apparatus was put into production in Qingdao Factory of Medical Apparatus and it won the second prize for the Achievements in Scientific Research in Shandong Province (P.R.C.) in 1980.

Since 1980, some factories concerned in Shanghai, Fuoshan and Chaoyang have worked in coorperation with the Shanghai Research Institute of Chinese Traditional Medicine and have developed Model SM-01 Animate Information Simulator, Model Zhongyan-II Qigong Infrared Information Medical Apparatus, Model SZY-1 and Model SZY-2 and Model SZY-3 Qigong Information Medical Apparatus. They have been turned out by factories in batches. Evaluations have proved that these apparatuses work well and have curative effect on chronic diseases such as hypertension, bronchitis, cardiopathy, pseudo myopia, etc. Up to now, many hospitals have applied those apparatuses to clinical practice to cure patients.

169. What Are the Properties and the Uses of Model SZY-1, SZY-2 and SZY-3 Qigong Information Medical Apparatus Developed by the Shanghai Research Institute of Traditional Chinese Medicine?

These models of apparatuses are all developed on the basis of the imitation of the "external Qi" emitted by Mr. Lin Hou-sheng, author of this book. This kind of "external Qi" is just the infrared electromagnetic waves under the control of the rise and fall in the low frequency.

With the permission of the government department concerned, they have been put into production and have been turned out and are still being turned out in batches. The major properties of the apparatuses are as follows: they make use of magnetic tapes for the transformation of Qigong information which is sent out in two forms — the form of electric pulses and the form of infrared radiation; they are light and handy, easy to be operated and convenient to be used in curing diseases; they produce rather good curative effects. Evaluations have proved that such apparatuses can produce the effects of killing pain, diminishing inflamation and removing spasm. In clinical practice, they produce rather good curative effects on hypertension, cardiopathy, bronchitis, pseudo myopia, periathritis of shoulder joint, acute sprain, muscular strain of the lumbar region, sequelae of brain concussion, and neurosis, etc. Besides, they can also produce the curative effects of alleviating dizziness, emesis, insomnia and various pains and symptoms. They can also be used in the rescue of dangerously or seriously ill patients of cardiopathy and other diseases.

The SZY-1 model is light, portable and easy to carry about. It is suitable for use in mobile medical teams. It has two functions: it can be used as a medical apparatus during treatment of patients; it may be used as an equipment to play music. Model SZY-2 and SZY-3 are of desk type. They are fit for use in the consulting rooms of hospitals. Moreover, Model SZY-3 can be used for treatment of two patients at the same time. These medical apparatuses are fit for use in medical research institutes, medical colleges, hospitals, clinics in factories as well as for use by individuals or families.

MISCELLANEOUS

170. What Is the "Internal Qi"? What Is the "External Qi"?

Qigong is a kind of physical exercises for a conscious control of the Qi and the mind. When one has reached the advanced stage of Qigong exercises, one will be able to sense the movement of Qi along the main and collateral channels as a network of passages through which vital energy circulates in the human body according to Traditional Chinese Medicine. This kind of Qi which moves in the channels inside the human body is called internal Qi. The ancient Chinese doctor Li Shi-zhen said in his book *Research on the Eight Extra-channels*: "Only those who are able to turn their minds' eye to the inside of their body can see the visceras and channels inside their own bodies." What Dr. Li said is a very vivid description of the experiences a man has learned from doing Qigong exercises. Photographs of the radiation field have provided us with indicators of the "internal Qi". We believe that the "internal Qi" is present inside the human body and functions as a kind of power or energy inside the human body.

Those who have mastered Qigong will have sufficient "internal Qi" and can send it out through a certain acupuncture point on his body by exercising his own mental power. Qi emitted out of a human body is called "external Qi". The "internal Qi" is the origin of the "external Qi". Without the "internal Qi", there will be no "external Qi". We believe that the "internal Qi" and the "external Qi" form a unity. The "internal Qi" is the basis of the "external Qi" while the "external Qi" is a reflexion of the "internal Qi" outside the human body. In ancient times, the emission of the "external Qi" in Qigong was called the "giving away of Qi". The emission of the "external Qi" for curing patients has been existing ever since ancient times and has been spreading among the folks long before.

According to Traditional Chinese Medicine, Qi is the essential material for the maintainance of life and activities of the human body. Although we can neither see nor touch both the internal and external Qi, it is undoubtedly a kind of matter. As to its material form, tests have proved that it is a kind of field, a biogenic energy, far-infrared radiation, infrasonic sound, a flow of certain material, a kind of information and its carrier, etc. Those who are interested in the nature of Qi shall go on working hard so as to discover all its mysteries.

171. What Is the Renmai and Dumai? What Is Xiao Zhou Tian?

The Renmai is a passage through which the Qi travels. The Renmai goes along the front middle line of the chest and abdomen of a human body. It comes out of Baozhong (that is the internal sex organ inside the pelvic cavity) and leads to perineum. From there it goes on to travel along the front middle line in the abdomen and passes mons pubis, abdomen, chest, neck until it reaches the middle of the lower lip where it breaks into two branches which pass over the face and end below the eye sockets. The Renmai is the sea of Yin channels. The three Yin channels of each foot intersect the Renmai at the lower abdomen and thus the Yin channels of the right foot are related to those of the left foot through the Renmai. Therefore, the Renmai has the function of adjusting the Yin channels and is accordingly called "the Yin Channel is Chief in charge of all Yin channels in the whole body". It has the functions of adjusting menstruation, nourishing the foetus and it is, therefore, also called the "guardian angel of the foetus".

The Dumai (Back Middle) is a passage through which Qi travels and it goes along the middle line on the back of the human body. It also comes out of Baozhong (that is the internal sex organ inside the pelvic cavity) and leads to perineum where it goes on to travel along the central line of the back and passes the sacrum, loin, back and neck until it enters the head and goes on to travel along the middle line of

the head before it reaches the top of the head and then goes down to
the forehead, the nose, the upper lip and ends at the center of the upper
lip. The Dumai has some branches which surround the kidney and lead
to the heart. It is also called "the sea of the Yang channels". The six
Yang channels intersect the Dumai at Dazhui. The Dumai has the
function of adjusting the Yang channels and is accordingly called the
Yang Channel in Chief in charge of all the Yang channels of the whole
body. The Dumai leads to the brain and its branches surround the
kidney. The kidney produces marrow and the brain is the marrow sea.
Therefore, the Dumai can reflect physiological and pathological
conditions of the brain and the marrow and its also connects the brain
and marrow to the internal sex organ.

The circulation of the Qi along Renmai and Dumai is called Xiao
Zhou Tian (the Small Circulation). That is to say, the Qi comes out
of Dantian and gradually goes down and passes perineum, Weilu (also
called Changqiang). Then, it goes up along the back of the body to
Dazhui (also called Big Vertebra) and continues to go on to Yuzhen
(also called Fengfu) before it reaches Niwuan Gong (also called Baihui)
at the top of the head. After that it begins to go down to Shengting
(also called Yintang) and travels along the middle line of the forehead
and the bridge of the nose and passes Suoliao (also called Bizhun) to
enter the Renmai. Sometimes, the Qi breaks up into two parts after
it has reached Shengting and goes down past the eyes and along the
cheeks to unite again within the mouth before it passes the tip of the
tongue to intersect Renmai. The circulation of the Qi in such a small
circle is called Xiao Zhou Tian (the Small Circulation) in the
terminology of Qigong.

172. What Is Meant by Qi Rushing Up Along Chongmai and Qi Running Through Daimai? What Is Da Zhou Tian?

The Chongmai is a channel which is in charge of the vital energy and blood in all the channels. The Chongmai goes up to the head and down to the feet. It can adjust the vital energy and blood in the twelve channels and is accordingly called the "sea of the twelve channels" as well as the "blood sea". It comes out of the Baozhong (that is the internal sex organ inside the pelvic cavity) and breaks into three branches there. One of the branches goes along the back wall of the abdomen and moves up along the inside of the spinal column; another branch goes along the front wall of the abdomen and its subsidiary branches go up close against the umbilicus and spread out in the chest before they go up past the larynx and finally form a cycle surrounding the lips; the third branch goes down and out of perineum and breaks into the subsidiary branches which move down along the inner side of the abdomen until they reach the inner side of the big toes. The rushing up of the Qi along the Chongmai refers to the sudden move of the Qi from the lower abdomen to the chest where it quickly spreads out. It is a common phenomenon.

The Daimai (also called the Belt Channel) forms a circle around the waist and resembles a belt. It can control the other channels. Therefore, it is said that "all the other channels are subject to the Daimai". The Daimai starts from hypochondrium, goes down slantingly to the Daimai acupuncture point and completes a cycle around the waist before coming out of the Daimai acupuncture point again to move forward and down to the upper side of the ilium along which it moves slantingly to the lower abdomen. The movement of the Qi along the Daimai refers to the fact that the Qi comes out of Dantian, moves towards the left and then turns to the right and returns to Dantian as if a string of beads rolls around the waist. This is the so-called movement of the Qi around the Daimai.

When one has reached the advanced stage of Qigong exercises, his Qi will circulate along the twelve channels and the eight extra channels to form a great circulation. This is called "Da Zhou Tian" (the Great Circulation) in the terminology of Qigong.

173.   What Are the Three Passes? Where Are They Located?

The three passes refer to the three places which are not easy for the Qi to go through when it moves in a small circulation (Xiao Zhou Tian). The book entitle *Jin Dan Da Cheng Ji* says: "Someone wants to know where the three passes on the back are. The answer is that the Yuzhen Pass is at the back of the head, the Lulu Pass is on the bilateral sides of the spine and the Weilu Pass is between water and fire."

The Yuzhen Pass is at the back of the head. In particular, it is located at the back of the head, right above the central point in the line between the Fengchi acupuncture points on the two sides, just touches the pillow when one lies down. This pass is the most difficult of the three passes for the Qi to pass and is therefore also called Tiebi (the Impenerable Fortress).

The Lulu Pass is located on the fourteenth vertebra on the back of the human body. That is the center of the line between the two elbow tips when a man is lying on his back.

The Weilu Pass is situated at the lowest point of a man's spinal column. Its upper part is connected with sacrum and its lower part is not associated with anything. The Weilu Pass is behind and above the anus. The Changqiang acupuncture point is located where the Weilu Pass is.

When the Qi is moving, sometimes it moves through the three passes naturally and without any difficulty. But sometimes it will be hindered. When it is hindered at the place where the bilateral Lulu Pass is, one can direct the Qi to move upward by exercising one's mental power and at the same time contract and raise one's anus so as to enable the Qi to go through the Weilu Pass on the one hand. And on the other hand, one can pat slightly and massage one's Jiaji acupuncture point and Weilu acupuncture point before one begins to do Qigong exercises. When one's Qi is hindered at the place where the Yuzhen Pass is, one can close one's eyes and try to direct one's line of sight upward and meanwhile consciously direct the Qi to move upward so that the Qi can go directly through the Weilu Pass. But one should never be overanxious for quick results and success in Qigong exercises. Otherwise, dangerous and harmful deviation will occur in the process of Qigong exercises. If one keeps on practising the exercises everyday, good results and curative effect will be achieved naturally.

174. What Is Dantian? Where Is It Located?

All the people who knew or know how to preserve their own health attach great importance to Dantian. They all place the hope for success in Qigong exercises on this part of the human body and think that it is a good place for them to make pills of immortality (as a Taoist practice) inside their own bodies. They do not think that Dantian is a small dot or an acupuncture point. Instead, they think that Dantian is an area or a field. A place for growing wheat is called a wheat-field and a place for growing rice is called a rice-field. A place where coal is found and dug out is called a coal-field whereas the place inside the human body where the pills of immortality (the name for such pills in Chinese is Dan and the word field is pronounced Tian in Chinese) are made is called Dantian (field for producing pills of immortality as a Taoist practice in ancient China). In ancient times in China, those Toaists who sought immortality put a kind of material like metal into an oven to make pills of immortality and took such pills. As a result, many of them got poisoned and died instead of enjoying longevity and immortality. Later on, some people who wanted and tried to preserve health thought of the idea of making pills of immortality inside the human body by doing breathing exercises and focusing one's mind on a certain part of the human body. If one wanted to make pills of immortality in the head, the corresponding part was called the Upper Dantian; if one wanted to make such pills inside the chest, this part of the human body was named the Middle Dantian correspondingly;

and if one wanted to make such pills in the lower abdomen, the part in the lower abdomen for the making of such pills was called the Lower Dantian.

People in ancient times thought that Dantian was an important place which could supply nutriment for the whole body. They also thought that breath came into and out of Dantian and that Yin and Yang (the positive and the negative or the male and female) closed and opened in this place. They believed that this place can warm every part of the body without fire and moisten the visceras without water. They held that life depended on this part of the body and if its relation with the other parts of the body was not cut off, life and vitality would be maintained. People who are good at Wushu (martial arts such as shadowboxing, sword-play, etc.) think that if a kind of vital force has been formed in Dantian, one can overpower others wherever one goes. This shows that people who practise Qigong exercises or martial arts attach very great importance to Dantian. But where is Dantian located? Books compiled or written in ancient times showed different opinions as to the position of Dantian. There were not only the Upper, Middle and Lower Dantian, but also Rear and Front Dantian. Moreover, the Upper, Middle and Lower Dantian might also refer to different places respectively. The Upper Dantian might refer to the place around Baihui acupuncture point or the place around Yintang acupuncture point, or Zhuqiao acupuncture point; the Middle Dantian might refer to the place around Danzhong (a position of the body surface in the center between the two breasts) or the place round the navel; and the Lower Dantian might refer to the center of the navel, or a place behind the navel inside the body, or a place 45 mm below the navel; the Lower Dantian might refer to a place 50 mm or even 100 mm below the navel. There were also some other people who think that the Lower Dantian refers to the place around perineum and that the Rear Dantian refers to the place round Mingmen acupuncture point. In all, opinions vary as to the position of Dantian.

We thought there are 3 Dantians: Upper Dantian at the place

between two eyebrows; Middle Dantian at the heart; and Lower Dantian at the abdomen below the navel. Keeping mind at Dantian as we often mention of means the Lower Dantian, that is, keeping mind at the area on the abdomen below the navel.

175. What Is Meant by Keeping One's Mind at Dantian? What Is the Purpose of Doing So?

To keep the mind at Dantian means to think of Dantian quietly and slightly.

The Upper Dantian is located in the head. Those patients who suffer from deficiency and collapse of the vital energy, or cerebral anaemia, or hypotension and the patient whose head has a fear for cold wind can practise the skill of keeping the mind at the Upper Dantian. Because the Upper Dantian is the headquarters of all Yang-channels. But a beginner in Qigong should not start practising the skill of keeping the mind at the Upper Dantian immediately. Otherwise, there will perhaps be overactive functional activities of the vital energy and harmful and dangerous deviation will occur in the process of Qigong exercises. If a patient is suffering from diseases such as excessive heart-fire flaming up or excess of liver-Ying, or hypertension, it is all the more necessary for him to avoid adopting the skill of keeping the mind at the Upper Dantian. Otherwise, the disease will become even more serious.

The Middle Dantian is inside the chest. A patient who is suffering from collapse of middle-warmer energy or women who are suffering from menorrhagia can adopt the skill of keeping the mind at the Middle Dantian. But those who have just begun learning to keep the mind at the middle Dantian should follow the directions of a teacher of Qigong exercises so as to avoid the occurrence of such phenomena as the feeling of oppression in the chest and shortness of breath, etc..

The Lower Dantian is in the lower abdomen. Most of the people who have practiced or are still practising Qigong all advocate the skill of keeping the mind at the Lower Dantian. By keeping the mind at Dantian, we usually mean keeping the mind at the Lower Dantian. Because this part of the body is most closely related to the life activities of a human body. It is situated in the middle of a man's body and in this area there are the acupuncture points such as Guanyuan, Qihai and Mingmen, etc. which have the functions of nourishing the kidney-energy and improving the function of the kidney. The Lower Dantian is also the place where the Qi goes out to move along the Renmai, Dumai, Chongmai and Daimai. It is also the hub where the healthy energy moves up or down and opens or closes. It is also the place where the seminal fluid of male is formed and stored and the place where a female nourishes the fetus inside her own body. Therefore, some people think that the Lower Dantian is the ''source of life'', the fundament of the five solid organs and the six hollow organs'', the ''root of the twelve channels,'' the ''confluence of Yin and Yang'' and the ''gate for the breath to go in and out of''. The reason why all the people who practise martial arts lay special emphasis on training themselves to achieve the ability to keep their mind on the Lower Dantian is that it is the place where the healthy energy is gathered, stored and controlled as well as the base where the healthy energy comes in or out. If one pays great attention to training himself to obtain the ability to keep his mind on the Lower Dantian, his health will be improved and diseases can be prevented or cured.

176. What Is Meant by the Convergence of the Qi into Dantian? What Is the Significance of This?

The convergence of the Qi into Dantian refers to a man's conscious action of converging the Qi into the area Dantian and his conscious action of making the Qi pushing towards Dantian with the help of the force he feels to be inside his chest when he breathes. Judging from the point of view of physiology and human anatomy, the air one breathes in and out will never be able to reach the area Dantian. But according to the theory of Qigong, the sensation of breathing one feels, the movement of the diaphragm and the expansion and contraction of the abdomen can help to form in the middle of the human body an excitive line established reflexly and leading directly to the area called Dantian. Once such an excitive line has been established, the stimulation of mental power on the Dantian is increased. Therefore, it can be said that the convergence of the Qi into Dantian is a means for strengthening the stimulation of mental power on Dantian.

Dantian is the source of life, the origin of vital energy and the root of the channels, therefore, the stimulation of mental power on Dantian increases the vital energy in Dantian. This has the good effects of fostering the predorminal energy and improving one's health.

177. How Does A Man Choose A Point Or An Area for Himself to Focus His Mind on?

The selection of a point or area for ourselves to keep our minds on should be based upon what type of humour we belong to, what type of Qigong exercises we do, what kind of disease we have and how seriously ill we are.

Selection based on humour type: If you belong to inert type, quiet and peaceful and easy to fall into tranquility when doing Qigong exercise, you may choose any point or area of your own body for yourself to keep your mind on. For instance, you may keep your mind on the area Dantian, or the acupuncture point Yongquan, or the acupuncture point Tanzhong. If you are of vivacious type, not easy to fall into tranquility in doing Qigong exercise, you may keep your mind on an imaginary scene of the sea, flowers or some other beautiful scenes or objects, or even an imaginary happy and gay scene.

Selection based on the type of Qigong exercises adopted: If you are doing the static Qigong exercise, it is advisable for you to choose a part of your own body for you to keep your mind on; if you are practising the dynamic Qigong exercise or the dynamic-and-static-combined Qigong exercise, you had better choose a scene away from your own body for you to keep your mind on. For example, when you are taking a walk outdoors, or doing the Qigong exercise in the standing posture, or when you are doing the Qigong exercise while walking, you had better adopt the method of keeping your mind on a scene or object away from your own body. Besides, it is only when the method of keeping the mind on a part of your own body is impracticable that you choose to keep your mind on a scene or object away from your own body.

Selection based on the type of disease: A patient with hypertension, for instance, should choose to keep his mind on a place in the lower part of his own body, such as the lower Dantian and the acupuncture point Yongquan, etc. so that the vital energy and the blood move downward and the blood pressure can be lowered. A patient with hypotension or anaemia should often choose to keep his mind on the middle or upper part of his own body so that it is advantageous for the blood pressure to rise and for the vital energy and the blood to move upward. (Of course, it is necessary that you have a doctor to instruct you while you are practising the method of keeping your mind on the head.)

Selection based on the seriousness of the disease: A patient, who has the symptom of excess-syndrome in the upper part and deficiency in the lower part, for example, should usually choose to keep his mind on the lower part of his body; while a patient who has the symptom of deficiency-syndrome in the upper part and excess in the lower part should usually choose to keep his mind on the upper part of his body. A patient who suffers from deficiency of kidney and decline of the fire from the gate of life may choose to keep his mind on the acupuncture point Mingmen(This acupuncture point is also called the Gate of Life), so as to improve the function of the kidney; a patient who suffers from deficiency of the spleen and stomach may choose to keep his mind on the acupuncture point Zusanli so as to improve the function of the stomach Channel of Foot-Yangming.

178. How to Master the Skill of Focusing the Mind on the Lower Dantian?

Most of the people who practise Qigong exercises choose to focus their minds on the lower Dantian. Various schools of Qigong all demand that one adopt abdominal respiration. When one begins to practise the method of abdominal respiration, he should try to direct the movement of his Qi with his own mental power so that his Qi moves closer and closer to the lower abdomen until it gradually reaches it. (That is to say his Qi converges into Dantian.) When he is inhaling and exhaling, he should concentrate his attention on the movement of the air in and out and silently focus his mind on Dantian in the lower abdomen as well as the expansion and contraction of the lower abdomen. This is what we call the focusing one's mind on Dantian. As to the position of Dantian, we should not regard it only as a tiny spot similar in size to a small aperture or acupuncture point. We should focus our minds on an area that is in the middle of the surface of the lower abdomen or on the area in that place in a three-dimensional sense. When one has fallen further into tranquility, he will feel only the slight movement of the lower abdomen up and down. He will feel relaxed and comfortable from head to foot and he will feel that everything is dim and distant as if unreal.

When one is trying to focus his mind on Dantian, it is unavoidable and quite natural that some distracting thoughts will appear. If so, one should not be too anxious. Instead, he should try to get rid of these distracting thoughts and always keep his mind on Dantian. He may also stop doing Qigong exercise for a short period of time and take a walk at a slow pace in a small area. He may also do a few sections of health-preserving exercises or a complete cycle of setting-up exercises to radio music. When he feels calm and tranquil again, he may proceed on to focusing his mind on Dantian again.

179. How Does One Exert Appropriate Efforts to Focus His Mind on Dantian?

By appropriate efforts exerted to focus one's mind on Dantian we mean the appropriate state of concentration of one's mind. This is often a great problem to one who is practising Qigong exercises. Not a few people failed to make appropriate efforts and as a result took a roundabout course or even made deviation harmful to their health. In order to be able to control the degree of concentration of one's mind, one must go in for the exercises to gain experience and keep on making adjustment until intensity of concentration rises to a suitable degree. Clinical practice has shown that if the intensity of the concentration of one's mind is too small, there will be many distracting thoughts and one will fail to focus his mind on Dantian; and it has also been shown that if the intensity of the concentration of the mind is too great, there will be fewer distracting thoughts, but it will cause one to have the feelings of headache, fullness in the head and nervousness as well as some other discomforts. Ancient Chinese people knew well from experience what a suitable degree of concentration of the mind was. They said: "One should do it neither too consciously nor too absent-mindedly; if one does it too consciously, it will cause some discomforts that are reflected in some physical symptoms and if one does it too absent-mindedly, one will fail to achieve the expected effects. One should maintain the concentration of the mind at a moderate level where the concentration is neither too low nor too high." We should follow such instructions given by our ancestors.

When one has just begun to practise the skill of concentration of the mind, one should exert comparatively greater efforts. It helps one to get rid of distracting thoughts. But the intensity of concentration should be limited to the extent that it does not cause headache, or the feeling of fullness in the head and nervousness. When this has been achieved, one may gradually lower the intensity of concentration of his mind as he goes on practising Qigong exercises for a longer and longer period of time until he reaches the moderate degree of concentration. Besides, the intensity of concentration should vary with the change in the number of distracting thoughts every time when one is practising Qigong exercises. If many distracting thoughts should appear, one should heighten the intensity of concentration on his mind; when there are fewer distracting thoughts, he should lower the intensity of concentration. If the intensity of concentration is too great and if this lasts for too long, the place on which one focus his mind will become hot and one may even feel that this part is swelling up. If so, one should stop focusing his mind on this part or choose another place to focus his mind on so as to prevent bad effects.

180.   What Is Meant by Falling into Tranquility?

The tranquil state refers to the state of mind where the workings of his mind are comparatively unitary and where there are fewer distracting thoughts in his mind and his reaction to the stimulation of outside factors is weakened. The degree of tranquility depends on how well one has mastered the skills of Qigong exercises. When one is in a state of tranquility, he often feels calm and that everything around him is dim and distant as if they were non-existent. As one masters the skills of Qigong better and better, the degree of tranquility heightens. The degree of tranquility varies greatly in accordance with the difference in the people who do Qigong exercises. Furthermore, it even varies each time when one practises Qigong exercises. When one has just mastered the skill of entering the state of tranquility, he usually feels calm and peaceful in the mind. His mind is often concentrated and few distracting thoughts occur to him. What he is focusing his mind on is comparatively stablized and his reaction to the stimulation from the outside world is weakened to some extent. When he goes further on with Qigong exercises, his mind will be all the more concentrated. He only feels a soft and continuous trace of breath. His mind is peaceful and concentrated. When he has arrived at a further state of tranquility, he will feel that everything around him is quiet and still as well as dim and distant as if non-existent. Everything seems so still to him that they were like stagnant water. He himself will feel as if he were transformed into a weightless wisp of smoke rising continuously and as if he were mounting the clouds and riding the mist. It is hard to describe the sense of comfort one has at this stage. But such a great tranquility does not occur very often. Once it has appeared, one should immediately seize this good opportunity to go on doing Qigong exercises. But one should not do it too consciously, nor should he try too hard to keep himself in this state. Otherwise, one's mind will be diverted by distracting thoughts.

181. What Physiological Effects Does the State of Tranquility Create?

The state of tranquility has great physiological significance to a man's health in a wide range. First of all, the state of tranquility has the positive effect on protecting a man's organism and his health.

As is known to all, the process of excitation and depression is the basic process of the activities of the higher nervous system. All reflexes, including the advanced thinking, depend on the process of excitation of the nerve cells. As excitation is always accompanied by the extraordinary consumption of biochemical elements, when the state of excitation has lasted for too long a period of time, or when it is excessive, it will cause functional disorder of the higher nerve center. The rules governing the higher nerves demand that the process of excitation should be in harmony with the process of inhibition to exercise its normal physiological functions. The internal inhibition which occurs when one is in a state of tranquility is the same as other kinds of physiological inhibition in that it not only guanrantees the exact realization of all kinds of reflexes but also has the effects of protecting, adjusting and restoring the biochemical elements and physiological functions of the brain cells. The human body is a biological control system of advanced and complex properties and levels. The cerebral hemispheres are the center which adjust the automatic control system. The activities of the whole human organism and the various organs of a human body as well as the biophysical process of the cells are all controlled and adjusted by the higher nerve center. Tests have shown that when a man falls into the state of tranquility in Qigong exercises, his encephaloelectric waves tend to synchronize and the electric activities of the brain cells become orderly. The functions of the higher nerves are improved and the adjusting function of the higher nerves is improved as well. So the whole human organism reaches a new state of dynamic equilibrium. When one is in a state of tranquility in Qigong exercises, his basal metabolism is reduced and the consumption of oxygen is decreased. The amount of the oxygen consumed by an ordinary man when he is asleep decreases by 10% than when he is awake. But when a man is in a state of tranquility in Qigong exercises, the amount of oxygen consumed by him is even smaller than when he is in sound sleep. Besides, the depression brought about by Qigong exercises has the functions of replenishing and retrieving the component parts of the brain cells. The state of tranquility in Qigong exercises can help to reduce the rate of increase of the entropy in the human organism. (If the rate of increase of entropy is greater than the rate of the discharge of entropy, it signals that the human organism is degenerating.) The increase in the steroid in plasma, the decrease in the somatotropin content and the improvement in the quality of the central nervous transmitter and serotonin, all these changes show that the falling into tranquility in Qigong exercises is a physiological process of the metabolism of small quantity of energy. Therefore, the state of tranquility is good for the storage of energy.

Tests have also shown that when one is in a state of tranquility, the tension of his sympathetic nerve is reduced and that of his parasympathetic nerve increases. The coordination between them is further improved so that the human organism is in a relaxed reflexive state. This is good for both prevention and cure of diseases.

182. What Will People Feel in the State of Tranquility? How to Deal with Them?

When a man has adjusted his breath, focus his mind on Dantian and gone through some other related exercises, his cerebral cortex falls into a state which is peculiar to a man who is in the process of doing Qigong exercises. This peculiar state has good effects on the main and collateral channels in the human body, on his vital energy and his blood and on his visceras and other organisms. In turn, there will be some physiological changes in the symptoms and signs of a man. These physiological changes are the very physiological basis for the sensations a man feels when he is in a state of tranquility in Qigong exercises. Obviously, the state of tranquility in Qigong exercises is also reflected in the multiple effects it produces.

In clinical practice, it has been found that when a man falls into the state of tranquility in Qigong exercises, he feels that he is clear-headed, peaceful in the mind and calm. He will also have the comfortable feelings that his whole body or part of his body becomes warm or cool, that the muscles are quivering or becoming numb and soft, etc.. He may also feel that his whole body or some parts of his body have expanded or contracted or feel as if he were riding the mist. He will feel that he has lost count of time as well. In brief, the feelings one has when he has fallen into the state of tranquility are varied. The ancient Chinese people summarized these varied feelings by calling them "the eight kinds of sensations": the sensation of movement, the sensation of itch, the sensation of coolness, the sensation of warmth, the sensation of lightness, the sensation of heaviness, the sensation of astringency and the sensation of satiny. Some other people interpreted "the eight kinds of sensations" as the sensation of swing, the sensation of clarity, the sensation of coldness, the sensation of hotness, the sensation of being afloat in the air, the sensation of sinking down, the sensation of hardness and the sensation of softness. It is not unusual for a man to have these eight kinds of sensations when he is in a state of tranquility in the process of doing Qigong exercises. Anyhow, he should neither try too hard to sustain such sensations nor should he be afraid of them. Instead, he should leave them to go on in the original way and he should meanwhile go on practising the Qigong exercises. When he hears a sudden scream or sees something horrible, he should try to remain calm and ignore them and continue to keep his mind on Dantian. If he manages to do so, he will not be harmed by them.

183. What Influence Do the Posture and the Way of Breathing Have on A Man's State of Tranquility?

Technically speaking, all types of Qigong exercises are composed of three parts posture, breathing and the mental power. These three parts are interrelated and have influence over one another. Therefore, the adjustment of one's own posture as well as his breathing contributes to both the formation of and the development in the state of tranquility.

The influence of posture over the state of tranquility is easy to be seen. When one adopts an incorrect posture, he will be unable to relax his whole body or some of his muscles and he will, therefore, be in a state of nervousness and tension which will in turn cause the cerebral cortex to send out a series of malignant excitative impulses of an afferent nature. Thus, he will fail to enter the state of tranquility. On the contrary, if one adopts a comfortable and natural posture and if all the muscles of his body are relaxed to the greatest extent possible, the excitation of the cerebral cortex will be lessened and it helps him to enter the state of tranquility more easily.

The way in which one breathes also has quite great influence on the state of tranquility. Focusing one's mind on something is a means for enabling oneself to enter the state of tranquility. Usually, one tries to keep his mind on his breathing first before he manages to keep his mind on Dantian. Therefore, whether one can successfully adjust his breathing directly decides if he can manage the concentration of his mind and it also directly affects himself as to whether he can successfully keep himself in the state of tranquility.

The above-mentioned relations can be summed up in one sentence — "Successful adjustment of the breath enables one to be calm and peaceful in the mind." A light, regular, thin and slow breath is a kind of benign stimulus which is helpful in bringing out the state of tranquility.

Whenever one is in a strained posture and his breath is irregular, he will be upset and distracting thoughts will arise. Consequently, he is unable to enter the state of tranquility. But the better he manages to keep himself in the state of tranquility, the more relaxed and comfortable he feels and the more regular and smooth his breath is. This is a concrete manifestation of the truth that the adjustment of the posture, the adjustment of breath and the adjustment of the mental power are helpful and complementary to one another.

184. What Is the Difference Between Being in the State of Tranquility and Being in A Drowsy State?

Both the tranquil state and the drowsy state are likely to appear in practice of Qigong exercises. We have to strictly distinguish the one from the other because the two have different physiological bases and produce different effects. The state of tranquility brought about by doing Qigong exercises refers to the peculiar state of the cerebral cortex when one is in the process of doing Qigong exercises. If one is in such a state, the benign excitative focus brought about subjectively by the mental power is in a dorminant position and all the other parts of the cerebral cortex are in a state of inhibition under the control of the mental power. This helps the brain to work in an orderly condition. But the drowsy state refers to the stage at which the cerebral cortex is when it is passing from a sober state into the sleeping state. This stage is characterized by a wide-range inhibition of the cerebral cortex.

When a man has fallen into the state of tranquility in Qigong exercises, he will feel that he is clear-headed and that there are fewer distracting thoughts. And his reflex to the stimulation from the outside world is weakened. After he has stopped doing Qigong exercises, he feels that he is much more high-spirited, vigorous and energetic than he was before. But if he is in a drowsy state, he will feel dizzy and he will be clear-headed at one time and unconscious at another. Sometimes, there are few distracting thoughts while sometimes he is temporarily dreaming and sometimes he will suddenly rise from the sleeping state. After he has stopped doing Qigong exercises, he will feel both mentally exhausted and that his whole body is aching.

One should be very careful in doing Qigong exercises and try to analyze in a detailed way what he feels in a state of tranquility. He should develop his ability in enhancing the degree of tranquility. If he finds himself to be in a drowsy state, he should make adjustment at once so as to rouse himself from it immediately.

185. What Are the Factors That Usually Affect One When One Is Trying to Enter the State of Tranquility?

There are many factors which may affect one when one is trying to enter the state of tranquility. On the whole, these factors can be divided into two categories. One category is helpful to the formation of the state of tranquility and the other hinders it. When one is doing Qigong exercises, he should make the best use of the favourable factors and try to get rid of as many disadvantageous factors as possible so that one can go on smoothly with his Qigong exercises and keep himself in the state of tranquility.

The factors which are helpful to the formation of the state of tranquility are as follows:

Quiet surroundings and soft light can help to diminish new and unfamiliar factors which stimulate the cerebral cortex, and, as a result, the formation of the state of tranquility will become easier.

If one does Qigong exercises in a room which is kept at a moderate temperature and where the air is fresh or if he is doing the exercises outdoors, he will often feel relaxed, carefree and clear-headed. This is of some importance to the formation of the state of tranquility.

The ease of the mind and a cheerful mood can make one feel calm and peaceful. This is also advantageous to the formation of the state of tranquility.

It is essential to the formation of the tranquil state that one masters the correct ways of doing Qigong exercises and the main points concerning the movements in Qigong exercises. If one does the exercises in the proper way, proceeds in an orderly way and advances step by step, he will be able to avoid detours and achieve the expected effect of falling into the tranquil state.

It is also necessary that one has confidence when doing Qigong exercises. Qigong therapy is a treatment of disease by the patient himself. It is only when one exercises his own subjective initiative and does the exercises carefully and manages to get rid of distracting thoughts can one successfully enter the tranquil state.

The factors which hinder the formation of the tranquil state are as follows:

When one is under a heavy mental burden, he will often feel upset and there will be many distracting thoughts. This is unfavourable to the formation of the tranquil state.

If one is overanxious for quick results and fails to exercise his own mental power in a proper way or, if he tries too consciously to sustain a particular vision and tries too hard and too consciously to enter the state of tranquility, he will feel strained and excited instead. This hinders him from entering the state of tranquility.

Pains caused by diseases upset people and cause physical discomfort. They are malignant stimuli and surely hinder a man from entering the state of tranquility.

If one does Qigong exercises in an improper posture, fails to breathe smoothly and is not able to concentrate his mind, he will surely fail to enter the tranquil state.

Besides, one who is better cultivated can manage to enter the state of tranquility more easily than one who is not well cultivated. Judging from a man's mental constitution, one who has good self-control enters the state of tranquility easily while one who is easily excited has difficulty in entering such a state. Other factors such as age and sex also have influence over the process of trying to enter this state. Anyhow, so long as one has confidence, he tries hard enough to master the main points concerning Qigong exercises and diminishes the distracting thoughts gradually, he will finally achieve the effect of entering the state of tranquility as one goes on with his Qigong exercises.

186. What Is to be Done If One Cannot Enter the State of Tranquility?

Failure to enter the state of tranquility refers to the fact that one fails to concentrate his mind and cannot enter the state of tranquility. The more eagerly one wants to enter this state, the more difficult it is for him to do so. It is because that the great wish itself to enter this state is a distracting thought and it may cause the cerebral cortex to be nervous and excited. Physiologically speaking, this is similar to what a patient of insomnia experiences. The more eagerly he wishes to fall asleep, the less chance there is for him to manage it. To enter the tranquil state, it is necessary for a man to keep doing Qigong exercises for quite a long period of time besides mastering the correct ways of doing the exercises. A man who has just taken up Qigong exercises naturally has difficulties in entering the tranquil state because on the one hand it is not long before he took up Qigong exercises and on the other hand he is overanxious for quick results, which causes many distracting thoughts. When a man is faced with this kind of difficulty, he should not be too worried. Neither should he be overanxious for quick results. On the contrary, he should be patient when doing Qigong exercises and advance step by step. It will not be long before the distracting thoughts diminish and he naturally manages to enter the state of tranquility.

Some people who are experienced in Qigong exercises may also find themselves being disturbed by many distracting thoughts and they will be so greatly upset that they fail to enter the state of tranquility. At this moment, they should stop doing the exercises at once and try to find out the cause. Things such as noisy environment, inappropriate temperature, anxiety, pains and discomforts caused by diseases, improper ways of doing the exercises, irregular breathing and being hungry or overfed will hinder one from entering the state of tranquility. One should try to eliminate such a cause. When there are more than two factors which hinder one from entering the tranquil state, he should decide which is the major factor that causes more trouble and try to eliminate it before getting rid of the others so as to reach the state of tranquil state and achieve curative effects.

187. What Are the Common Methods Used To Help One Reach the Tranquil State?

People who practise Qigong exercises all take it as an important step in Qigong to reach the state of tranquility. Summing up the methods used and the clinical instructions given as well as the experiences learned from practice both in the past and at present, we present to you some of them which are common in use for you to choose from.

The method of keeping the mind on something: To help himself enter the state of tranquility, one who does Qigong exercises often chooses to keep his mind on Dantian or the acupuncture point Yongquan. It means that one focuses all his attention on Dantian or the acupuncture point Yongquan when he is doing Qigong exercises so as to help himself to enter the state of tranquility.

The method of counting one's breath: When one is doing Qigong exercises, he may count the number of his own breath to a hundred or a thousand. A complete cycle of breathing is made up of one action of exhalation and one action of inhalation. This helps one to enter the state of tranquility.

The method of listening to one's own breath: This refers to the method of listening to the sound of the air coming in and going out when one breathes to help induce himself to fall into the state of tranquility. This method is adopted on the condition that one has mastered the method of counting the number of his own breath.

The method of following one's own breath: On the condition that one has mastered the method of listening to one's own breath, he may adopt the method of following his own breath with his mind when he inhales and exhales. This helps to induce him to reach the state of tranquility.

The method of imagining some beautiful scenes: When doing Qigong exercises, one may imagine some beautiful scenes unfolding before one's eyes. For example, the scene of the rising sun, the bright moon, a blue sky with some white fluffy clouds, great hills and beautiful waters, a vast stretch of sea, wonderful flowers and plants and verdant pine trees and sypress, etc..

The method of recalling to one's memory some pleasant sounds: It helps to induce one to fall into tranquility to recall to one's memory some soft and pleasant music, songs or the rhythmic and pleasant ring of a bell, etc. when one is doing Qigong exercises.

The method of repeating some words silently: It means that one may choose and repeat silently some words with good meanings or the names for some parts of the body on which one keeps his mind on. For example, say words such as "relaxed", "pleasant" , "healthy", or Dantian or Yongquan, etc.. When one has fallen into tranquility, he will naturally forget to go on repeating such words. When distracting thoughts come back, one may use this method to eliminate them again.

The method of relaxation and calmness: This is a method of relaxing oneself in order to reach tranquility. During Qigong exercises, one may imagine that the different parts of his own body are becoming relaxed one after another (as in the method of relaxing all parts of one's body from head to foot or in the method of relaxing oneself following three lines). He may also think of tranquility when inhaling and of relaxation when exhaling, and repeat this cycle time and again to induce himself to fall into tranquility.

The method of keeping both one's mind and one's eyes on some part of one's own body: When one is doing Qigong exercises, he may keep both his mind and his eyes on his nose, and then let the line of sight pass over the nose to the navel or simply focus his mind's eye on the navel so that the line of sight, the nose and the navel are connected along the same line. This helps to induce one to fall into tranquility.

The method of using inducements: This refers to the method of inducing one to fall into tranquility by oneself or with other people's help. He may lay his hands on his lower abdomen and massage it with both of his hands or he may be induced to fall into tranquility with the help of suggestions from other people.

One may try out the above-mentioned methods while doing Qigong exercises and choose any one which is fit for oneself.

188. Which Way of Breathing Shall One Adopt When Doing Qigong Exercises?

There are many different ways of breathing and each of them is adopted to fit one of the many types of Qigong. For instance, there are abdominal respiration, thoracic respiration, deep respiration, holding breath respiration, breathing with large gulps of air coming in and out of the mouth, one inhalation and one exhalation, two inhalations and one exhalation, respiration imitating that of a fetus, respiration as if one were hibernating, natural respiration, and so on. One may choose one of these ways of breathing for his Qigong exercises according to his own habit or to the particular diseases he has. For example, a patient who suffers from stomach diseases or the diseases of the intestines may adopt the method of abdominal respiration while a patient of some heart disease or disease of the lung may adopt the method of thoracic respiration. Each of the various methods of respiration has its own merits. But if there is not a coach to instruct you, you had better adopt the method of natural respiration and gradually pass on to other ways of breathing. When doing Qigong exercises, people should on the whole inhale through the nose and exhale through the mouth for it is not only people's general habit to breathe in this way but it is also in keeping with the demand of physiology and health. A beginner in Qigong should not adopt the method of holding-breath respiration, or the method of respiration imitating that of a fetus, or the method of respiration as if one were hibernating. Otherwise, dangerous and harmful deviations may occur. These methods are only fit for those who have laid down a rather solid foundation in Qigong exercises and those who have achieved a rather advanced command of the skills of Qigong and reached a rather advanced stage in the exercises.

189. Which Posture Shall One Adopt for Doing Qigong Exercises?

The postures for Qigong exercises include lying posture, sitting posture, and standing posture. One may also do Qigong exercises while walking. One should decide on a particular posture according to the kind of illness he has, the stage of his illness and his own physical constitution, his age and his habits and customs.

Decision made according to the type of illness: A patient of gastroptosis had better adopt a lying posture; a patient of hypertension had better adopt a sitting posture; a patient of bronchitis had better adopt either a sitting or a standing posture; a patient of neurasthenia had better adopt a standing posture; and if a patient of lung cancer is still rather strong in physical constitution, he had better choose to walk while doing Qigong exercises. Those patients who are rather weak had better adopt a lying or a sitting posture and gradually go on to adopt a standing posture or choose to do Qigong exercises while walking.

Decision upon the posture based on the stage of illness: Those patients who are seriously ill, weak or have even been confined to the bed for a long time had better adopt a lying posture. A patient whose illness is less serious and who is comparatively less weak had better adopt a sitting posture or a half-standing posture. Those patients whose illness is not serious at all and who are strong in physical constitution had better adopt a standing posture at the middle position or low position.

Some patients who are seriously ill, such as patients of gastric haemorrhage and patients of hepatomegaly and ascites and those patients who have been confined to the bed should generally first practise the static Qigong in lying posture until they have regained physical strength and health to some extent. Then he may begin to practise dynamic Qigong or the dynamic-and-static-combined Qigong.

Decision upon the posture based on the type of diseases: Static Qigong and dynamic Qigong produce different effects. Therefore, people should decide upon one of the types of Qigong according to the kind of disease they have. For instance, patients with gastroptosis or nephroptosis had better practise static Qigong in the lying posture. Patients with coronary heart disease or hypertension should generally practise static Qigong in the sitting posture and in a relaxed manner. Patients with arthritis or patients with cancer in the first stage of the disease should generally practise dynamic Qigong. They should especially practise Qigong Walking Exercise.

Of course, one should also choose between dynamic and static Qigong according to his own physical constitution and health. For instance, patients who suffer from the same kind of disease of cancer of the lung should choose between various types of Qigong according to their own physical constitution and health. Those who are in the early stage of the disease are physically stronger, and therefore should choose to do Qigong exercises in a walking-at-a-quick-pace manner while those who are in the advanced stage of the illness should choose to do Qigong exercises in a walking-at-a-slow-pace manner or choose to practise static Qigong.

Decision upon the posture based on one's age and one's liking: Young people who like to move round may practise dynamic Qigong or static-and dynamic-combined Qigong. Old people usually like to be quiet and remain still may practise static Qigong or dynamic-and-static-combined Qigong as well.

Decision upon the posture based on habits and customs: In ancient China or India, for instance, people were used to sitting cross-legged or with one of the legs crooked. But Japanese people are used to sitting in a kneeling posture.

Decision upon the posture based on whether one feels comfortable or not: Whatever posture you adopt, you should keep on doing Qigong exercises in the posture you have chosen if you are comfortable to do the exercises in the chosen posture. If you feel uncomfortable to do the exercises in the posture you have chosen and if you have tried this posture out for a period of time and still feel uncomfortable, you should choose some other postures.

190. What Method Shall One Use to Concentrate His Mind While Doing Qigong Exercises?

Concentrating one's mind in Qigong exercises is also called adjusting one's mind. There are a variety of methods to concentrate one's mind. There are, for example, the method of repeating some words silently, the method of relaxing oneself, the method thinking of being quiet when inhaling and being relaxed when exhaling, the method of counting one's own breath, the method of keeping one's mind on some particular vision or object, the method of directing the movement of the Qi and the method of repeating some words or ideas which have positive meanings. Whatever method one chooses, he should make the decision according to his disposition and the type of disease he has. For instance, people who can manage to enter the state of tranquility easily may choose the method of keeping the mind on some particular vision or object; people who are likely to be disturbed by distracting thoughts may choose the method of repeating silently some words or ideas which have positive meanings. So far as the type of disease is concerned, patients with cardiopathy or hypertension may choose the method of relaxing oneself;patients with diseases of the stomach or the intestines may choose the method of keeping the mind on Dantian; patients with diseases of the liver or the spleen may choose the method of directing the movement of the Qi; and patients with neurasthenia should usually choose the method of counting the breath or the method of thinking of being quiet when inhaling and being relaxed when exhaling. Therefore, we say that we should make the decision upon a posture on the basis of differentiation of the types of diseases.

191. Which Kind of Qigong Exercises Is Better, the Static Qigong Or the Dynamic Qigong?

There are two major types of Qigong, the static type and the dynamic type. Qigong exercises in the lying, or the sitting, or the standing posture belong to the type of static Qigong. Qigong exercises done in a walking manner, the Five-Animal Play and Taiji Qigong, Shiduanjin (ten-section) Qigong Exercise, and the Spontaneous Moving Qigong Exercise belong to the dynamic Qigong. The distinction between dynamic and static Qigong is based on whether the limbs move or not in Qigong exercises. As a matter of fact, static Qigong does not imply complete motionlessness. On the contrary, it is motionless seen from the outside while dynamic in the inside. For instance, one who is practising the Qigong exercises in the standing posture seems to be standing in a place fixedly without moving a bit. But actually, he will feel hot and be sweating all over after having done this kind of Qigong exercises for a while. And the motion of his viscera such as the heart, lungs, liver, stomach, kidney, etc. are strengthened. Therefore, static Qigong is only relatively motionless in comparison with dynamic Qigong. When choosing between static and dynamic Qigong, one should also base his choice on the type of disease he has, the stage of his illness, his physical constitution and his age. For example, patients who are weak and seriously ill should practise static Qigong first and then proceed to dynamic Qigong. Sometimes, such a patient can also practise static Qigong and dynamic Qigong at the same time. Static Qigong and dynamic Qigong have their own respective merits and we cannot pass a simple judgement on either of the two types of Qigong by saying which is good and which is not.'We have to choose from the two according to particular conditions.

192. Which Is Better, To Close Eyes Or To Open Them When Doing Qigong Exercises?

Generally speaking, when you are practising the Intrinsic Nourishing exercise or the Relaxing Qigong Exercise, you had better close your eyes gently so that the optic nerve will not be stimulated and the cerebral cortex will not be excited. In this way one is able to concentrate his mind and it is possible for him to reach the state of tranquility. Since it is one of the important steps in Qigong exercises to reach the state of tranquility, the significance of closing the eyes (to shut out the stimulation from the outside) is quite remarkable.

Sometimes, some people fail to concentrate their attention in Qigong exercises by closing the eyes. On the contrary, they are disturbed by many distracting thoughts. When one is faced with such a problem, he may close his eyes slightly, leaving a very narrow passage for the light to come in. This helps one to concentrate his mind. Besides, sometimes some people feel sleepy when doing Qigong exercises. They may also close their eyes slightly and leave a very narrow passage for the light to come in and for himself to gaze at a point of his own body.

This may help to prevent and eliminate sleepiness.

When one is practising the Qigong exercises in a standing posture and is employing the method of repeating some words or ideas which have positive meanings, he shall usually do the exercises with his eyes open. When one is practising dynamic Qigong or dynamic-and-static-combined Qigong, he must keep his eyes open. Therefore, one bases his choice between opening and closing his eyes on the type of the Qigong exercises he is doing and on his own particular needs.

193. How Long and How Often Should One Practise Qigong?

People should decide how long they should do Qigong exercises each time and how often they shall do the exercises each day according to their respective constitutions (those who are strong may do it for a longer period of time and comparatively more often in a day and vice versa), their respective ages (those who are younger can do it for a longer period of time and more often and vice versa), the respective stages of their diseases (those people whose illness is less serious can practise it for a longer period of time and more often and vice versa). In brief, one should base his decision about the length and number of time of Qigong exercises on the differentiation of his particular diseases and cases and it is hard to make any generalization concerning the length and number of times of Qigong exercises. Anyhow, it should be remembered that one should always advance step by step and lengthen the time and increase the frequency as well as the intensity of Qigong exercises gradually. The general principle for one to keep in Qigong exercises is that he should limit the length, the number of times and the intensity of Qigong exercise to such an extent that one feels cheerful and relaxed after having done the exercises (that is quite natural, anyhow, for those who have just taken up Qigong exercises to feel that their muscles are aching after doing the exercises each time). Those people who are ill when doing Qigong exercises should especially avoid overstraining themselves. When people who are ill have recently taken up Qigong exercises, they should avoid practising the exercises too hard. Otherwise, they will be exhausted and the consequences will be bad.

Usually, one should do the exercises twice a day, once in the morning and the other in the evening. At the beginning one should usually do the exercises for 10 — 20 minutes each session. Later on, it may be prolonged to 40 — 60 minutes each session. The frequency and the intensity of Qigong exercises should also be increased gradually. It will be better for one to do the exercises half an hour before or after the meal. Those who are physically stronger may do the exercises for a longer period of time each time and do it more often each day. But it does not imply that the longer, the better or the oftener, the better. One should, anyhow, do the exercises to such an extent that one is not overstrained. So long as the posture and the methods adopted are correct and one keeps on doing the exercises, remarkable effect will be achieved.

194. What Preparations Shall One Make for Qigong Exercises?

Preparations before Qigong exercises are meant to make it easier for one to start Qigong exercises and to help one achieve the expected effects.

The preparations before Qigong exercises are as follows:

One should first be mentally prepared for the Qigong exercises one is going to do. It means that one should first calm down and stop doing or thinking about what one had been doing or thinking up to that time.

He should choose a comparatively quiet place and the place should not be too bright whether it is indoors or outdoors. There shall be fresh air in the place and it should be convenient for the air to circulate. But one should be protected from being got in draught. He should keep warm so as to avoid catching cold.

A bed, or a chair and a suitable site should be prepared for one to do the exercises and they should be as comfortable as possible.

The site one chooses for Qigong exercises should be away from great noise.

One should take off his coat, loosen his belt and take the hard objects out of his pockets and put them aside.

Before beginning to do the exercises, one should defecate or urinate if necessary.

195. What Cautions Should One Bear in Mind About Doing Qigong Exercises?

When one is doing Qigong exercises, he should take a note of the following things:

One should do the different sets of the exercises in meeting with special demands and points for attention set for each different set of exercises.

All the postures in the exercises should be comfortable, correct and one should keep a smiling expression when doing the exercises. Every part of his body should be as relaxed as possible, especially the muscles on his forehead. He should breathe in a natural way and his breath should be light, regular, thin, long and slow. He should avoid making especially great efforts to lengthen or shorten his own breath consciously.

He should exercise his mental power lightly, slowly and gently and avoid making especially great efforts consciously to retain various kinds of sensations.

If one is suddenly struck with a cry or a big noise, he should not be nervous. He should ignore it and go on doing the exercises or gradually proceed to the end of the exercises so as to prevent harmful and dangerous deviations caused by sudden surprise.

196. What Are the Good Effects That Occur After Qigong Exercises?

Those who have managed to do the exercises well receive good effects after the exercises.

When one is doing the exercises, his upper limbs or even his whole body become warm and numb and he feels bloated in the upper limbs or even all over his body. He also feels as if some ants were crawling under his skin, and he feels as well that some muscles are trembling. After the exercises, he feels clear-headed, cheerful, energetic, relaxed and his physical strength is increased.

After the exercises, he also feels that his gastric peristalsis is strengthened. His appetite is improved. He eats more than he did before and his digestive function is bettered.

After the exercises, he feels calm and it becomes easy for him to fall asleep.

Those who were originally fat lose weight and their physical constitution becomes normal after the exercises.

After the exercises, their limbs coordinate with one another better, the flexiblity of their limbs is improved and they walk more briskly.

197. Must One Do the Closing Movement to End a Qigong Session?

Whatever kind of Qigong exercises one does, either dynamic Qigong, or static Qigong, or dynamic-and-static-combined Qigong, one must make the ending movement in their Qigong exercises well. If one pays adequate attention to the ending movement in Qigong exercises and do it well, it will help him to achieve better results and meanwhile it enables one to prevent the occurence of harmful deviations. Therefore, it is very important to make the ending movement well. For instance, the last few movements in the kind of Qigong exercises practised in a still and sitting posture are carried out by laying the palms of one's hands on Dantian for some time before one ends the exercises. When one is practising the Qigong exercises in the standing posture, he usually ends his exercises by gradually straigthening his legs and meanwhile he raises his hands with palms facing the sky and finger s facing one another in order. At the same time, he should inhale. When he has raised his hands to the front of his neck, he turns over his hands so that his palms face the ground. Then he gradually lowers his hands and at the same time he exhales. He should repeat these actions in a complete cycle for 3 — 5 times. When one is practising the dynamic-and-static-combined Qigong, he usually ends his exercises by rubbing the palms against each other until they are warm and then rubbing his face and head with his palms several times.

If one carries out the ending movement in Qigong exercises in a good way, he will feel comfortable and relaxed after the exercises and he will also be able to achieve good results.

198. Is It Necessary for One to Focus His Mind on Dantian and Adopt Abdominal Respiration in All Kinds of Qigong Exercises?

Some people think that one should keep his mind on Dantian and adopt the method of abdominal respiration no matter what kind of Qigong exercises he does. Such an opinion is incomplete and is, therefore, incorrect.

It is of course important to keep one's mind on Dantian. Some people who are weak can increase the vital energy in them by practising the skill of keeping their minds on Dantian. Abdominal respiration is important, too. People who have diseases of the stomach or the intestines may strengthen their gastric peristalsis by putting into practice the method of abdominal respiration. They are both good for one's health. But there is a great variety of Qigong exercises. There are many different postures and different ways to help one to concentrate one's mind and many different ways of breathing. So far as keeping one's mind on some objects or visions is concerned, there are two major ways, one is to keep one's mind on some external scene and the other is to keep one's mind on some internal scene (that refers to some part of one's own body). When one adopts the latter method, one should determine which acupuncture point he should keep his mind on. In terms of breathing, besides abdominal respiration, there are natural respiration, thoracic respiration, deep respiration, holding breathing and breathing which imitates that of a fetus, and so on. In brief, one should determine the place to keep his mind on and the method of respiration on the basis of differentiation of the types of diseases, the stages of illness, the degree of tranquility and his own habits and customs. For instance, patients with hypertension had better choose the acupuncture point Yongquan to keep his mind on and patients with pulmonary emphysema had better adopt the method of thoracic respiration.

199. How Long Shall One Keep on Doing Qigong Exercises Before One Is Able to Emit the "External Qi"?

Many people are interested in being able to emit the "external Qi" because the "external Qi" can be used to cure other people's diseases without touching them physically and it can set some apparatuses in motion without touching them, too. Therefore, many people tend to ask: will the adults be able to emit 'external Qi' after they have learned Qigong exercises? How long shall people keep on doing Qigong exercises before they are able to emit 'external Qi'? We think that it is better for people to begin to do the exercises at about the age of ten so as to develop the ability to emit the "external Qi". Although it is also possible for people who start doing the exercises at an older age to obtain the ability to emit the "external Qi", it takes a longer period of time for them to obtain such an ability and the amount of the "external Qi" they can emit is comparatively smaller. But it is really very good to the health of the adults if they practise the skills which will enable them to emit the "external Qi".

It is not easy to tell how long one should go on doing Qigong exercises to be able to emit the "external Qi". It depends on how hard one does the exercises. It also depends on his age, his health, the original foundation he has laid for Qigong exercises. It also depends on whether he does the exercises in a correct way or not. Generally, it takes a man about 3 years to achieve the ability to emit the "external Qi". But there are some people who begin to feel the movement of the Qi inside his own body after 2 — 3 months' training. But he should not try to emit the "external Qi" out of curiosity. Because in nine cases out of ten, they will fail, and moreover, they will impair their own health if they do so. For instance, once a man who took great interest in Qigong exercises tried to emit the "external Qi" only after practising the skills of emitting the "external Qi" for less than a month. As a result, he failed. Moreover, he damaged his own vitality and always felt tired after trying to do so. He was confined to the bed for a week.

Therefore, we think that people should at least go on doing Qigong exercises for 2 — 3 years in order to be able to emit the "external Qi" without doing any harm to his own health. And we believe it to be necessary for one to be tested with some particular apparatuses to confirm that he is able to emit the "external Qi" before he really does so for clinical purposes. We also hold that the major purpose of one's practising the skills of emitting the "external Qi" is to build up his own physique instead of using the "external Qi" to cure other people of their diseases because a kind of medical apparatus designed on the basis of bionics has already been developed to replace human beings in performing the task of emitting the "external Qi".

200. What Should One Take Special Notice of When Practising the Qigong Skill of Emitting the "External Qi"?

When people are practising the Qigong skill of emitting the "external Qi", they should pay attention to the following things:

They should adopt a correct posture and be relaxed and should persist in doing so.

When they have adopted a correct posture, they may talk or listen to light and pleasant music. But they should not move any more.

When doing Qigong exercises, they should breathe naturally and adopt the method of saying some words which have benign meanings. They should avoid swearing or being angry.

They should not do Qigong exercises on an empty stomach. Neither should they eat too much before doing the exercises. They should have some hot drink instead before doing the exercises.

They should do some warming-up exercises before beginning to do the Qigong exercises. They should first practise the Qigong exercises in the standing posture in a low position with the palms facing the ground and each time they should do it for about an hour. After having practised this skill for a year, they may proceed to practising the skill of Flying Sword in the Sky. This kind of exercises should also last for a year. Then, they may practise the stepping movements imitating a dragon or an eagle.

When they have assumed the necessary posture and begun to do the exercises, they should go on naturally without making too great an effort to retain or pursue some particular sensations.

It is a good phenomenon to feel warm in the palms or to feel warm all over the body and even perspire a bit when one is doing Qigong exercises. But if one feels cold when doing the exercises, he should do the ending movement and then stop. He may resume the exercises the day after.

One should do the exercises for a proper length of time and the intensity of the exercises should be appropriate as well. When one has just taken up the exercises, he should not overstrain himself, otherwise, he will be too exhausted. It is natural that one's knee joints ache after one has done the exercises. But one should restrict the amount of

334

exercises. If the amount of exercises he does is too great, bad results will occur.

When one has just taken up the exercises, one should do the exercises for a comparatively shorter period each time and he should choose the less difficult skills to practise. The length of time and the degree of the difficulty of the exercises should be increased gradually and one should advance step by step.

After one has finished doing the exercises, he will perspire. But he should not have cold drinks or wipe away the sweat with a cold towel. Instead, he should wipe away the sweat with a hot towel and have hot drinks.

201. What Kind of Diet Is Suitable for A Man Who Practises Qigong?

Our ancestors held that people who practise Qigong should be on a vegetarian diet and that they should give up smoking and drinking. What our ancestors have said is correct in certain ways. It is known to all of us that many people who prefer a vegetarian diet and who live a regular life and do physical exercises are able to keep fit and enjoy longevity. We believe that it is good for people who practise Qigong to eat light food. However, it is also necessary that they increase to a proper extent the amount of nourishments they take. Human beings need such nutriments as sugar, fat, protein, vitamins and inorganic salt, etc.. Therefore, if they want to absorb various nutriments, they should take in fat and protein besides sugar and vitamins. People who practise Qigong should determine what kind of food they should eat more on the basis of differentiation of their diseases. For instance, patients of hypertension or coronary heart disease should eat more vegetables and take in less fat when they are practising Qigong; patients of anaemia or hypotension should take in more fat and protein besides sugar and vitamins during Qigong exercises; and patients of diabetes mellitus should take in less sugar during Qigong exercises.

People who practise Qigong must quit smoking because there are toxins such as nicotine in tobacco smoke. The purpose of doing Qigong exercises is to remove the toxins in the human body while smoking means to take in toxins. Therefore, smoking does harm to people who practise Qigong and they must be determined to give it up. Patients of rheumatic arthritis may drink a little wine or medical liquor every day.

In brief, people who practise Qigong should eat light food, take in various nutriments and give up smoking. These will be good to their health.

202. Is It Good to Do Qigong Exercises on An Empty Stomach Or Immediately After A Meal?

It is not good for one to do the exercises on an empty stomach. Nor is it good for him to start doing Qigong exercises immediately after a meal. Qigong exercises help to strengthen gastric and intestinal peristalsis whereby the digestion and absorption of the food is improved. This means a lot to patients who have diseases of the digestive system. When a patient is practising Qigong on an empty stomach, the peristalsis of his stomach and intestines is strengthened all the same. But comparatively speaking, his stomach and intestines are empty now. Therefore, he feels intense hunger. When he feels so, he should eat something immediately. Otherwise, it will be difficult for him to keep tranquil and to regulate his breath. So we may say that it is improper for one to practise the Intrinsic Nourishing Qigong Exercise on an empty stomach. But it is not proper to do the exercises immediately after a meal, either. It is because that one's stomach is full and heavily burdened immediately after one takes a meal. This also makes it difficult for one to regulate his breath, to keep tranquil and it causes one to feel uncomfortable as well. Therefore, we say that people had better avoid doing Qigong exercises either on an empty stomach or immediately after a meal.

203. What Good Do Qigong Exercises Do to Healthy People?

It is a common sense known to everyone that physical exercises help to build up one's health. But whenever the term physical exercises is mentioned, people are likely to think of only running, jumping, playing ball games, mountaineering, swimming and playing gymnatics which require the movement of the limbs help to build up people's health. Such an opinion is incomplete. As a matter of fact, Qigong exercise is also a kind of physical exercise and it helps to improve people's health, too. Static Qigong is particularly devoid of visible movement of the limbs. But in static Qigong, viscera are all in motion. This kind of movement is called internal movement. Qigong exercise is a kind of physical exercise for medical purpose and it is unique to the Chinese nation.

The function of Qigong is to promote the intrinsic subjective initiative of the human organism, to dredge the main and collateral channels, to regulate the blood and vital energy, to support the healthy energy and to eliminate the evil factors and to build up people's health. It can also serve to adjust the function of the cerebral cortex, to build up the resistance of the human organism against the attack of diseases, to remove the imbalance between the human organism and its surroundings and to promote the adaptability of the human organism to the surroundings. Therefore, both ill people and healthy people can practise Qigong. Those who are ill may be cured of their diseases by doing Qigong exercises and those who are healthy may preserve their health and prolong their life span by doing the exercises. Clinical practice has proved that many people who had originally suffered from diseases for a long time regained health by doing the exercises and those who were weak though not ill become stronger and those who were strong become ever stronger and more healthy.

Healthy people have good physique and rather great physical strength. They may, therefore, adopt the standing posture in the low position or the middle position when practising static Qigong and many of them can practise dynamic Qigong or dynamic-and-static-combined Qigong. Qigong exercises add pleasure to people's life and help to build up people's health.

204. If One Fails to Keep His Mind on A Chosen Object, Will the Effect of Qigong Exercises Be Impaired?

When practising Qigong, a beginner may often be faced with such a problem: sometimes, the more he wants to be tranquil, to keep his mind on Dantian and to concentrate his mind, the more distracting thoughts he has. For example, when one is trying to keep his mind on Dantian, he manages it at this moment and fails at another and distracting thoughts arise and disturb him in consequence. This of course impairs the effect of Qigong exercises and the curative effect. But after a period of exercises (2 — 3 weeks), this phenomenon will occur less often and disappear gradually. The effects vary with the degrees of persistency of the distracting thoughts and with the degrees of its influence over the state of tranquility.

In brief, distracting thoughts have bad effects on Qigong exercises more or less and if one fails to keep his mind on a chosen object, the effect of Qigong will certainly be impaired as well.

205. Can People Practise Several Types of Qigong Exercises At One Time?

Generally speaking, a patient of chronic disease should choose one or two types of Qigong exercises to practise in order to improve his health. The one or two types of Qigong exercises should suit the state of his health and he should cling to the type of Qigong exercises he has chosen so as to achieve good results.

If he learns several types of Qigong exercises at one time when he has just taken up Qigong and when he has not yet reached a proper stage, harmful and dangerous deviations will occur. In particular, disorder of the Qi will occur. If one has practised Qigong for a considerable period of time and has reached a proper stage, he may start practising several types of Qigong exercises at the same time. But even so, he should not be practising too many types of Qigong exercises at the same time and he should pay special attention to the time of Qigong exercises so that it is appropriate. For instance, he should practise Taiji Qigong early in the morning, the Qigong exercises in the standing posture in the afternoon and the Relaxation Qigong Exercise in the evening. Besides, some people who have practised several types of Qigong at the same time for a long period of time and yet do not have any uncomfortable feeling at all may continue to practise Qigong in the original way. But we hold that it is better for people to choose few types of Qigong exercises and try to do these few types of Qigong exercises well than to try too many types of Qigong exercises at one time.

206. Must One Finish Doing the Whole Set of Qigong Exercises When Practising the Eighteen-Section of Taiji Qigong?

Generally speaking, one should finish doing all the eighteen sections when he is practising the Eighteen-form of Taiji Qigong. By doing so, the different parts of one's body may all have some physical training and it is good to one's health. But some people have a weak physique and their illness is rather serious. They cannot finish all the eighteen sections at one go. They may choose to do a few of the sections of the exercises according to the state of their own health and the stage of their illness. For instance, patients with cardiopathy or pulmonary emphysema may do some movements such as Expanding Chest, churning up waves and billows and pigeon spreading wings, etc.. A patient whose back and waist are aching can choose to do some movements such as turning torso to look at the moon, Turning waist and pushing palms and dredging from the sea and looking at the sky, etc.. Patients with neurasthenia or neurosis may choose to do some movements such as holding a ball before the shoulder, wild-goose in flight and Waving like rainbow, etc.. In brief, a patient who cannot finish the whole set of the Eighteen-form of Taiji Qigong may determine which few forms of the exercises he should do according to the kind of disease he has, the stage of his illness and his own disposition, etc.. Good results may also be achieved by doing so.

207. What Other Kinds of Physical Exercises Can One Do in Combination with Qigong?

Some people think that one should give up other kinds of physical exercises when he is practising Qigong. It is wrong to think so. Because Qigong exercises were developed by the Chinese people during the long course of their fight against diseases and Qigong itself is a kind of physical exercises for medical purpose. And it is unique to the Chinese nation. Therefore, people can do other kinds of physical exercises when they are practising Qigong. However, one should determine what other kinds of physical exercises he could do according to the actual conditions. He may choose to take a walk, play ping-pong, play badminton, or to practise shadow-boxing or shadow-fencing, mountain-climbing or swimming. The amount of the exercises can either be decided by the doctor for the patients or by the patients themselves according to the patients' circumstances. But the time for Qigong exercises and that for other kinds of physical exercises might as well be arranged in such a way that each of them is done at a different time. For instance, one may do running exercises and practise shadow boxing in the morning and do Qigong exercises in the evening, or he may do Qigong exercises in the morning and other kinds of physical exercises in the afternoon. If one does the exercises in this way, they will not interfere with one another. On the contrary, they will complement one another and bring out the best in each other.

208. How Can One Coordinate Qigong Exercises with Taijiquan?

Both Qigong and Taijiquan (shadow-boxing) are means of building up one's physical strength and improving one's health. Therefore, people who practise Qigong may practise shadow-boxing as well. But they should make arrangement so that they do the two kinds of physical exercises separately because these two kinds of exercises should be done in different ways and demand different methods of respiration, different postures and different ways of using one's mental power. Besides, in these two different types of physical exercises, one's blood and vital energy circulate along different channels and move in different directions. For instance, one may practise shadow-boxing in the morning and Qigong exercises in the evening; or he may practise Qigong in the morning and shadow-boxing in the afternoon. If one does the exercises according to such schedules, Qigong and shadow-boxing will not contradict each other. On the contrary, they will complement each other and hence one's health improves more greatly. Those patients who are rather seriously ill, weak and who cannot stand up may practise Qigong exercises in a lying posture or sitting posture until his physical strength has become greater, his physique has been built and he has taken a turn for the better. Then he may begin to practise shadow-boxing at the same time when he is practising Qigong.

People who practise Spontaneous Moving Qigong Exercise may do without shadow-boxing because the movements in shadow-boxing have already been made spontaneously in the process of Automatic-movement Qigong exercises.

209. Does One Need A Coach for Qigong Training?

The advantage of having a coach to guide oneself in Qigong exercises is that one will be taught the correct posture and the correct methods so that he can avoid detours. If one does not have a coach to guide oneself, he will sometimes adopt inapproriate posture and methods. Then, he will not be able to achieve great effect although he has done the exercises for a rather long period of time. Besides, if one is instructed by a coach, he can prevent harmful and dangerous deviations. Clinical practice has proved that many side-effects will be produced if people do Qigong exercises in improper ways and if one does not correct himself immediately, harmful and dangerous deviations will arise. For instance, the Qi will gather at one place and its movement will be hindered; the disordered activities of the human organism cannot be stopped; one will feel dizzy, headache and in some parts of his body there will be a swelling feeling, pain and other discomforts. Thus, the curative effect is not achieved. On the contrary, one's health is impaired. But it is actually impossible for everyone who practises Qigong to have a coach. So some people have to study by themselves by reading books on the subject. But they must follow strictly the principles concerning Qigong exercises and keep in line with the correct methods; or they should go to a coach sometimes to seek advice in order to make corrections in time. Those people may also write to convalescent hospitals, clinics, or other kinds of medical institutions concerned to be taught by correspondence instead of being instructed by coaches in person. Of course, it is the best and more beneficial for those who can manage to call on experienced coaches to seek their instructions.

210. How Do People Choose Qigong Coaches for Themselves?

Qigong came into being in China tens of hundreds of years ago and it has been very popular with the public. There are many different schools of Qigong and a lot of Qigong coaches in China in different places such as hospitals, schools, factories, government institutions and physical training centers. How should one choose a coach for himself? We think it necessary for him to take into account the following things as he is choosing a coach for himself:

He should inquire to know how long the coach has been teaching Qigong and if he has been well acquainted with the basic knowledge of Qigong and if he has mastered rather well the skills of several types of Qigong.

The coach should have some basic knowledge of medicine. Such a coach will be able to give instructions to a patient and determine treatment on the basis of differentiation of diseases. Patients should be on guard against those people who deliberately mystify Qigong. Otherwise, harmful and dangerous deviations as well as malpractice will occur.

A patient should choose a coach who is particularly fit for himself. For instance, a patient who is fit to do static Qigong should choose a coach who is good at teaching Relaxation-and-static Qigong and the Intrinsic Nourishing Qigong Exercise; and a patient who is fit to do dynamic Qigong should choose a coach who teaches Taiji Qigong, the Five-Animal-Play and the Qigong Walking exercises. Thus, one may practise Qigong exercises with a definite purpose in view.

People should also choose coaches according to the different purposes they have in mind. For instance, those who practise Qigong for the purpose of preventing and curing diseases should choose a Qigong doctor to teach themselves and those who practise Qigong for the purpose of building up their physical strength and defending themselves against violence should choose a coach who majors in Qigong as a kind of martial arts or a coach belong to the school of Shao-lin Martial Arts.

In brief, one should choose a Qigong coach on the basis of his own particular needs and circumstances.

211. Is It Good for One to Change from One Type to Another Very Often When Practising Qigong?

It is not good for one to change from one type of Qigong to another very often. Because it is similar with the case of learning calligraphy. When one changes from one style of calligraphy to another before he has mastered the style he originally studied, he will surely fail to master either style. There are many different schools of Qigong and each school has its own theory, and its own particular methods. Each school has its own merits. The purpose is invariably to help build up one's health. But some people tend to follow any new coach that comes into their way and change their mind very often, hoping to learn many different types of Qigong. The result is that it leads them to nowhere and time is wasted. Moreover, bad effects result from the failure to grasp the essential points of each type of Qigong he studied. Therefore, he who takes up Qigong should be determined to study only one or two types of Qigong exercises which are fit for himself and persist in his practice with determination and confidence. In this way, he will soon achieve the desired effects. But if the disease he has makes it necessary for him to change to another type of Qigong, he may do it. Yet, he should give it careful consideration and he had better change to another type of Qigong exercises under the instruction of a doctor so that better effects can be achieved and harmful and dangerous deviations can be prevented.

212. What Should One Do When Feeling Sleepy During A Qigong Session in Lying Posture?

When doing Qigong exercises in a lying posture, some people are inclined to fall asleep and sometimes even into sound sleep. This is because one's eyes are closed when one is doing the exercises and because he is doing the exercises lying in a very quiet surrounding. Such a problem often occurs in patients who have a weak physique and tend to fall into inhibition easily. The effect of Qigong exercises is impaired and the formation of the "internal Qi" is hindered if one falls into sleep when doing Qigong exercises. So this problem must be solved. The method of solving the problem is that he closes his eyes slightly and naturally, leaving a very narrow passage for the light to come in. The light that comes in stimulates the optic nerves constantly and prevents him from falling into sleep. After a period of exercises, most people will get rid of the phenomenon of feeling sleepy and falling asleep when practising Qigong. If this problem can not be solved after one has practised the exercises for a long time, he may change from the lying posture of Intrinsic Nourishing Qigong Exercise to a sitting posture. Anyhow, it is good for a patient with neurasthenia or hypertension to feel sleepy when doing Qigong exercises. Such a patient should let himself fall asleep naturally because it is good for the treatment of his disease.

213. Can One Change from Lying on One Side to the Other When Doing Qigong Exercises in the Sideway Lying Posture?

When practising Qigong, a patient with gastric or intestinal disease often lies on his right side; a patient with liver disease often lies on his left side.

Can one change from one side to the other in one instance of practising Qigong in the posture of lying on his side? We say yes. Because one will feel tired after doing Qigong exercises in any single posture for some time. And those who fail to relax his muscles and joints will more easily get tired. He may change his posture or turn to lie on the other side if he feels tired. He must grasp the essential points concerning the movements in Qigong exercises and relax himself all over so that he does the exercises in a comfortable and natural way.

Beginners should not do the exercises for a long time each time. Anyhow, people should not change from side to side too often in one single session of doing the Qigong exercises in the posture of lying on his side. Otherwise, the degree of tranquility will be reduced and the effect of the exercises will be lessened.

214. Is It Better to Breathe Through the Mouth Than Through the Nose When Practising Qigong, Or Vice Versa?

There are many ways of respiration in Qigong exercises. For instance, one may breathe through the nose, or inhale through the nose and exhale through the mouth or vice versa. We think that it is better for people to breathe through the nose or inhale through the nose and exhale through the mouth. Because there is vibrissae, turbinate and upper and lower nasal passageways inside the nose. When one inhales air through his nose, these component parts of the nose filtrate the air, warm it up and moisten it; besides, respiration through the nose makes it easier for people to regulate their breath because they are accustomed to breathing through the nose. Therefore, breathing through the nose is more appropriate judging from either the demand of physiology and health or the demand of Qigong. If one is breathing deeply in Qigong exercises, he may inhale through the nose and exhale through the mouth. But it is not proper for him to inhale through the mouth and exhale through the nose because such a way of breathing is against the common sense concerning physiology and hygiene.

If there is something wrong with the nose and one cannot breathe through the nose, he may temporarily breathe through the mouth instead. But he should rid himself of the nasal disease as soon as possible so that he may breathe through the nose again.

215. Can One Stuff Up One's Ears with Cotton

When Practising Qigong in A Noisy Environment and Not Easy to Enter the State of Tranquility?

It is very essential that one should enter the state of tranquility if one is practising the Intrinsic Nourishing Qigong Exercise or the Relaxation Qigong Exercise. A quiet enviroment is helpful to a man when he tries to enter the state of tranquility, but it is not the decisive factor.

Usually people should choose a quiet place where he practises Qigong. In a quiet place, he may shut out strong and frequent stimulations from the outside world and this helps him to enter the state of tranquility. When it has been some time since one took up Qigong, one can soon reach the state of tranquility though he is doing the exercises in a noisy environment because a kind of conditioned reflex peculiar to people who have mastered Qigong has been developed. It is obvious that the degree of a man's Qigong accomplishment decides how soon he can reach the state of tranquility. Although noise from the outside can be diminished or totally shut out if he stuffs up his ears with materials such as cotton, but this does little good to a man in his developing his ability to reach the state of tranquility in a natural way. The reason is the same as that why it does little good for patient with insomnia to depend on sleeping pills to send himself into sleep. So we say that it is better for one to make use of his own mental power to induce the state of tranquility.

If one cannot manage to reach the state of tranquility after one has done Qigong exercises for a long time, he may try the method of keeping the mind on some chosen object, the method of relaxing himself, or the method of saying some words silently to induce the state of tranquility. If he fails to reach the state of tranquility though he has tried these methods, he may practise dynamic Qigong or dynamic-and-static-combined Qigong for a change. He may also try the method of saying some words which have good meanings.

216. Why Does One's Saliva Increase When Practising Qigong? What Significance Does It Have?

When one is practising Qigong, especially the Intrinsic Nourishing Qigong Exercise, the tip of his tongue rises and falls or the tongue is pressed against the palate. Such actions stimulate the endocrine system and causes the increase in the secretion of saliva. Besides, the digestive organs are more active. The peristalsis of the stomach and intestines become especially more active. This also causes the salivary gland to secrete more saliva. The most important reason for the increase in saliva is that the parasympathetic nerves are more excited when one is doing Qigong exercises. The increase in saliva in the process of Qigong exercises helps digestion and promotes appetite on the one hand, and on the other hand one can strengthen the stimulation of his own mental power to Dantian with the help of the sensation he feels when he swallows the saliva. So he should swallow his saliva instead of spitting it out when his saliva increases while doing Qigong exercises.

217. Shall One Regulate His Breathing Consciously If His Breath Is Irregular When He Adopts the Method of Natural Respiration?

The answer to the question is no. If one tries to regulate his breath consciously, it is no longer called natural respiration. Natural respiration is also called quiet breathing. Its requirements can be summed up in five words: light, regular, thin, slow and quiet. But it is not easy to fulfil the requirements in a short time. One should not be overanxious for quick results. He who exerts too great efforts to control his own breath will not achieve the result of regular and smooth breath. Instead, the consequence is that his breath will become irregular and difficult. When one adopts the method of natural respiration, he should breathe naturally, and based on this he may slightly induce his own breath to become light, regular, thin, slow and quiet only a bit consciously.

218. Some People Hold That the Tongue Should Be Pressed Against the Palate or Moved Up and Down, and Some Others Don't. Which to Follow?

Some people hold that when one is practising the Tonic Qigong, he should press his tongue against his palate and the purpose is to improve the circulation of the Qi along the Renmai and Dumai. They also hold that when one is practising the Intrinsic Nourishing Qigong Exercise, he should move his tongue up and down. The up-and-down movement of the tongue is one of the means in Qigong exercises and it serves the following two purposes: one is to help a man to concentrate his mind and the other is to excite the autonomic nerve to help improve the digestive ability of the digestive system and to enable it to make good conditioned reflexes. But we don't think that a beginner should press his tongue against his palate or move his tongue up and down when he is doing Qigong exercises. Because a beginner has not yet become skillful enough and he will become very nervous if he is asked to do so. This kind of nervousness hinders him from being relaxed and entering the state of tranquility. Another reason is that some people press their tongues against their palates in such an awkward way because they have not grasped the essential principle that the tips of their tongues become stiff or some other bad consequences follow.

219. Why Does Not One Need to Press His Tongue Against His Palate When Practising Standing Qigong Exercises in A Low Position?

When one is practising Qigong, especially the Intrinsic Nourishing Qigong Exercise, it is gradually required that his Qi is first able to travel through Shao Zhou Tian and then it travels through Da Zhou Tian. It is known to many people that if one presses his tongue against the palate, the Renmai and the Dumai can be connected and it helps the Qi to travel through Shao Zhou Tian. Therefore, when one is practising Qigong, he should press his tongue against the palate. Beside, he should also move his tongue up and down. The significance of doing so is that the up-and-down movement of the tongue helps one to concentrate his mind and helps to excite the nerves of the digestive system and it in turn improves the digestive function. But the Qigong exercises in the standing posture in a low position requires that the Qi goes through Da Zhou Tian directly without going through Shao Zhou Tian first. One only needs to do the exercises for some time according to the set rules concerning the postures, the methods of exercising his mental power and the method of respiration and then the Qi will be able to circulate in Da Zhou Tian. Therefore, when one is practising Qigong exercises in the standing posture in the low position, it is unnecessary for him to make his Qi circulate in Shao Zhou Tian. So it is also unnecessary for him to press his tongue against the palate and to move his tongue up and down.

220. Why Are the Movements of Raising and Lowering the Hands and Stretching Out and Drawing Back the Arms Preferred in Dynamic Qigong?

The action of raising and lowering the hands in dynamic Qigong is carried out in the following way: One places his palms in front of the lower abdomen and the fingers of the two hands face one another. The palms face upward. One raises his hands gradually and inhales at the same time. It is also called the raising of the Qi. And the purpose is to raise the refined substance (refined Qi); when the two hands are raised to the nose, one turns his hands over so that the palm face downward. Then he lowers his hands. This is also called the lowering of the Qi. The purpose is to lower the turbid substance (the turbid Qi). And it is the best that one manages to lower the turbid Qi consciously down to one meter below the earth surface. The action of stretching out and drawing back the arms is carried out in the following way: one places his hands in front of his chest in such a way that the backs of his hands face each other. Then he gradually stretches out his arms so that all the parts of his body limber up. Meanwhile, he should inhale as if to take in a large amount of the healthy energy from the universe; then he turns his hands over so that the palms of his hands face each other. And the two hands move toward the chest until they meet before the chest. At this moment, it seems that one has taken in the true energy and has kept it inside his body by exercising his mental power.

By making the movements of raising and lowering one's hands and stretching out and drawing back one's arms, the refined Qi is raised and the turbid Qi is lowered and the true energy is taken in and kept inside one's body. This makes him feel comfortable and cheerful and it is good to his mental as well as physical health. That is why dynamic Qigong often includes the movements of raising and lowering the hands and stretching out and drawing back the arms.

221. Is It Normal That Some People Have Difficulty in Sensing the Rise and Fall of the Abdominal Wall When He Adopts Abdominal Breathing?

A patient with stomach or intestine diseases is often advised to adopt the method of keeping his mind on Dantian and the method of abdominal respiration. The degree to which one senses the up-and-down movement of his own abdominal wall when he adopts the method of abdominal respiration varies from person to person. Some people sense it clearly while other people have difficulty in sensing it. This is quite normal. But it is wrong and incorrect for one to change his posture which was originally correct in order to be able to feel the movement of his own abdominal wall. For instance, he will bend forward or lean backward. But whether one senses the up-and-down movement of his own abdominal wall has little to do with Qigong exercises. So one does not need to trouble himself with it and to change his posture.

222. Why Is It Good to Say Some Words Silently When Practising Qigong? Why Can Not the Number of Words Exceed Nine?

When practising Qigong, people often say silently some phrases such as "song jing" (a phrase in Chinese and it means "relaxation and calmness"), "Yu kuai" (it means "happy"), "Quan shen shu fu" (it means "comfortable in every part of the body"), "Shen ti jian kang" (it means "healthy"), "Da jia dou lai lian Qigong" (it means "Join us in our Qigong exercises, everyone.") and "Wo men de jia ting he mu xing fu" (it means "our family is harmonious and happy"), etc.. The function of doing so is as follows:

Judging from the meanings of these phrases such as healthy, happy and relaxation, they are all positive stimulation. They produce the effect of inducing tranquility or the effect of making one feel healthy and happy.

One can diminish the distracting thoughts, concentrate his mind and lessen the degree of sleepiness by saying these expressions silently. Besides, the rhythm of these expressions also helps to regulate one's breath.

The experience of our ancestors and clinical observations tells us that the number of the words in each of such phrases should not exceed nine usually. Because one will feel headache, or he will feel stuffed in the chest, or his breath will become unsmooth and blocked, or he will

352

be anxious and upset if the action of inhalation or exhalation lasts for too long when one is trying to utter a complete and long expressions.

223. Which Is Important for Intrinsic Nourishing Exercise, to Regulate One's Breath or to Reach the State of Tranquility?

Regulating the breath and reaching the state of tranquility are of equal importance in the Intrinsic Nourishing Qigong Exercise. So patients who practise this kind of Qigong in order to cure his own disease should pay equal attention to both of them. Regulating the breath and reaching the state of tranquility interact on each other and they should not be treated as if they were separated from each other.

Reaching the state of tranquility helps one to breathe regularly and naturally; and when one's breath becomes regular and smooth, his mind will calm down and it helps him to reach the state of tranquility. Ancient Chinese people said: "Whenever one's breath is irregular, his Qi will be turbid. If one fails to regulate his breath, distracting thoughts will arise." When distracting thoughts arise, the effects of Qigong will be impaired. So it is obvious that both to regulate the breath and to reach the state of tranquility are two important steps in Qigong exercises and one should lay equal emphasis on both of them in doing Qigong exercises.

224. What Is Meant by Focusing Eyes on the Tip of the Nose? What Is Its Significance?

"To focus the eyes on the center of the nose" means to fix one's eyes on the tip of the nose lightly. The purpose is to concentrate one's eyes on something so that it is easier for one to concentrate his mind and reach the state of tranquility. But it also helps to prevent one from falling asleep when he is doing Qigong exercises. If one feels sleepy or falls into sleep when he is doing Qigong exercises, he should prevent himself from doing so by adopting the method of "focusing the eyes on the center of the nose". But he should not make too great exertion when he does so. Instead, he should focus his eyes on the tip of his nose only slightly so that he sees only a pale light.

The method of focusing the eyes on the tip of the nose is only one of the means employed in Qigong exercises and it does not fit everyone. If this method is put into practice in a correct way, it will be very beneficial; but if it is put into practice in an improper way, it will cause headache, dizziness and the feeling of fullness in the eyes, etc.. People who are not fit to use this method can use the method of closing the eyes slightly and keeping the mind on Dantian. Or he may use the method of saying some words which have positive meanings. By using other methods, he is spared the trouble of carrying out the rather difficult action of focusing his eyes on the tip of the nose and he also manages to avoid the side-effects that may be brought about by this movement.

225. What Is Meant by Turning One's Mind's Eye Inward? What Is Its Significance?

To turn one's mind's eye inward is also called "to look at a part of one's own body". That is to shut one's eyes or close one's eyes slightly and look at a part of one's own body such as a main channel, or a collateral channel, or an acupuncture point. After a period of such training, one can generally develop a kind of ability of seeing with his mind's eye the interior of his own body. That is to say that he seems to be able to see his internal Qi moving along the channels. This is just as what Li Shi-zhen said in his book *Research on the Eight Extra-channels*: "Only those who are able to turn their mind's eye can see the interior channels."

The significance of turning one's mind's eye inward is that it helps one to concentrate his mind, to reach the state of tranquility and to give the human organism certain stimulation so that some changes will be brought about in the human organism and the internal Qi is formed and circulates in the body more easily.

226. What Are Xing Gong and Ming Gong?

Qigong can be divided into dynamic Qigong, static Qigong and dynamic-and-static-combined Qigong according to the difference in the manners of movements adopted. Static Qigong may be further divided into Xing Gong and Ming Gong according to the difference in the purposes for practising the static Qigong and the difference in the methods one adopts when practising this kind of Qigong.

"Xing Gong" emphasizes the strengthening of the mental power. By mental power, we mean the consciousness of the brain and the mental activities. Xing Gong emphasizes the mental power, the cultivation of the ability to concentrate one's mind and the formation of the state of tranquility.

Ming Gong emphasizes the building up of the Qi. That is to emphasize the forming, storing and circulating of the Qi. And the greatest emphasis is on the replenishment of the essence and vital energy as well as the true energy inside the human body and the circulation of the "internal Qi" along the channels.

Although Xing Gong and Ming Gong differ from each other in that the methods of practising the two kinds of Qigong are different and each of the two kinds of Qigong lays particular emphasis on different things, they are closely related to each other. Both the Qi and the mental power should be promoted when one is practising Qigong. The Qi is the very foundation of Qigong and the mental power has the function of directing the movement of the Qi. Therefore, we hold that "both of the two should be promoted together." One should not only promote the Qi but also develop his mental power. The Qi should be directed by the mental power and the two of them should cooperate with each other and unite together so that the true energy, the Qi and the spirit are all promoted and diseases are prevented or cured and health is improved.

227. What Are the Six Magical Powers?

The term "the Six Magical Powers" was created by ancient Chinese people. They thought that Qigong exercises could enable people to see clearly, hear sharply and walk briskly. They also held that Qigong exercises could enable one to reach the state of caring about or caring for nothing and to obtain foresight. Such abilities mentioned above are called "the Six Magical Powers".

The Magical Eyesight: This is the ability to discern what ordinary eyes can not see. For instance, the ability to see with naked eyes the visceras of a human body or objects that are covered up.

The Magical Hearing: This refers to the ability to hear what ordinary ears cannot hear and the ability to hear a very faint sound at a far distance away.

The Magical Power of the nimble limbs: This refers to the nimble quality of the limbs and the ability to walk very fast as if one's body were weightless and one were riding the mist.

The Magical power of knowing things before others do: This refers to the ability to have inspiration which ordinary people do not have and the ability to foretell things.

The Magical Foresight: This is the ability to sense things which happened in the past or to foretell things that will take place in the future.

The Magical power of preventing the true energy, the Qi and the spirit from leaking out: When one has reached the advanced stage of Qigong, he will be able to be care-free, indifferent to whatever that is going on around him and even be able to forget about his own being. And the true energy and the Qi will not leak out.

The book entitled *Ancient Saints. Zhong-ni* tells about a story of a student of Lao Zi's. The student's name is Yuan Cang-zi. When he was practising Qigong, he was able to see things without looking at them and to hear without using his ears. He could see things or hear sounds that were very tiny and a long distance away. He had the ability of remote sensing. This is exactly the magical powers produced by Qigong exercises.

228. What Is Bio-Feedback? How Is It Different From Qigong Exercises?

Bio-feedback is based on conditioned reflexes. It is a means for helping people to control some of the biological functions of their organs. It is mainly meant to train people so that they develop the ability to control their organs' secretion and contraction. The concrete steps of doing so are as follows: an apparatus of bio-feedback is made use of to transform the minute changes in the biological functions into acoustic or optic signals. The signals are told (fed back to) the person being tested so that he knows the functional state which a part of his body is in. He then tries to control or adjust the state and turns it towards desired destination. And the result of the efforts made to control or adjust the state is transformed by the apparatus into acoustic or optic signals and fed back to him again so that he knows the changes going on fairly well and is able to make adjustments in response in time.

Qigong exercises is different from bio-feedback. Qigong exercises require that one's mind enters the state of tranquility and the central nerves are under subjective inhibition and in a relaxed state. But bio-feedback demands that the person being tested keeps a close watch over the increasing consolidation of the signals fed back to him. So there are no changes in the indicators of the above-mentioned subjective inhibition and relaxation.

Qigong exercises themself include the element of bio-feedback. If one does Qigong exercises with the help of bio-feedback, he may consciously adjust the relations between the biological systems inside his own body by using his own mental power. And he may get control of the time and intensity of Qigong exercises and remove the functional disorders successfully.

229. Is Qigong the Same Thing As Hypnotism?

Qigong is different from hypnotism.

Qigong is a legacy of the Chinese traditional medicine and it has a history of several thousand years. People can prevent or cure diseases and improve their own health by themselves through doing Qigong exercises. But hypnotism is adopted in western countries. The psychiatrist uses hypnotism (the stimulation of some words or hints) to achieve curative effects on his patients.

The Qi in Qigong is in fact a kind of material. Chinese traditional medicine teaches that "the Qi is the fundamental energy to maintain the life of human beings." Tests carried out with scientific apparatuses have also proved that the "external Qi" in Qigong is actually materials such as the infrared electromagnetic waves under the control of the rise and fall of the low frequency, magnetism and the static electricity. But hypnotism mainly depends on the words, hints used by the psychiatrist to stimulate the second signal system in order to achieve its curative effects.

Qigong therapy improves one's health on the basis that he persists in doing Qigong exercises to cultivate the potential energy inside himself. So in using Qigong therapy one is active. But hypnotism relies on the hints given by the psychiatrist. The patient is "manipulated" by the psychiatrist and is therefore in a passive state.

230. What Is the Difference between Hard Qigong and Keep-Fit Qigong?

Hard Qigong and Keep-Fit Qigong have something in common, but they also differ from each other in certain respects. What is common

358

to them is that they have the same final aim to build up people's health in different ways. They differ from each other in the methods adopted in practising the two kinds of Qigong and in the immediate purposes they serve respectively.

Hard Qigong is also said to be Qigong as a kind of martial arts. It is based on the training in the basic skills of Wushu (martial arts such as shadow-boxing, sword-play, etc.) and besides, it includes patting and striking, etc.. This helps the Qi to move to a certain part of the body and infuse the muscles and bones in this part with unusual resistence. It is said that this part can stand the attack of a knife or a spear and it can endure piercing, great pressure, fire and scalding. Therefore, hard Qigong can serve the purpose of a kind of performance as well as a means for self-defence. But Keep-Fit Qigong, as the term suggests, is meant to keep a person fit, to cure diseases and to prolong life. Although it is divided into three kinds — dynamic Qigong, static Qigong and dynamic-and-static-combined Qigong, the physical movements included in it are generally tender and slow and it is required that the man who is doing this kind of Qigong should reach the state of tranquility. Its effect of preserving people's health is achieved mainly through the promotion of the true energy and the Qi.

231. What Are the Wonderful Performances of Hard Qigong?

There are many wonderful performances of hard Qigong. In July 1979, many famous Qigong and Wushu performers in China gathered in the Xiyuan Guest House in Beijing and entertained some leaders in the State Council of China and some scientists as well with a lot of wonderful performances. For instance, in one of the items, an iron rod of one meter long and 4 centimeters wide was fixed. Mr. Hou Shu-ying, a Qigong performer, gathered all the Qi in his body and sent it to his hand. Then he struck the iron rod with his hand. The iron rod was broken into two. When he sent all his Qi to his forehead and struck the iron rod with his head, the iron rod broke into two immediately once again. But Mr. Hou Shu-ying's hand and head were not hurt a bit. Next, Mr. Hou gathered his Qi again and lay on the ground. 20 strong young men lifted 2 prefabricated concrete slabs (about 1.5 tons in weight) and placed them on him. His wife, Wang Shu-ying, jumped onto the slabs composedly and uttered: "Rise!" The concrete slabs waved back and forth against Mr. Hou Shu-ying's body when he was directing his Qi and the slabs rose and fell twice. At last, Wang Shu-ying jumped off and the young men lifted the slabs off Mr. Hou Shu-ying and he jumped to his feet. People could see that even the colour in his face didn't change a bit.

Another man from Guangdong Province, Mr. Zhu Biao gave a performance of "breaking stones with the hand and the fingers". He put on the ground a flat piece of pebble of 3 centimeters thick and 8 centimeters wide. Then he directed his Qi to the side of his palm and struck the pebble with great force. The pebble broke into two with a crash. Then, he directed his Qi to his index finger and his middle finger and struck another pebble with the two fingers. It broke into two as well.

A man from Hunan Province whose name is Zhao Ji-shu gave the performance of "Turnig on the sharp tip of a fork." After he had directed his Qi to the belly, he lay on his lower abdomen which was pressed against the tip of the fork. His whole body was supported and lifted off the ground by the tip of the fork. Moreover, he turned round on the tip of the fork. The pressure on the point of his lower abdomen which was pressed against the tip of the fork was about 3000 kg/cm^2.

Mr. Liu Jin-rong from Wuxi in Jiangsu Province held a broadsword in his hand and pressed its blade against his chest where he had gathered his Qi. Then he asked a strong man to hit repeatedly the back of the blade with a thick wooden stick about 5 kilograms heavy. The strong man became exhausted, yet the blade of the broadsword didn't even cut one milimeter into Mr. Liu's skin. Laying down the broadsword, Mr. Liu picked up a piece of steel plate 4 milimeters thick, 5 centimeters broad and 70 centimeters long. He struck his own side very violently for 3 times with the piece of steel plate and the piece of steel plate was bent into the form of an arch. Then, Mr. Liu directed his Qi to his head and struck his head with the same piece of steel plate. The piece of steel plate became straight once again.

Two Qigong performers from the Guangxi Zhuang Autonomous Prefecture, Mr. Dun Pei-zhi and Mr. Zhu Zhong-fu, gave the performance of "pushing against the sharp point of a spear with one's throat". Before giving the performance mentioned above, they gathered their Qi and struck each other's chest, belly and costal region with bare hands, bricks and three-section cudgels. After that, each of them directed his Qi to the throat and began to push with his throat the sharp point of a spear which had a sharp-pointed metal head on each end of the shaft. But the Qigong performers pushed so hard that the shaft which was made of tree bough was bent into the shape of a semicircle. It was estimated that the pressure on the throat of each of them was about 500 kg/cm^2. But their throats were not hurt a bit.

On July 1981, two Qigong performers, Mr. Shun Da-fa and Mr. Li Li-qun, gave a performance to the first group of students enrolled in the training course on "Chinese Qigong" as well as some foreign visitors from America, Japan and Peru and some other countries. The performance took place in Zhongshan Medical College in Guangzhou. The performance included items such as "Lying on the lower abdomen which is pressed against the sharp tip of a fork," "Pulling a car with the mouth", "Pushing an reinforcing bar with the throat", "Walking over glass" and "Sliding the hand on a flame-red iron chain". The wonderful performance won great applause from the audience.

How does it come about that the flesh and bones become harder than stone and steel? Qigong performers give the uniform answer that it is because the Qi is directed to a certain part of the body. Therefore, it is very necessary to make a study of the Qi in Qigong.

232. Shall Patients with Hypertension and Patients

with Hypotension Adopt the Same Methods in Qigong Exercises?

Patients with hypertension and patients with hypotension practise Qigong exercises for the same purpose of regaining health. But there are differences between the methods they adopt in doing the exercises. The differences are as follows:

The parts which they keep their minds on are different: A patient with hypertension should choose a place in the lower half of his body to keep his mind on when doing Qigong exercises. For instance, he should keep his mind on Dantian or the acupuncture point Yongquan, etc.. But a patient with hypotension should choose a place in the upper half of his body to keep his mind on. For example, he should keep his mind on the acupuncture point such as Danzhong and Baihui.

The Qi moves in different directions: When a patient with hypertension is practising Qigong, his Qi should move from the upper part of his body towards the lower part. For instance, it should move from head to foot. But when a patient with hypotension is practising Qigong, his Qi should move from the lower part of the body to the upper part. For instance, it should move from foot to head.

The last movements of the hand at the end of the exercises are different: When a patient with hypertension is coming to the end of the exercises, he raises his hands towards his chest, the palms of his hand facing upward. Meanwhile, he inhales. When the hands are raised to the chest, he turns over his hands so that the palms face downward and lower his hands. Meanwhile, he exhales. But when a patient with hypotension is coming to the end of his exercises, he does not turn over his hands and his palms still face downward when he raises his hands to his chest and meanwhile inhales. Then he lowers his hands and meanwhile he exhales. By doing so, he prevents his Qi from going upward. Therefore, the blood pressure will not rise too high.

233. How Shall One Regulate Sexual Life

During the Course of Qigong Training?

When a patient has done Qigong exercises for some time and has made some progress in Qigong, he will take a turn for the better and his health will be built up. And therefore his sexual desire will become stronger. So a person who is doing Qigong exercises often raises or should take into consideration the question that how he shall treat his own sexual intercourse. Our ancestors held that when one is doing Qigong exercises, he should be moderate in having sexual intercourse. Our ancestors were right to some extent in saying so. But when one is faced with the actual situation, it becomes rather difficult to get control of oneself. A husband and a wife who live in different places have little difficulty in stopping having sexual intercourse. But a couple who live together have rather great difficulties in controlling themselves. When a couple live together, they should decide how often they should have sexual intercourse according to their own health. Those who are comparatively stronger should not have sexual intercourse too often and those who are weaker should have as fewer sexual intercourse as possible. Those who are very weak and whose illness is very serious should make up their minds to refrain from having sexual intercourse for a certain period of time. In this way, Qigong exercises can produce better curative effects and the patient can regain health more quickly.

When a patient has a strong sexual desire in the period of time when he does Qigong exercises, he should remind himself that strong impulse will make his illness become more serious. When one is doing Qigong exercises, he should concentrate his mind and get rid of distracting thoughts. In order to get rid of the sexual impulse, he may move to another place to do the exercises or change the methods of doing the exercises. For instance, he may go out of the room and do the exercises outdoors or he may replace static Qigong with dynamic Qigong or with the dynamic-and-static-combined Qigong so that he may continue doing the exercises and achieve better results.

Besides, the husband and the wife should be considerate towards each other and coorperate with each other. The husband or wife who is healthy should especially take the health of his or her spouse and their mutual happiness into consideration and refrain from demanding sexual intercourse for some time or have fewer sexual intercourses with his or her spouse. This is the correct attitude toward sexual intercourse.

234. How Shall One Do Qigong Exercises When He Is Travelling by Train Or by Sea?

One may practise Qigong even when he is travelling by train or by sea. Those who are sitting may do the exercises in the sitting posture and those who are lying in bed may do the exercises in the lying posture. This is a vigorous means for relaxing oneself when a traveller is mentally or physically tired. Usually, he should adopt the Relaxation Qigong Exercise. When one is trying to reach the state of tranquility, he should be prepared for sudden and big noise which often appears on a train or a ship. And he should not be too deep in tranquility. Otherwise, he will be frightened by big and sudden noise such as that made by siren and he will be greatly harmed.

If one can manage to do Qigong exercises when travelling by ship or by train and achieve the desired results, it means that he has obtained the ability to adapt himself to stimulations from various kinds of environments. If so, he will achieve even better results when he is practising the exercises in a quiet environment.

235. Can A Woman Do Qigong Exercises During Menstruation?

Women may do Qigong exercises during menstruation. But some women's menstruation change after they have done Qigong exercises. For instance, the period of menstruation shortens or the amount of menstruation increases. Such phenomena are caused by keeping the mind on Dantian because the mental power directly stimulates the womb. Besides, observations of the blood flow after Qigong exercises show that the blood flow of some women increases by 30% when they adopt the method of keeping the mind on Dantian. In order to eliminate such phenomena, they may adopt the following methods:

Lessen the stimulation on Dantian by replacing the method of keeping the mind on Dantian with the method of saying some words with positive meanings.

Keep one's mind on a place which is far away from the womb. For instance, one may choose to keep her mind on the acupuncture point Yongquan.

During the period of menstruation, a woman should practise Qigong for a shorter period of time and she should lessen the intensity of the exercises. If the amount of menstruation is still very great, she may stop doing the exercises for several days until the menstruation is over.

Women should not practise the Spontaneous Moving Exercise during menstruation.

236. Why Should People Choose Appropriate Kind of Qigong According to Their Particular Needs and Circumstances?

People who are just picking up Qigong are often faced with such a question: What kind of Qigong shall I practise?

Because there are many kinds of Qigong and they serve different purposes, a person who is just taking up Qigong should choose from them one particular kind which is fit for himself. For instance, one should choose to practise the setting-up Qigong, the Relaxation-and-calmness Qigong, the Intrinsic Nourishing Qigong, or Taiji Qigong if he wants to get rid of a kind of disease to improve his health. This is because the kind of Qigong can cure diseases. If one wants to reach a more advanced stage of Qigong, he should choose to practise the Shaolin Internal Qigong, or practise Qigong in the standing posture in a low position so as to lay a solid foundation for further exercises. If people are old or weak, they may mainly practise the static Qigong. Those who are young may mainly practise dynamic Qigong or the dynamic-and-static-combined Qigong. In short, people should decide what kind of Qigong they should practise according to their own particular situation so that they may easily achieve the expected results.

237. Why Is It Better for People to Sit on A Hard Stool Or Lie on A Plank Bed When Practising Qigong?

What is most important in doing Qigong exercises is that the posture should be correct. A correct sitting posture in a Qigong session demands that one should sit straight and his neck should be straight as well. He should sit in a relaxed and natural way. When one is practising Qigong in the lying posture, he should also be relaxed and remain natural in this posture. The advantage of a plank bed and a wooden stool is to keep people straight and make it uneasy for a man's spinal column to bend. This in turn helps people to concentrate their minds and regulate their breath. But it is not absolutely necessary that one should sit on a wooden stool or lie on a plank bed to do Qigong exercises. So far as he can do the exercises in the correct posture and he grasps the essential points as to how to concentrate the mind and how to regulate the breath, the desired results can be achieved as well.

238. Why Should People Cultivate Their Moral Character Before Doing Qigong Exercises?

It is Mr. Ma Chun who put forward in the book *Qigong for Building up People's Fitness* the idea that one should cultivate his own moral character before doing Qigong exercises. He thinks that a good moral character is the basis for mastering Qigong. A man who practises

Qigong should have a noble moral character and he should not harm
others to benefit himself. Speaking in concrete terms, one should respect
one's teachers and parents; he should care for the old and the young;
he should be upright and ready to take up the cudgels for a just cause;
he should be ready to sacrifice his own benefits for the sake of others.
If one does not have a good moral character, it is impossible for him
to reach a high level in Qigong exercises. We agree to such an opinion.
The purpose for doing Qigong exercises is to prevent and cure diseases,
to build up the physique and to improve the health. Besides, one can
master the skills for defending himself by doing Qigong exercises. Our
ancestors held that when one is doing Qigong exercises, he should
cultivate his own moral character, get rid of unhealthy desires and treat
others kindly. Only in this way can he manage to get rid of distracting
ideas, to develop the true energy and to reach the state of tranquility
and become both mentally and physically healthy. If he has a lot of
selfish ideas and personal considerations and is intolerant and if he has
a lot of evil intentions and is always thinking of doing harm to others
to benefit himself, it will be very difficult for him to reach the state
of tranquility.

239. Which Diseases Can Qigong Cure and Which Others Not?

Qigong therapy is a therapy which treats the human organism
as a whole. Qigong exercises can help to cultivate the potential energy
in a human being and it can bring into play the positive factors in a
human being. It helps to dredge the main and collateral channels, to
regulate the blood and the vital energy, to bring about a balance between
the Yin and the Yang, to support the healthy energy and eliminate the
evil factors. So it has the function of improving a man's
immunonological function and resistance to prevent and cure diseases,
and the function of building up a man's fitness and improving his
health. That is why Qigong can cure many kinds of diseases, especially

chronic diseases such as hypertension, cardiopathy, arthritis, pulmonary tuberculosis, pulmonary emphysema, gastric and duodenal ulcer, gastroptosis, chronic hepatitis, chronic nephritis, allergic colitis, neurasthenia, neurosis, schizophrenia, backache, periarthritis of shoulder joints, the disease of slipped disk of lumbar vertebra, the sequelae of the concussion of brain, stroke, constipation and paraplegia, etc.. Qigong also has the effect of supporting the true energy in patients with cancer.

Those who are patients with manic psychosis, or patients with hemorrhgic diseases and those patients with suppurative skin diseases should be forbidden to do Qigong exercises.

240. Will Diseases Which Have Been Cured by Qigong Exercises Recur?

Although Qigong therapy has curative effects on various kinds of diseases, especially chronic diseases, clinical observations which have accumulated in many years have also shown that in some cases, the diseases recur. But Qigong therapy should not be looked down upon simply because of this.

There are various and complex causes which may induce the recurrence of some diseases. For instance, infection caused by germs, disordered life, great mental tension and overtiredness, etc. may cause the recurrence of diseases. Under the influence of the above-mentioned factors, even originally healthy people will fall ill, let alone a man who has just recovered from obstinate illness. If a man has proper food and drink, and if he leads a regular life and remains in a calm, unruffled mood and keeps on doing Qigong exercises, usually the diseases will not recur. If they should recur, he may still cure it by doing Qigong exercises again. Of course, if western medicine and Chinese traditional medicine are employed together to cure the diseases, the patient will recover more quickly.

241. If One Wants to Enjoy Longevity, What Else Shall He Pay Attention to Besides Doing Qigong Exercises?

Qigong can enable one to enjoy longevity. This has been proved by the practice of mankind in several thousand years. But if one wants to enjoy longevity, besides doing Qigong exercises earnestly, he should also pay attention to the following points:

Remain optimistic: During the Ten Years of Disturbance, not a few people became inflicted with cardiopathy, hypertension or cancer. This had a lot to do with great anxiety, nervousness and depression. So people should try to remain optimistic, tolerant and treat their own troubles and cares as light-heartedly as possible.

Live a regular life: One should live a regular life and develop the habit of "early to bed and early to rise". He should make arrangements so that work, study, house-work and physical exercises can be carried out in an orderly way.

Eat light food: One should eat light food such as vegetable and bean products as often as possible for the three meals every day. An excessive amount of fat does harm to old people. But a patient who is especially weak should take in a bit more nutriments.

Give up smoking and drinking: In tobacco smoke there is nicotine and other kinds of poisonous things. They will cause various kinds of diseases. Therefore, smoking does people no good but harm and people should make up their minds to give up smoking. So far as drinking is concerned, we think that people may drink a small amount of wine which contains little alchohol. But excessive drinking harms people's health.

Do physical exercises: There is a common saying — Life depends on physical movement. It does good to people's health to do physical exercises often. Therefore, besides doing Qigong exercises, one should also do other kinds of physical exercises. For instance, taking a walk, playing ball games, playing shadow-boxing, climbing mountains and swimming, all do good to people's health and help to build up their fitness.

Taking part in physical labour: People should do a suitable amount of physical labour. This applies particularly to people who are weak in physical constitution and those who are mental workers. Doing some light physical labour does good to people's physical health as well as their mental health. But people should not be over-worked.

Get contol of one's own sexual desire: People should not have excessive sexual intercourse. Otherwise, too much true energy will be consumed and one's health will be impaired.

Pay attention to hygiene: Many infectious diseases are caused by ignoring hygiene. Therefore, it is very important to pay attention to personal hygiene and to public hygiene.

Breathe in fresh air: The rooms should be often aired so that the air in the rooms is always fresh. Besides, people should often go to places where there are many trees and flowers early in the morning. There is a lot of fresh air for people to breathe in.

Get cured of one's own diseases as early as possible: When people fall ill, they should always be examined and treated as early as possible. Sometimes, both western and Chinese traditional medicine can be applied. In this way, the illness can be put under control in time and the patient can recover before long.

242. If the Patient Does Not Take A Turn for the Better After Doing Qigong Exercises for Some Time, What Shall He Do?

The effect of Qigong exercises has a lot to do with the patient's age, his physical constitution, his mood, the nature of the disease he has, the course of the disease he has and the confidence he has in Qigong. The curative effect of Qigong varies with these factors.

According to clinical observations, it usually takes about 2 weeks to eliminate the pain caused by peptic ulcer. In two weeks, the patient's appetite will be improved and other symptoms will be alleviated. Some patients don't take very obvious turn for the better after doing Qigong exercises for one or two months. And a few patients do not take any turn for the better after a three-month course of treatment. Some patients' health improves very quickly at the beginning of the exercises. But later on, the curative effect becomes less obvious. People who practise Qigong should first of all have confidence in Qigong. Besides, they should grasp the methods and essential points in Qigong exercises. If the patients do not take a turn for the better in one or two months, they should not lose their hearts. Instead, they should keep on doing the exercises. And they should try to find out the cause and eliminate it. At the same time, he should ask to be treated with both western and Chinese traditional medicine to achieve better results. Patients who have taken a turn for the better after a course of treatment with Qigong but who have not yet recovered completely should keep on doing the exercises until they recover completely. If a patient does not take any turn for the better after having completed a course of treatment with Qigong, he should be treated with some other methods for a change according to how serious the illness is. Or he may stop doing the exercises for a week to take a rest.

243. Some People Do Not Gain Or Gain Little Weight after Having Done Qigong Exercises for Some Time. What Is the Cause of This?

After having done the exercises for a certain period of time, most of the people will gain weight because their appetite is enlarged, their digestive function is improved and their ability to assimilate nutriments is enhanced. Besides, their symptoms are alleviated. But a few people do not gain weight or gain little weight after having done the exercises for some time although their symptoms are gradually disappearing. This is anyhow a normal phenomenon. The main cause of this is that when one is doing the exercises, especially the Qigong exercises in the standing posture, there is rather violent internal movement. His whole body warms up and he perspires a lot. A part of his subcutaneous fat is consumed. The result is that his muscles are more sturdy. We think that the increase in the weight brought about by Qigong exercises is one of the indicators of the curative effects produced by Qigong. But it is not the sole indicator nor the major indicator. The major indicator is that his illness is alleviated or eliminated and he becomes stronger. Therefore, people who practise Qigong should not lose confidence in Qigong because they do not gain weight. Neither shall they have any doubt about it.

244. Why Do Some People's Lower Abdomens Swell Up after They Have Done Qigong Exercises for A Long Time?

Some people's lower abdomens swell up after they have done the exercises for a long time if they have used the method of keeping their minds on Dantian and the method of abdominal respiration. This is a normal phenomenon. Abdominal respiration is a special kind of respiration adopted in Qigong exercises. In abdominal respiration, the muscles in the abdominal region move greatly. After one has done the exercises for a long time, abdominal muscles will be more resilient. Besides, keeping the mind on Dantian fills the lower abdomen with the Qi. So the lower abdomen will naturally become larger. This is a good phenomenon brought about by doing Qigong exercises. It is because when people do Qigong exercises, their autonomic nerves become more excited, their gastric peristalsis becomes stronger, and their muscles and skins become more resilient. Meanwhile, their lower abdomens are filled with the Qi and it increases the abdominal pressure. This has a good curative effect on patients of astroptosis and patients of nephroptosis.

But it should also be pointed out that it is wrong for some people to keep their mind on Dantian with too great an exertion. This will also cause the lower abdomen to swell up. Such a phenomenon is abnormal. So people should pay attention to it and correct their mistake in time.

245. Why Does One Side of the Body Become Cold While the Other Side Becomes Hot When Doing Qigong Exercises?

When someone is doing Qigong exercises, the left side of his body becomes hot and the right side of his body becomes cold or the upper part of his body becomes hot and the lower part of becomes cold, or the vice versa. With some other people, the thumb and the index finger of one of their hands become hot and the other fingers become cold. Such phenomena occur because these people were in a ruffled and uncalm mood before starting the exercises, or because their postures are incorrect when they are doing the exercises, or because they are not feeling well and it causes their blood and vital energy to be in disorder, their channels to become blocked and it also causes the imbalance between the Yin and the Yang. When such phenomena occur, one should not be upset. Instead, he should calm himself down further and check to see if he is doing the exercises in the correct posture. If he finds out that his posture is incorrect, he should make corrections immediately and continue to do the exercises. The physical imbalance will be alleviated and eliminated. If it lingers on, he should do sufficient warming-up exercises to warm up his own body or have a cup of hot drink next time before he begins to do the exercises. In this way, such a kind of imablance will gradually be eliminated.

246. Why Do Some People Have A Headache Or Pain in the Eyes When Doing Qigong Exercises?

The cause of headache in Qigong exercises is that one cannot reach the state of tranquility after doing the exercises for a long time and he keeps his mind on Dantian with too great an exertion. Or it is because that his posture is incorrect, he is not relaxed or he breathes too forcefully. The pain in the eyeballs or the eye-sockets are caused by one's making too great an exertion when he is looking at an object outside or a part of his own body. Therefore, when one is doing Qigong exercises, he should close his eyes lightly and refrain from making too great an exertion in looking at something. He should also do the exercises in the correct posture and his breath should be soft, regular, thin, slow and quiet. When he is keeping his mind on something, he should not make too great an exertion. Instead, he should do it properly. When he hears a sudden cry or big noise, he should not be frightened, he should ignore them and continue to do the exercises. If he manages to do so, he will not have headache or the pain in his eyes. If the causes of the headache and the pain in the eyes have been eliminated and the headache and the pain linger on, the patient should ask to be examined and then treated with both western and Chinese traditional medicine.

247. Why Do Some People's Limbs Or Even the Whole Body Tremble When Doing Qigong Exercises?

When some people are doing Qigong exercises, especially when they are practising Qigong in a standing posture, their limbs tremble and their bodies sway. Sometimes, their limbs even move greatly. This is because that the functional activities of the vital energy start and they stimulate and excite the motion analyzers of some parts of a man's body so that these motion analyzers set the muscles in some parts, especially the muscles of the limbs, into motion without being directed by the man's brain consciously. Another reason why a man's limbs or his body tremble or move is that some muscles are used for a long time and they become tired after a man has done Qigong exercises for a long time. When the muscles become tired, they will also tremble. Sometimes, they tremble for a moment and then the trembling stops. This shows that the muscles become relaxed after making self-adjustment. But in some cases, people's limbs keep on trembling and it does not come to an end. These people may continue to do the exercises until they are sweating all over. After the exercises, they may wipe themselves with hot water and they will feel comfortable. If a man is practising the Spontaneous Moving Exercise, he should end his exercise according to the rule set for this kind of exercises. He should not move his limbs or any other part of his body consciously. Otherwise, harmful effects and deviation would occur.

248. Why Does One Feel Warm Or Even Sweat When Doing Qigong Exercises?

Whether a man practises Qigong in winter or in summer, early in the morning or at night, he will feel warm and sweat. This is a good phenomenon and it is a good result of doing the exercises.

When one is practising Qigong, there is a great internal movement although he does not seem to move a lot. The internal movement causes the autonomic nervous system to become more excited and it causes the motion analyzer as well as the skin analyser to become excited, too. Therefore, the metabolism of the human organism becomes more active and the circulation of the blood becomes quicker. The sweat glands also gains a strong ability of secretion and the skin temperature rises. These cause the man to display normal phenomena of feeling warm and sweating.

The author of this book has made experiments with a thermograph in Shanghai Ruijin Hospital and Shanghai Research Institute of Hypertension. The experiments showed that when the author has practised Qigong in the standing posture for 3 minutes, the temperature at the acupuncture point Laogong rose by 2.8°C. When the skin temperature rises, a man will feel warm and when the heat radiates, the man will sweat. But when a man feels very hot and is sweating too much, he should try to control it. The way of doing so is as follows: He may shorten the duration of the exercises on the one hand, and on the other hand, he may lower the intensity of the exercises or the stimulation on a certain part of his body.

If one feels hot and sweats when doing the exercises, he should wipe off the sweat and put on his coat immediately after the exercises to keep himself warm. He should not get a draught directly either by sitting in front of an electric fan or sitting in a draught. Neither should he wash his hands or take a bath in cold water. Instead, he should wait for a moment before doing so. Otherwise, he will catch a cold and deviations will occur.

249. Why Does One Feel on His Skin and in the Muscles the Sensations of Pain, Numbness, Puffiness, Warmth, Heaviness and Itch When Doing Qigong Exercise?

When one is doing Qigong exercises, he will feel such sensations because of the following reasons: The excitation and inhibition of the sympathetic and parasympathetic nerves are gradually balanced because the whole body is undergoing both physiological and biochemical changes after the functional activities of the vital energy start. For instance, before doing the exercises, one's sympathetic nerve was excited because he was in an excited mood and the inhibitive function of his parasympathetic nerve was weakened. But when a man is doing the exercises, he is rather calm and he is in a calm and unruffled mood. So the excitation of his sympathetic nerve is accordingly inhibited and the excitation of his parasympathetic nerve becomes greater. At the same time, the blood circulation becomes quicker and the function of the metabolism is improved when one is doing the exercises. Because the nerves, the blood and the vital energy are being regulated and because the channels are being dredged and the electrical potential of the muscles is changing, the man will have in his skin and muscles the sensations such as aching pain, bloatedness, warmth, coolness, numbness, heaviness, itch and so on. These sensations are called "the Eight Sensations" in Qigong and they are normal phenomena. So people should go on doing the exercises and good results will be achieved.

250. Why Do People Have Various Illusions During the Practice of Qigong?

Sometimes the exercisers of Qigong can see scenes and objects in different colors and of various shapes during practice. This is called "illusion" in Qigong. It is not anything mysterious. Only when the cerebral cortex is kept in a state of inhibition can the exerciser have this sort of illusion. It is the same with dreaming. Things experienced in the past have left impressions in the brain. They will recur under specific conditions. But illusion is different from dream since the former occurs when one has entered the state of tranquility during exercise while the latter occurs during sleep. Therefore, one should not get nervous or frightened about such illusions nor pursue them during the exercise. Let them go naturally and they will disappear in the course of time. If the illusion lingers around and affects your practice, you can change into some other exercises, and it will disappear gradually.

251. Is It Proper to Go on with the Exercise When You Feel Cold All Over?

Generally speaking, the exerciser will feel comfortable or warm up and slightly sweat. But some others will feel cold all over because of psychological factors, such as nervousness, fear and anger. If he goes on practising, he will feel colder still. He should stop practising the exercise for a day or two. Or, he can change into some light limb exercises, or other activities temporarily until he has become calm and the psychological factors are removed. If he again feels cold all over the body when he picks up the exercise, he must take some measures such as drinking a cup of hot milk, hot coffee, hot soya-bean milk, or hot water to keep the body warm before practising the exercise. By doing so the phenomenon of cold can be removed. The exercise will be more effective when the cold has disappeared or lessened. If you feel cold when you practise Spontaneous Moving Exercise, you can go on practising Standing Qigong Exercise (at middle position or at low position) and you will feel warm all over.

252. Is It Normal to Feel Sore at Knee Joints During Practising Standing Qigong Exercise?

This is a normal phenomenon. You have to take a required posture while practising the Standing Qigong Exercise although you try to keep your body as relaxed as possible. You can only get relatively relaxed. The knee joints that are bent in a curve have to bear great weight, especially when you stand at middle position or low position. In addition, the movements of inner organs are strenuous during Standing Qigong Exercise, and reactions of certain organs and portions are great. Therefore, after Qigong exercise, you will sense soreness or pain over the body, especially at the knee joints, which is a normal occurrence. With time for the exercise increased, soreness and pain will disappear gradually, similar to other physical training. "There is no physical training without soreness and pain." Similarly without such reactions in Standing Qigong Exercise you cannot attain the purpose of building up physique. Therefore, it is normal to warm up, sweat slightly, and ache at knee joints. It can only be taken as a good phenomenon.

253. Will Varicosis of Lower Limbs Be Induced

by Long Standing Qigong?

Practising Standing Qigong Exercise over a long time will not induce varicosity in lower limbs. There are shallow veins and deep veins in lower limbs, including the large saphenous vein and the small saphenous vein. Deep veins include the anterior tibial veins and the posterior tibial veins the popliteal vein and the femoral vein. Both shallow veins and deep veins are linked by communicative branches. The deep and shallow veins or their communicative branches of lower-limbs all have valvula venosa, which can prevent reverse flow of blood when it is flowing to the heart along the veins. Varicosis is caused by the fact that veins have lost elasticity, and changes have ocurred in their valvula venosa, which fails to prevent the reverse flow of blood effectively, so that blood circulation is hindered. As a result, the blood in lower limb veins cannot flow back to the heart smoothly, but coagulate at the lower-limbs, resulting in varicosis.

The Standing Qigong Exercise seems to require you to stand without moving the lower-limbs. However, after practising for some time, you will feel the lower-limbs warming up, which proves that the Standing Qigong Exercise not only helps enhance muscle strength, but also improve the elasticity of the wall of blood vessels and the function of valvula venosa of the vein. So it can promote blood circulation in the lower limbs. That is to say, the Standing Qigong Exercise cannot cause lower limb varicosis. On the contrary, it can enhance back flow of blood in lower limbs.

254. Can We Listen to Music When Practising Standing Qigong Exercise?

When practising Standing Qigong Exercise, you are required to take a correct posture, keep the body relaxed, breathe naturally, keep calm in the mind, or think of pleasant things. In order to prolong the time for the Standing Qigong Exercise, some people choose to listen to light music while they are regulating the body, the breath and the mind. Listening to light and pleasant music can make you happy and relaxed, and can remove harmful stimulus and tension from cerebral cortex. It can help you get rid of distracting thoughts and relieve tiredness without your noticing the time. Therefore, listening to music is advisable. But it should be light music in low volume. When listening to music, attention should be paid to the "three regulations", not to appreciating music only. Otherwise, it won't serve the purpose of Qigong practice. Listening to light music during practice can bring better effects as well as prevent deviations.

255. How to Deal with Involuntary Movement When It Occurs During the Practice of Standing Qigong Exercise?

Standing Qigong Exercise is used as an exercise for people to keep fit and cure diseases, as are the trees deeply rooted in the ground and growing steadily. When practising this exercise, you are required to keep relaxed, natural, and correct in posture. You should not move about at will, but be even in breathing and happy in mood. But occasionally some exercisers can suddenly wave about unconsciously. This results from the work of Qi mechanism, and matters nothing at all. Generally, it is not advisable to wave about when practising this exercise. If this should occur suddenly, let it go naturally. If you feel comfortable when waving about, you can let it be so, but never pursue it intentionally. Otherwise, it may cause deviations. If you sense discomfort, you can bring it to an end by following the closing movement for Spontaneous Moving Exercise. If you prefer waving about, you should follow the principles and points to remember for Spontaneous Moving Exercise (Refer to Question 89 for details).

256. How to Deal with Finger Tips Becoming Thick after Finishing Qigong Exercise?

Tests have proved that the capacity of blood vessels increases and finger tips become thicker when one is doing Qigong. This is caused by increase of blood volume and blood flow amount at the finger tips' capillaries. After finishing the exercise blood stagnates at the finger tips because it does not flow back immediately. Therefore, we suggest rubbing palms, hand backs and fingers right after practice to cause blood to flow back in time, so as to prevent finger tips from becoming thicker. If they have already become thick, the problem can also be solved in this way.

257. What to Do If Someone Gets Frightened During Qigong Exercise?

Some people can be frightened by a sudden explosion from outside or sudden appearance of illusions while keeping in quiet meditation and concentration. The sufferer may appear panic-stricken, with arrhythmia and unusual feelings in body organs. The fine phenomena he normally feels, such as quick entering into tranquility, gentle and long breathing and comfort all over the body, will disappear with the fright. If this should occur, you must stop practising at once, press ears with two palms and practise "sounding heaven drum" 10 times, or drink a cup of hot tea, wash face with hot water, immerse two hands in hot water for one or two minutes; or better still, take a hot bath to relax your muscles, calm your emotions and get rid of tension. It should be mentioned that you must not be nervous for a sudden occurrence when practising tranquil exercise. You must keep calm, take no notice of it and go on practising. Thus, you can avoid getting frightened or inducing deviations.

258. How to Treat Acute Sprain with Qigong Therapy?

People frequently get hurt on the skin, muscle, joints or bones, especially get strained at soft tissues in daily activities. Some sufferers at once resort to hot compress, or fumigating and washing therapy by means of Chinese medicines, such as safflower, Speranskia tuberculata, Lycopodium clavatum, schizonepeta tenuifolia, saposhnikovia divaricata, and the like; or Qigong mind-keeping method and Qigong massaging therapy at the strained portion. We consider these treatments to be able to cause expansion of blood vessels, increase of oozing, worsening of the swelling and tissue injury. They are not helpful for curing an acute strain.

Generally speaking, when soft tissues get sprained capillaries in the injured portion such as muscle or ligament or joints are likely to be injured as well. The first thing to do at the preliminary acute stage is to use cold compress so as to cause blood vessels to contract to reduce internal haemorrhage and ease swelling gradually. Twenty four hours later you can use hot compress therapy, fumigating and washing therapy, Qigong mind-keeping method or Qigong massaging therapy according to the changing state of the injury.

Usually two or three days after the sprain, swelling will disappear and acute stage will be over. If the injury lasts for many days, part of the soft tissues will become adhesive, joint function will be restrained, or extravasated blood will appear at the injured area. Only then can the use of hot compress therapy, fumigating and washing therapy and Qigong therapy (including mind-keeping at the injury and Qigong massage) help actuate the main and collateral channels, stimulate the circulation of blood and Qi to cure the sprain. Therefore, it is more effective to use Qigong therapy on the sprain after its acute stage.

259. What Is the Regular Pattern of External Movement in Spontaneous Moving Exercise As Described in This Book?

The Spontaneous Moving Exercise introduced in this book can

382

cause the exerciser to move spontaneously when he is in a highly tranquil state. This is a normal phenomenon referred to as "extreme tranquility brings movement". Body movement brought about by this exercise is spontaneous and regular. The external movement tends to change from small range to large range, from partial movement to that of the whole body, from violent movement to gentle movement, from moving irregularly to moving regularly, and from moving with pause to quietening and moving at one's own will. The movement includes various kinds, similar to movements of boxing exercises or movements of gymnastics, martial arts, and dancing. The exerciser will involuntarily massage and pat himself, point to the acupoints or indicate the main and collateral channels. He will even spontaneously take the postures of "Five Animals": tiger, bear, deer, bird, and ape, and imitate their movements and sounds. Each exerciser displays different spontaneous movements (including those of five animals).

The regular pattern of body movements follows:

Keeping tranquil → Spontaneous external movement → Moving with pauses → Quietening and moving at one's own will → In a state of nothingness.

That is to say, irregular movements become regular.

260. Why Do People Feel Dizzy and Sick after Finishing Spontaneous Moving Exercise? How to Deal with It?

Some people feel dizzy and sick after the exercise simply because they are not skillful at this exercise, or do not follow the principles and points to remember. If the exerciser fails to follow the rules either intentionally or unintentionally, he will feel dizzy and sick after finishing the exercise. For instance, the weak persons choose to practise this exercise at a standing posture (they should take a lying posture or sitting posture); the external movement becomes violent without restrain; external movement lasts too long causing fatigue; the exerciser looks inside at the point of Zuqiao or nose tip instead of naval with closed eyes; turning-round movement takes place without being controlled (turning-round should be controlled or stopped by means of reverse turning or sitting down); practising the exercise with the wind or in a draught leads to a cold, and so on. All these manifestations will likely lead to dizziness and sickness after finishing the exercise. To prevent such happenings, the exerciser should take proper posture and choose proper time for practice according to his own physique and state of illness. He should control the extent of external movement, and practise in strict accordance with the procedures and points to remember for Spontaneous Moving Exercise.

261. Why Do People Find Their Hands and Feet Ice-Cold after Finishing Spontaneous Moving Exercise? How to Deal with It?

This often occurs to those whose hands and feet are relatively colder, mostly caused by their special regulation of body temperature. Some people are weak in physique, and the blood-circulation at the finger tips is poor, so that they have cold hands and feet. They probably sweat a lot, and their skins of hands and feet are always wet. Those who feel cold at hands and feet after the exercise often sweat a lot. The reason may be that the tiny arteries of limbs contract and blood flow decreases in order to keep body heat (sweating is a process of releasing heat from the body) and to maintain body temperature.

This phenomenon is temporary after finishing Spontaneous Moving Exercise. It will be improved with the external movement becoming gentle and the exerciser entering tranquility. It is advisable for the exerciser to wipe the sweat, avoid a place with wind, rub the hands and the point of Yongquan after the exercise, and go on practising the Standing Qigong Exercise at middle position or low position for a while. Thus, the above-mentioned phenomena will be removed.

262. If External Movement Occurs before One Finishes the Procedure of Regulation of Mind During Spontaneous Moving Exercise, How to Deal with It?

As is said in this book, the exerciser will have external movement when he is in a real state of tranquility. The first time spontaneous external movement takes place naturally, the exerciser is likely to induce external movement whenever he practises this exercise. Some people have had much practice, and they will spontaneously move about when they enter into tranquility without finishing regulation of the mind. If this occurs, they should restrain themselves, and try to finish mind-regulating procedure before inducing external movement. Otherwise, it will lead to deviations. They tend to move about even at ordinary time whenever they quiet down. Or they will move about violently and find it impossible to close the exercise. Therefore, they must pay attention not to take this phenomenon as a sign of superb skill.

263. Some People Have No External Movement When Doing Spontaneous Moving Exercise. But Tend to Move About At the End of the Exercise. Why, and How to Deal with It?

This is because they want to close the exercise before they have had enough practice, and the Yang Qi has not been stirred up. Another reason is: the exerciser has not focused the mind on the required area, that is, on the point of Dantian during the process. Only when he intends to close the exercise and only by this time does he focus his mind on Dantian to cause Yang Qi to stir slightly and induce external movement. To overcome this defect, the exerciser should keep really quiet during practice, look inside at Dantian, listen to Dantian and think of Dantian. In other words, he should keep his mind at the area of Dantian without much effort, to stir up Yang Qi for external movement. At the same time, it is better for him to prolong the time for practice (to an extent that he feels comfortable after the exercise) so as to have enough time to stir up Yang Qi.

264. Some People Feel Hot Mass Or Hot Stream of Qi Inside the Body after A Period of Practice of Qigong. Why? How to Deal with It?

After a period of practice of Spontaneous Moving Exercise introduced in this book, some people often feel a hot mass or a hot stream of Qi inside the body. This reflects the existence of "inner Qi", and it is a good phenomenon. The mass of hot Qi occurs at certain portions of the channels. When you have reached a higher level of proficiency and your inner Qi becomes abundant, the mass of hot Qi will develop into a stream of hot Qi circulating along the channels. This is the reaction of what is meant by the Qigong terms as Large Zhoutian and Small Zhoutian being opened. When there is the reaction of hot Qi mass running about, do not control it, nor to pursue it, nor to induce it with the mind. Leave it as it is and go on practising to increase inner Qi. The inner Qi running through the acupoints in the body will bring the same curative effects as acupuncture and moxibustion at these acupoints. When one's inner Qi grows, his health will be improved naturally.

265. Some People Feel "A Gust of Wind Covering the Ears" During the Practice of Qigong. Why? How to Deal with It?

When practising Spontaneous Moving Exercise, some exercisers, who have trouble at the five sense organs or infection in the upper respiratory tract, will have such phenomenon. This is the reaction of Qi attacking the diseased area. Do not worry about it, and go on practising. Do not close the exercise until it has been removed (usually it will disappear by itself). If it stays after you have finished the exercise, you can open and close your mouth for several times, or cover your nose and spurt out a gust of Qi with your mouth. This will relieve the trouble. The exerciser who has such phenomenon should practise more Qigong exercise to get rid of the disease and bring good health.

266. How to Coordinate Mind Concentration At Dantian with Natural Breathing When Practising Spontaneous Moving Exercise?

The area for mind concentration in Spontaneous Moving Exercise introduced in this book should be at Dantian. Adopt natural breathing method, that is, the exerciser is required to breathe naturally. He should not pay attention to exhalation and inhalation, but breathe naturally. It is helpful for him entering into tranquility, and preventing difficulty in breathing. When the exerciser has kept his mind at Dantian and entered into tranquility, his breathing will become deeper, longer and slower without his awareness (this exercise can help develop natural breathing without the necessity of intention). This is a fine reaction of practising the exercise. The exerciser has only to keep his mind at Dantian, and takes no notice of breathing. He must not forget to keep the mind at Dantian. He should not pursue the speed and depth of breathing as he himself requres it, and should let it develop naturally.

By doing so he will feel comfortable at the thoracic cavity after the exercise. (Those who have trouble at the respiratory system will feel the effect more distinctly.) With constant practice the exerciser will find his breathing frequency per minute reduced and the depth of breathing increased gradually, and the physiological function of his respiratory system improved.

The writer of the book has instructed some patients with silicosis to practise Spontaneous Moving Exercise in the hospital and required them to follow the principles to deal with the reactions mentioned above, he has brought satisfactory curative effects.

267. Can the Spontaneous Moving Exercise Bring Curative Effects If No External Movement Occurs?

The exerciser who knows the method of Spontaneous Moving Exercise introduced in the book will start to move spontaneously after entering into tranquility and his Yang Qi being stirred up. If he has more practice, there will occur various reactions in his body, and the reaction of inner Qi will also appear gradually. This is common with the exercisers. But some exercisers display no spontaneous external movement whatsoever, even though they have had a lot of practice and various reactions have occurred in their bodies, including the reaction of inner Qi. This is because they have inner movement first and it is not easy for them to induce external movement. We have made clinical observations over a long time, and found those exercisers to have also achieved good curative effects though they display no external movement during practice. The physiological parameters taken from them prove this fact. We maintain that if the exerciser really enters into tranquility, he can achieve the same effect as practising quiet Qigong exercise though no external movement is displayed temporarily. Through observation, we have also found out that if these exercisers go on with constant practice, they will have spontaneous external movement, even more intense and regular.

268. Why Do People Feel Painful At the Diseased

Part of the Body During the Spontaneous Moving Exercise? How to Deal with It?

If a patient knows the method of Spontaneous Moving Exercise introduced in this book, he often feels painful or uncomfortable at the diseased area during practising the exercise. The lasting time and extent of the pain vary with each time of practice. Sometimes he finds it hard to tolerate the pain. This is a fine reaction of the Qi attacking the diseased area. The exerciser should not fear such phenomenon, nor to stop practising the exercise. (If he feels too painful to stand, he can change standing posture into sitting or lying posture.) He should improve mind-concentration, and go on with the exercise until the pain has been relieved completely. Observation over long-period has revealed that the pain caused by the Qi attacking the focus of infection will disappear with continuous practice. It has also been found from the observation that each time the Qi attacks the focus of infection during Qigong exercise, the patient's state of illness turns a step further for the better.

269. Why Does Liquid Come Out from Eyes and Nose During Spontaneous Moving Exercise? How to Deal with It?

Some patients, who have trouble with eyes, nose, infection of upper respiratory tract, stagnation of hepatic Qi, often find liquid coming out from eyes and nose when practising Spontaneous Moving Exercise. One should not fear this symptom, as it is the fine reaction of Qi attacking the disease. Go on practising until liquid stops coming out. It is helpful for the exercisers to recover health.

270. Can One Bring Violent External Movement to An End During Spontaneous Moving Exercise?

The exerciser should understand that range of external movement should not exceed the two hands raised up horizontally at two sides. The intensity of external movement should not be so great as to make one tired when he finishes practising the exercise. If you know all this, no violent external movement will occur during practice. If that should occur, do not stop practising at once. You should bring the movement to a stop gradually. Stop practising the exercise when the external movements of the limbs have come to an end. If you stop the violent external movement suddenly, you will feel uncomfortable, and your limbs will move recklessly even after you have brought the exercise to an end. You will even move recklessly in the subsequent practices without a proper way to stop. Therefore, much attention should be paid to the method of bringing an exercise to an end.

271. How to Deal with Cough and Phlegm During Spontaneous Moving Exercise?

Those who have trouble in respiratory system often cough and have a lot of phlegm when practising Spontaneous Moving Exercise introduced in this book. This is the fine effect of Qi attacking the disease. The exerciser should not restrain coughing if he wants to cough, and must spit the phlegm that comes out. When the coughing ceases, the exerciser can go on keeping the mind at Dantian and practising the exercise. He should not stop practising the exercise before he has ceased coughing. Doing in this way over a period of time, the disease can be lessened and the patient will become better gradually.

272. What Are the Contents of the Ancient Literature — *Xing Qi Yu Pei Ming*?

Xing Qi Yu Pei Ming (Jade Ornament with Inscription of Qigong) is a relic recently unearthed, on which there is the inscription recording how ancient people practised Qigong. It proves that the Chinese people had accumulated rich experience in practising Qigong as early as the early Period of Warring States (4th century B.C.).

In the book of *The Era of Slave-Owning System* Guo Mo-ruo has studied this unearthed relic and given an explanation of the inscribed record. He says that the inscription is about the process of deep breathing. He maintains that when you inhale deeply, you draw in a large amount of air. The air goes downward and gets stored up. And then when you exhale, the Qi goes up, as if a plant began to sprout in the direction opposite to the route by which the Qi comes in. The Qi retreats to the utmost. The Heaven mechanism moves upward while the Earth mechanism moves downward. To breathe with the circulation of Qi can promote growth, whereas to breathe against the circulation of Qi will lead to death. This is what ancient people called as Daoyin, and what present-day people call as Qigong.

We regard this inscription by the ancient people as a detailed and vivid description of breath-regulating process of Qigong and an illustration of the circulating route of inner Qi flowing along the main and collateral channels. It further proves that Qigong is a splendid heritage of the Chinese medicine, and a science for people to keep fit and attain longevity.

273. What Important Relics on Qigong Were Unearthed from the Han Tomb At Mawangdui?

Among the relics unearthed from the No.3 Han Tomb at Mawangdui near Changsha are two important pictures on Qigong. They are the earliest relics of the early Western Han Dynasty ever found so far. Among those relics there is one colored silk painting, which contains more than forty figures in various exercising postures: sitting in repose with eyes closed, holding head with both hands, squatting

391

down with belly contracted, bowing and bending waist, standing with head lifted up, pressing down with knees bent, all of them lifely. It is of great value to the research of the source and development of Qigong. The other one is the picture of "Pi Gu Method of Taking in Qi" attached to the "Daoyin Picture", which is characterised by its skills. The method suggests selecting suitable place in accordance with the change of seasons, and practising "Taking in Qi", which will shed some light on these points of Qigong exercise for the later generations.

CORRECTION OF DEVIATIONS

274. What Is the Deviation in Qigong Exercise?

The purpose of practising Qigong is to prevent and cure diseases, enhance one's physique and build up health. But some people do not follow the fundamental principles and points for attention for Qigong in practice. They want to find a short-cut and are overanxious for quick results, which inevitably cause deviations, such as dizziness, feeling of distension or heaviness of the brain, stickiness at forehead, distension at Daitain, swelling up at vertebra, mass of Qi binding the body, chest distension and breathing with difficulty, numbness in the leg, palpitation and restlessness, stiffness of the tongue, uncontrolable movements, sleepiness, heat and chill at chest and back, rushing up of Qi, leakage of Qi and emission, increased sexual libido, etc. These symptoms are deviations known in Qigong circles, or referred to as "going too far and getting infatuated." Whenever a deviation occurs, one must find a remedy for it, or ask for help from an experienced Qigong master. Otherwise, it will cause sufferings to one's body and mind.

One should remember that it is not the Qigong itself that causes deviations. It is the exerciser who has not followed the principles and rules of the exercise that induces deviations. Therefore, one should not negate the essentials of Qigong simply because some exercisers' suffer from deviations during practice.

275. What Are the Causes of Deviations?

It is normal for an exerciser to have some fine feelings during the course of practising Qigong. But some beginners have uncomfortable feelings in practice, which are called deviations. Causes of deviations vary greatly. Details follows:

(1) Tne exerciser has selected an exercise regardless of his physical

conditions, state of illness, deficiency-excess and Yin-Yang, and function of the viscera. If the exercise does not suit the exerciser's specific condition and state of illness, it will not bring curative effects, but result in deviations.

(2) The exerciser takes up Qigong just out of curiosity. He does not ask for guidance from a teacher and has no plan of gradual progression. He changes his mind the moment he sees something new. He changes the forms of exercises frequently. He follows one teacher for some time, and goes to another when he wants a change. He gives up one exercise after another at his free will. Doing in this way without a basic exercise to follow is apt to result in deviations.

(3) Some people pursue blindly various effects and phenomena, which is the incorrect way to Qigong practice commonly-seen among exercisers. In other words, this is the way to cause deviations. For instance, when practising the Spontaneous Moving Exercise, if one does not practise naturally, but pursues the taste of moving, he unconsciously increases the extent of motion and will move violently. He will find himself out of control.

(4) Some people have been too rigid and mechanical about the practical method. They have failed to get the body and the mind relaxed. As a result, they run counter to the rules of keeping lively, natural and relaxed. For instance, when practising Standing Qigong Exercise, if one does not relax his lower back and goes on doing the exercise, his lateral or bilateral ligamentun sacrospinosum will be injured, causing deviations.

(5) Someone tries to lead the Qi Mai to circulate with the mind intentionally and wrongly messes up the main and collateral channels, and thus violates the circulation of the main and collateral channels along the right route. For instance, if one pursues with the mind to open up the large and small Zhoutian before he has had enough training, he will never achieve the purpose. On the contrary, he will suffer from Qi stagnation, with a feeling of bearing down with the weight of Mount Taishan, and deviations result.

(6) Some people are afraid of seeing and having some illusions during practice, such as images, shadows or scenes with various colors floating along before their eyes. Or they are superstitious about such things and are not scientific in the analysis of such phenomena. They go off into wild flights of fancy, and even tremble with fear. These belong to another kind of deviations.

(7) While practising the quiet Qigong exercise, one can be interrupted by a sudden cry or an explosion, and feel frightened. This will bring about great fright, faster heartbeats, arrhythmia, and even panic. This is also deviations.

(8) Some people misbelieve some so-called Qigong masters or doctors who have no genuine knowledge of Qigong, and mistake the deviations occurring in Qigong practice for fine phenomena, and pursue them with effort. As a result, the deviations grow more serious.

(9) While practising, one suddenly gets angry for certain reasons, which will cause the Qi mechanism to go in a reverse direction, causing deviation. For instance, if you suddenly scold or beat a child during the exercise, you will feel uncomfortable at certain portion of your body, causing deviation.

(10) You do not pay attention to the principles and points of attention for Qigong exercise and run counter to prohibitory rules. For instance, when you have practised the exercise streaming with sweat, you go right away for a cold bath. You will feel uncomfortable or even fall ill after the bath.

Deviations occur during practice simply because one does not follow the principles and points of attention for Qigong exercise. It is never a problem brought about by the Qigong therapy itself. We should not one-sidedly deny the advantages of Qigong therapy or doubt its effects simply because some deviations have taken place. In order to avoid deviations, one should first select a proper exercise suitable for one's own physical conditions, and follow the principles and points to remember in practice. He will achieve good results if he keeps on practising as directed above.

276. How to Make Preliminary Correction of A Deviation?

Generally speaking, if the exerciser follow the principles, essentials and points to remember for Qigong exercise, no deviation will occur. When one senses dizziness, stickiness at forehead, heaviness or distension in the head, swelling at Dantian, distension at chest and breathing with difficulty, palpitation and restlessness, deviations result. If one cannot find a Qigong master to help correct the deviation, he can first do it by himself. The method follows:

Change into another form of exercise: Stop the Qigong exercise you are doing. Find out the cause to the fault. Change into Relaxing Qigong Exercise. Relax the body part by part or wholly. Practise Moving Qigong Exercise with pleasant thoughts, such as Taiji Qigong Exercise, Shiduanjin Exercise, etc.

Use Patting Relaxing Method: Pat the body from head to feet with your own hands in coordination with relaxation, and, at the same time think of the portion you are patting and relaxing.

Rub Yongquan Point (At the sole): Rub the soles with your own palms, and lead the Qi downward to soles intentionally. Rub two soles 300 times each day.

Take part in recreational and physical activities: To stop doing the Qigong exercise alone will not help correct a deviation. Besides the methods mentioned above, you can take part in some recreational and physical activities beneficial to health and do some light physical work. Keep a happy mood, and do away with anxieties. Listen to light music, and change into exercises with pleasant thoughts (never practise the exercise of keeping the mind at a certain point). By doing in this way over a period of time, some deviations will be lessened or disappear.

277. How to Correct the Deviation of "Heavy Weight on the Head"?

Deviation occurs to a few exercisers who feel Qi accumulating at the headtop as if "to be weighted down with the heaviness of Mount Taishan", and sense compression and distension in the head. This is caused by concentrating the mind with too much effort. The exerciser should change into Relaxing Qigong Exercise along Three-Lines, Relaxing Qigong Exercise Part By Part and Wholly Relaxing Qigong Exercise, which can usually remove deviations. Moreover, he can press gently the two Taiyang points with two middle fingers, and rub them 100 times in clockwise direction, and then press gently the points of Fengchi with two middle fingers and rub them 100 times in clockwise direction.

Corrections by a Qigong master in the following way: Touch the point of Baihui of the sufferer with the tip of the thumb of a half-clenched fist, point at this point and emit the "external Qi" to push down a little, and with the pushing down movement turn the thumb tip in half-circle at the same time. When the sufferer feels his head relaxed, the sense of the heavy "Mount Taishan" is removed.

278. How to Correct the Deviation of "Stickiness At Forehead"?

Deviations sometimes occur to individual exerciser. He feels Qi accumulating at forehead as if there were a paste sticking to the forehead, and he feels uncomfortable. At this moment, if the exerciser changes into Relaxing Qigong Exercise Along Three-Lines, the deviation can be removed. He can also ask a Qigong master to help correct it. Methods for correction follow: The Qigong master may take the point of Yintang (between two eyebrows) with two thumbs. He points at Yintang with thumb tips, the other fingers and palms gently holding the forehead. Then move two thumbs leftward and rightward to the points of Taiyang (at the hollow places near the brow ends), emit "external Qi", turn thumb tips in a circle 10 times at Taiyang points and then move them back to the point of Yintang. Move back and forth about 10 times, and then knead lower eye sockets for a while with thumbs until the sufferer feels relaxed at the forehead as if "the paste" were taken away.

279. How to Correct the Deviation of "Distension At Dantian"?

Some exercisers may suffer from deviations. One may feel Qi accumulating at Dantian. He feels the lower abdomen swelling up. When he breathes out and in, his abdomen sinks like a hollow pit or swells out like a balloon. He feels extremely uncomfortable with distension at the belly all the time.

Self correction: The sufferer should slightly press the area about 40 mm below the naval with right middle finger tip. Push downward with the finger tip pointing downward leading the Qi downward with the mind. Several minutes later, he will feel the Qi flowing downward and the distension lessened. Then he should repeat the movement for some more time, and distension at Dantian will be removed.

Correction by a Qigong master: Hold the two thick tendons about 150 mm from the naval with thumbs and index fingers (the thick tendons, each about 130 mm long, slanting in the shape of "\ /"). Hold the middle of the tendons, and emit "external Qi", and pull the two tendons sideways horizontally until a grumbling sound in the abdomen is heard. The distension is thus lessened, and the sufferer returns to normal.

280. How to Correct the Deviation of "Swelling Up At the Big Vertebra"?

The deviation sometimes occurs to a certain exerciser. He feels Qi accumulating at vertebra (at the seventh cervical vertebra), swelling up as big as a ping-pong ball.

Self correction: The sufferer should stand naturally, get the whole body relaxed and slightly shake the body intentionally. A few minutes later he will feel the swelling at the vertebra lessened.

Correction by a Qigong master: Touch the acupoint of Dazhui with middle finger, the finger tip pointing upward, and emit "external Qi", and then hold the swollen part with index finger and middle finger, push up and pull down. Doing in this way for several times and the sufferer's symptom will be gradually lessened.

281. How to Correct the Deviation of "Mass of Qi Binding the Whole Body"?

The deviation sometimes occurs to a certain exerciser. He feels a hot mass of Qi binding the whole body as if to be burned.

Self correction: The sufferer should stop concentrating the mind on a point or pursuing certain feelings. He may change into Relaxing Qigong Exercise or Keep-Fit Qigong Exercise, and the hot mass of Qi will gradually disappear.

Correction by a Qigong master: Touch the sufferer's vertebra with index finger and middle finger, pull downward with "external Qi" along the spine. Repeat the movement 8 — 10 times, and the hot mass of Qi will flow down and disappear.

282. How to Correct the Deviation of "Chest Distension and Difficulty in Breathing"?

Some exercisers practise breath-regulating exercise in the wrong way. They blindly pursue the unusual effects of breath-regulation. As a result, they sense dizziness, distension at chest and difficulty in breathing. If this deviation occurs, the exerciser should use natural breathing method or walking breathing method at once. He should stop other methods of breath-regulation, and then the above-mentioned symptoms will be removed.

283. How to Correct "Numbness in the Leg" When Practising Cross-Legged Qigong Exercise?

Numbness in the leg often occurs while practising cross-legged exercise, especially with the beginners. Some exercisers even practise double cross-legged "Wu Xin Chao Tian" Exercise at the preliminary stage. As they are not sufficiently relaxed and quieted down, they feel numb in the leg or even all over the body. They cannot stand up within several minutes. Though the consequence may not be serious, they will suffer from pain.

Correction: If you feel numb in the leg during or after cross-legged sitting, straighten the legs with the help of hands, and sit with legs hanging down. Massage legs and feet with both hands, from leg to instep for two or three minutes, and numbness will be removed.

284. How to Correct the Deviation of "Palpitation"?

Some exercisers do not know the correct method to use the mind. They keep the mind at certain acupoint or try to enter tranquility with much effort when practising sitting or lying exercise. Consequently, they are apt to become shocked and to palpitate because of sudden influence from outside.

Correction: Change into Standing Qigong Exercise. Do not keep the mind at certain portion of the body, but think of some pleasant scenes outside, such as beautiful flowers, blue sea, green woods, or some sights beneficial to one's health, or happiness in life. Doing in this way over a period of time, the symptoms will be lessened or removed.

285. How to Correct Deviation of "Tightness of Head and Stiffness of Tongue"?

Some exercisers try to do differently and run counter to the principles for Qigong exercise, resulting in troubles. There was an exerciser who had learnt from books about Qigong that touching one's tongue to the upper palate could get Ren Mai and Du Mai connected. The exerciser was mechanical in his application of this rule, and stuck his tongue to palate all the time every day without a moment's release. Eventually his tongue nerve became stiff and he found the tongue unable to move and even found it difficult to speak.

Self correction: Massage gently the point of Jiache with two middle fingers, three minutes each time. Fifteen times or so will make the stiff tongue gradually return to normal.

Correction by a Qigong master: Massage gently dozens of times the points of Chengqi, Dicang, Jiache and Xinshu by emitting "external Qi". The tongue will gradually return to normal. After correction, the sufferer should never do this exercise any more.

286. How to Correct Deviation of "Being Out-of-Control"?

It is normal for the exerciser to move the head or even the whole body slightly while practising Tranquil Qigong Exercise. But a few exercisers pursue moving effects intentionally. They move along so much that they have failed to control themselves. This is the deviation of getting out-of-control.

Self correction: If this deviation should occur, one should not use the mind to conduct the movement. If he cannot control himself effectively, he must stop practising the exercise and do some light physical work instead, or take part in some recreational and physical activities beneficial to health. He should suspend practice for a time and then go on with the exercise.

Correction by a Qigong master: Massage gently by emitting "external Qi" at the sufferer's points of Dazhui, Quchi, Hegu, and Jianjin, causing the Qi to circulate along the route of main and collateral channels, that is, causing the Qi back to the right route. Thus, the deviation of being out-of-control will be corrected gradually.

287.   How to Correct Deviation of "Drowsiness"?

Some exercisers become drowsy or even fall into sleep unconsciously while practising sitting or lying exercise. Do not worry about this fault and correct it in time to solve the problem.

Correction: First, let the exerciser go on sleeping. When he wakes up and becomes spirited, he can pick up the exercise again. Secondly, let the exerciser not close his eyes. He should keep his eyes slightly open to receive slight stimula from outside constantly. Thirdly, let the exerciser change into Standing Qigong Exercise or Walking Qigong Exercise. By doing so, he can remove drowsiness.

288.   How to Correct the Deviation of "Rushing Up of Qi"?

Some exercisers are conscious of the Qi mechanism rushing up while doing Sitting Qigong Exercise. That is, he feels a stream of air spurting out from the mouth while exhaling, and a stream of air going straight to Dantian while inhaling. He feels nervous and uncomfortable.

Self correction: The exerciser should first stop practising the exercise, change cross-legged sitting posture into natural sitting posture, take natural breathing method instead of other breathing methods. By doing so, he will come to normal, and this deviation will gradually come to an end.

Correction by a Qigong master: Knead the sufferer's points of Jianjin 36 times with two hands, and put right palm on the point of Dazhui to push the Qi mechanism downward along the spine by means of "external Qi". This phenomenon will be lessened or removed completely.

289. How to Correct the Deviation of "Heat and Cold At Chest and Back"?

It is abnormal for the exerciser to feel hot or cold at the chest and back while practising sitting exercise.

Correction: If you feel cold, stop practising the exercise till the next day. Wash face with hot water, and immerse hands and feet in hot water for a while. Then the cold will disappear gradually. If you feel hot, raise up two palms facing upward to the level of eye brows, and then turn palms over and press them downward, at the same time say the word "Ha" while exhaling. Then the heat will grow less or disappear.

290. How to Correct Deviation of "Leakage of Qi and Spermatorrhea"?

Some male exercisers are conscious of the Qi leaking out from the front private part or private part when they keep the mind at the point of Huiyin. This is called leakage of Qi. If this goes on over a long time, the Qi will escape even when one is not practising exercise. It will develop into constant spermatorrhea.

Self correction: The exerciser should knead and rub the area of Dantian and Shenshu until he feels warm there. After doing in this way for some time, leakage of Qi and spermatorrhea will be lessened and removed gradually.

Correction by a Qigong master: Let the sufferer lie supine, emit "external Qi" with middle finger and index finger at the points of Qizhong and Guanyuan until he feels warm at the belly.

291. How to Correct Deviation of "Increased Sexual Libido?

Some male exercisers find sexual libido increased and penis becoming erect when they keep the mind at Dantian. This occurs even at night when one is not doing the exercise. Some people mistake it for good phenomena and even try to develop them, resulting in too much sexual intercourse. If you believe in such absurd theory, you can never keep fit and live longer. On the contrary, it will bring great harm to your health. One should always keep alert against this kind of fallacy.

Correction: If one's sexual libido should increase during exercise, change into other Qigong exercises immediately, such as natural sitting exercise, keep the mind at the point of Yongquan, or ask a Qigong master for help. He will seize the sufferer's points of Hegu and Laogong with thumbs and middle fingers, emit "external Qi" to remove this phenomenon.

INTERNATIONAL TRENDS

292. What Research Institutions on Qigong Have Been Set Up in the World?

In Europe and the United States, research institutions on Qigong have been set up in a number of renowned universities, such as Massachusetts Institute of Technology, Harvard University, State University of New York, St. Diego Naval Hospital, and Stanford Research Institute in the United States; and London University and London Boorbick Institute in Britain. They have been doing research work on Qigong. In Maharishi Research Institute in Switzerland more than 80 academic symposiums on Qigong were held in 1978. They have worked out an aspiring project for comprehensive research of Qigong, and invited scientists from different countries to join in their research work. Many learned societies of Qigong have been set up in Europe, Asia, Africa, Latin America and North America, which have trained more than 2,000,000 Qigong enthusiasts. The China's Qigong Scientific Research Society was set up in 1982 which has helped to develop the research and popularization of Qigong.

293. How Many International Scientific Conferences on Qigong Have Been Held?

Qigong in the foreign countries is known as "Yoga", "Ling Zi Exercise", "Bio-feedback Method", "Parapsychology", "Relaxation Training", "Flying Technique", "Kung Fu", "Zen", and so on. Recently, with the development of research on Qigong mechanism and growing fear of side-effects of medicines, people hope to find better methods to treat diseases without the need of taking medicines. Therefore, Qigong, the ancient exercise, has caught people's attention all over the world. Three international conferences on Qigong were held respectively in Prague in 1973, in Morocco in 1975, and in Rome in 1977, where exchanges of experiences on an extensive scale were carried out. As a result, they have made contributions to the promotion of the research work on Qigong theory and its popularization.

294. How Many Well-Known Scientists in the World Are Involved in Qigong Research?

In 1974 Sir Kerpokes, a British chemist and physist, used mordern scientific method to study the theory of Qigong's effects. By observation of experiments over a long time, he was the first to announce the actual existence of Qigong's phenomenon of parapsychological energy. 300 medical doctors of Ontario Medical Association in Canada have become interested in Qigong therapy and taken part in its research work. World-famous scientists Josephson, winner of Nobel Prize of physics in 1974, and Bragoukin, winner of Nobel Prize of chemistry in 1977, have also joined in the research and discussion of Qigong. Professor Jiang Tao, vice director of Dunsink Astronomical Observatory in Northern Ireland, spoke highly of the essay entitled "Preliminary Results of Experiments on the Material Basis of Qigong Therapy" published on the initial issue of China Nature Magazine in May of 1978. He said, "Their discoveries are of pioneering nature." "They are creative achievements." Chen De-ren, an American scientist, suggested to cooperate with the Chinese Qigong doctors in using scientific methods in research of Qigong therapy. Qian Xue-sen, a famous scientist in China, has taken part in the scientific research of Qigong and given full support for the work.

295. What Qigong Performances Have Been Miraculously Made in the World?

According to a report from the American Science News in 1974,

Professor Hanster and Palmer, physists of Dunplebick Institute in Britain, were in charge of an experiment on Qigong performed by Galler, an Israel Qigong Master. More than ten scientists witnessed the process. Galler began to emit Qi with a gauge in hand, which recorded intense signals corresponding to 100 — 150 particles per minute from the hand (the basic record was one particle per minute). Galler also emitted Qi toward a monocrystal metal disk. He put his hand gently on the hand of a physist, and in between the metal disk and the palm there is a plastic board keeping the two apart. Two minutes after Galler had emitted Qi, the monocrystal metal disk was distinctly bent. The scientists present at the experiment proved it to be true, and the two professors of physics signed the experiment report. According to a report of the year 1978, from Maharishi Research Institute in Switzerland, the Qigong master in that research center was able to rise high into the air (which is called Qigong Flying Technique) when he emitted Qi. By using electroencephalogram in the experiment, they found the maximum coherency shown in the electroencephalogram at the time when the Qigong master rose high into the air. They have carried out research work on physiology, physics, biochemistry and psychology of the Qigong exercisers, and published more than 100 essays.

296. What Clinical Qigong Practices Have Been Made in the World?

Clinical Qigong practice is developing in Europe and America. In Canada there are over 3,000 people taking part in clinical Qigong practice. They have not only cured some functional diseases caused by mental factors, but cured organic diseases as well. In the recent few years, Harvard University of the United States has been constant in the observation of the curative effects upon hypertension brought by Qigong. It has been reported that of 36 hypertension sufferers, whose systolic pressure and diastolic pressure had been 146/94.6 mm Hg., joined in an experiment made by Dr. Panter to reduce pressure. They were required to take either Qigong or silent sitting on a chair (imitating the posture of Qigong practice), and achieved different results. The patients practising Qigong had reduced their systolic pressure and diastolic pressure as many as 20.4/14.2 mm Hg. after a course of treatment, while the latter method only reduced blood pressure by 0.5/2.1 mm Hg. According to a Chinese-American professor Niu Man-jiang's introduction, 500 people in Rockefeller Foundation University in New York performed Qigong to treat hypertension, and over 75 percent of them achieved good curative effects after half a year's practice. Research results from some health organizations have proved that Qigong is effective for premature ventricular contractions due to ischemic heart disease. They observed the patients day and night by means of a remote control monitor device, and found that eight patients out of eleven had turned better, and the frequency of premature systole reduced from 151.5 times per hour before the treatment to 131. Naval Hospital in St. Diego has adopted Qigong in military training. For instance, they have used Qigong to train soldiers to raise their hand temperature in cold weather, so as to be able to work without gloves on.

297.　How Are Qigong Instruments Used In Some Countries?

In 1960 Dr. Marrinance and Holland of the United States discovered in their treatment of a patient with stroke and peripheral nerve injury, that when the electromyogram of patient's injured tissues was turned into signals which acted on the patient himself and through his own mental activities his state of illness turned better more quickly. In 1964 Dr. Andrews used the same method to observe 20 patients with hemiplegia and obtained the same effects. This attracted great attention in the medical circles of the United States and Canada. Since 1969 they have developed a series electronic monitoring instruments, such as EDG biofeedback apparatus, blood pressure feedback apparatus, skin temperature feedback apparatus, EMG biofeedback apparatus, etc. While doing the exercise, the patient can get information of the changes in or on his body feeding back to the patient himself through these instruments, so that he can control the time and intensity of the exercise, correct deviations, and lead to tranquility. This is called "Biofeedback". The method is in fact the use of modern instruments to help the patient in practising Qigong, and to bring better results. According to a report by Germuth and Browns of Canada, they have used this method to treat 200 patients. As a result, 60 percent have been cured, 32 percent have turned better, and only 8 percent achieved no result. Bradley of the United States applied this method to 114 cases, of which most turned better after 8 to 12 weeks gradually. All these patients had received normal treatment over a long period of time without any good effects. At present, this method of treatment is developing rapidly. In 1970 the Association of Biofeedback was set up in the United States with more than 1,000 members. In 1974, the first issue of a journal of the association was published, and since then an annual book of research work has come out each year.

298.　How Does Qigong Develop in Asia?

Yoga was originated in India thousands of years ago, which was passed on by Buddhist monks from the Ganges River to the Himalaya Mountains over many years. In India, Yoga Institute was opened in honor of this art and for further developing its research work. Now there are several Yoga Research Centers in India. Scholars and experts from different countries often go there to study and learn their experience. Yoga masters have made a lot of marvelous performances in other countries. In Japan, Qigong also has its long history. It is said that Ling Zi Exercise of China was imported into Japan as early as the time of Gin Emperor. Later on, Jian Zhen of Tang Dynasty crossed the sea eastward to introduce Buddhist doctrine. Yin Yuan of Qing

Dynasty crossed the sea eastward to spread Buddhism. All this exerted great influence upon Qigong in Japan. Now, the Qigong accepted by the Japanese people includes "Okada silent-sitting method", "Ema popular practice", "Fujita regulating heart and harmonizing method", "Moritai Tanaka's Ling Zi Exercise", and so on.

299. How Does Qigong Develop in Europe?

In Europe, Qigong was taken as one of sport items to train athletes in Poland and Czechoslovakia, and they won good records in the Olympic Game of 1964. Later on many countries paid great attention to it. Cloakes, chairman of the London Royal Association in Britain, was the first to use scientific method to study Qigong. After a long period of observation, he announced the actual existence of "parapsychological energy", and said that Qigong was not inconceivable, but had its material basis. Records have it that the art of Chinese massage was introduced to France in Tang Dynasty. In 1930s Maspero, a sinologist, gave an introduction on "foetal breathing method" and "holding breath method" of the Chinese Qigong in the Asian Journal. Breathing and Self-training method has become popular in West Germany. In some primary and middle schools, Qigong exercises are practised during the break as effective means to remove tiredness. In May of 1974, Maharishi Research Institute in Switzerland made an interesting experiment on measuring the change of Qigong master's brain wave, and discovered that Qigong was able to reduce the frequency of brain waves, and increase wave range by three times and more. It shows that human function can return to the slow wave of a child, causing the reversion of the biochemical senile index, and causing the wave shape in the brain areas to become synchronized, that is, electromagnetic activities of brain cells being in good order. In 1975, Maharishi Research Institute made a comprehensive research on Qigong in physiology, biochemistry, psychology, sociology, and so on.

They invited some scientists from other countries to take part in their work and published Collected Works entitled Transcendental Meditation and Flying Skill. In Austria, medical professor Schults for the first time published his essay in 1958, explaining the importance and detail methods of Qigong as physical exercises. He called this training method as "Autogenic training", which was later translated into "Relaxation Training" by many countries.

300. How Does Qigong Develop in America?

At present there are more than ten training courses teaching Qigong in the United States. For instance, "Transcendental Meditation Program", "Erherr Training Class", "Physiological Feedback Program", "Behavior Modification Program", etc. In New York City alone there are over eighty Yoga Schools. In the United States, Qigong is taken as one of the required courses for astronauts. In Canada Qigong therapy has been widely accepted. The Ontario Medical Society has over 800 medical doctors engaged in Qigong therapy. They are active in research and clinical work of Qigong. Since 1969 they have used a series of electronic surveillance instruments, which help to feedback to the patients themselves, to correct deviations, and to lead to tranquality. This is called "Biofeedback Therapy".

粤新登字 **04** 号

气功三百问

林厚省　骆佩钰　著

愈耀生　丁廷敏　竺蕊　译

卓大宏　校

责任编辑　陈素施　黄达全

*

中国广东科技出版社出版

（中国广州环市东路水荫路 11 号 13 楼）

中国广东新华印刷厂印刷

（中国广州永福路 45 号）

中国国际图书贸易总公司发行

（中国北京车公庄西路 35 号）

北京邮政信箱第 399 号　邮政编码 100044

1994 年（大 32 开）第 1 版（英文版）　1994 年第 1 次印刷

ISBN 7—5359—1269—9

R · 232　（外）

02400

14—E—2846P

图书在版编目（CIP）数据

300　QUESTIONS ON QIGONG
EXERCISES/林厚省、骆佩钰著；愈耀生等译
·一广州：广东科技出版社.1994.7.
ISBN7－5359－1269－9

Ⅰ.3…
Ⅱ.①林…②愈…
Ⅲ.气功－中国
Ⅳ.R247.4